CONTENTS

Section	Title	Page
	FORWARD	3
1.0	Introduction - The Photographers	4
2.0	'A Huddle of Red Tiles & Chimney's'	13
3.0	'Cobles, Caps & Clay Pipes'	19
4.0	Whats In a Name (Part 1)	29
5.0	Fishermen of Staithes	33
6.0	Whats In a Name (Part 2)	40
7.0	Smock Jackets	44
8.0	Master Mariners	47
9.0	Staithes Parliament	48
10.0	The Fish Sales	50
11.0	Staithes Working Women	53
12.0	Bonnetts & Buns	58
13.0	'The Seven Deadly Sins'	62
14.0	'The Five Virtues'	70
15.0	Shopping on the High Street	75
16.0	The 'Brothers' Club Walk	85
17.0	'The Butchers of Staithes'	87
18.0	The 'Staithes Co-operators'	89
19.0	Café Culture in Staithes	91
20.0	Beckside	96
21.0	Yards & Nicks of Staithes	98
22.0	'Steps of Staithes'	107
23.0	'Barefoot on the Barrass'	110
24.0	'Coffin Lane – 'The Road to Seaton'	114
25.0	'Life in the Gutter'	118
26.0	Seaton Garth – The Foreshore & The Staith	120
27.0	T'awd Trestle Bridges over Roxby Beck	127
28.0	'O'wer' The Beck' - Cowbar	132
29.0	For Those in Peril on the Sea	136
30.0	'Rockers and Wreckers'	141
31.0	Gateway to the German Ocean	144
32.0	Rough Seas – And Fewles O' Muck	149
33.0	Between Two Nabs	155
34.0	Northern Holiday Resort – Unspoilt By Modernity	158
35.0	'Digs' in Staithes	162
36.0	The Banks of Staithes	166
37.0	'Up-Top' – Staithes Lane End	169
38.0	Wartime in Staithes	172
39.0	Staithes Holiday Fellowship Camp	174
40.0	'The Halls of Staithes'	176
41.0	The Railway & Viaduct	179
42.0	Staithes Sporting Hero's	182
43.0	The Arts	186
44.0	'The Knights of Staithes'	188
45.0	Dale House	193
46.0	Boulby	197
	Staithes and District Annals	198
	Acknowledgements	200

A 'World Exclusive' photograph of Laura Johnson (the Dame to be) in the Beck of Staithes with fellow Staithes Group Artist, Frederick W. Jackson. This being the only known photograph of Laura and Fred in Staithes.

FOREWORD

The purpose of this book is not to write so much about the history of Staithes, and surrounding areas, as this has already been well covered in such excellent books as 'Staithes Chapters from the History of a Seafaring Town' by John Howard and 'Yorkshire Fisher Folk' by Peter Frank. The aim is to celebrate the photography and the photographers who had the foresight and energy to capture images of people, places and events that will stir memories for all those people who have an affinity with the North Yorkshire Coastal village of Staithes and its neighbouring districts such as Boulby and Dale House.

However all relevant research and related history has been included in order to ensure that this book becomes a reference for the future and that each heritage image has a thorough annotation.

THE REGULAR KODET.

The photographs within this book in the main are just part of the vast personal collection of Rod Jewell who has had an affinity with the North Yorkshire coast, in particular Staithes for the past 30 years. Most of the images have never been published in book form and include the cream of a recently discovered glass magic lantern slide collection, that have remained undiscovered in a Derbyshire 'lock-up' for many years. There are some ground breaking unpublished images in this vast collection which included in excess of 200 wonderful photographs of Staithes, Runswick & Sandsend taken between 1890 and 1908. (Further books on Runswick & Sandsend to be published in the near future). These 'glass positives' include a fascinating insight into the hard life of the Staithes Fishermen and women in the local fishing industry at Staithes, with individual rare photographs taken 10-14 years prior to the publication of local photographic postcards.

The main thrust of this book is Staithes, the village and its hardworking fisher men and women and their equally hard working cobles, together with the eminent photographers, who captured the important heritage images in this book.

SECTION 1.0 – INTRODUCTION TO THE PHOTOGRAPHERS:

 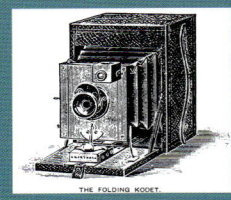  

We owe so much to the following photographers, who all captured important heritage images of Staithes and for their important contribution in forming such a unique archive of social history, events and people:

HENRY CHARLES MORLEY

H.C.Morley was not the first photographer in Staithes, as we know that a Mr A. Goodchild, photographer in the town, opened up his studio during the Staithes Fair week of 1863, which would have been predominantly for portrait photography.

H.C. Morley, Artist and Photographer, STAITHES.

Henry Charles was born in 1875 at Nottingham, and the 1911 census shows that he was 36 years of age and that he had been married to Liverpudlian Ellen Alker Brownell (34yrs) for just one year, he was recorded as both artist and photographer.

Morley may not have been the first, but he certainly was the best and this artistic man produced some significant heritage images. He was both an accomplished artist as well as a photographer, producing several paintings and many important photographs. One of his own large early paintings of Staithes Bank, hangs in the Staithes Heritage Centre for all to see.

He was not listed in Kelly's Directory of 1897, but was listed in the 1904 Directory. He opened his studio sometime in 1903, trading initially in portrait photography, in the form of the small carte de visite and the larger cabinet photographs. The above 'nameplate' was used exclusively on his portrait carte-de visite's and cabinet photographs, whereas his postcards carried his name as an indent mark on the front, in the bottom right hand corner, with later cards from c1909 carrying 'The Studio' Post Card mark on the reverse side. Some of his early photographic viewcards carry his name on the reverse side in green or purple colour.

Morley's real strength was his photography, published in the form of real photographic post cards and sold almost entirely from within the village of Staithes. His photographs were very atmospheric, well composed and had striking clarity and were eagerly sought by the Staithes locals & visitors alike.

We can assume he commenced his postcard local scenes around 1903, when he was just 28 years old. It is rare to find any Morley cards pre 1905 and the bulk of his real photographic postcards were produced between 1905-1912, but he spasmodically produced some fine quality images until around the end of WW1 in 1919. Morley did not wait for customers to come to him, Henry Charles was out nearly every week with his camera, capturing the fishermen and women at work and he must have taken almost every Staithes coble & crew during his peak period of 1905-1912. He also accepted private commissions for family photographs, in the form of postcards.

Plate 1. H.C.Morley c1908
Morley's house was called 'The Studio' and this was etched into the glass panel, above his doorway.
'The Studio' was situated off the High Street, being the end house of Brown's Terrace, not far from Morley's Steps, which were named after him.
Mr William Sowerby Smales previously trained as a tailor under Israel Jefferson in Hinderwell, in his drapery and grocers shop. William became a woollen draper/merchant tailor in his own right and in 1864 he married Hannah Rodham Trattles, who worked as a telegraph clerk. Their son William was a 'Letter Carrier' in 1891 and younger son John George was a telegram messenger in 1901.
William Sowerby Smales was also a valuable member of the postal service industry and he was the Staithes postman for at least 20 years.
In 1911 at the age of 68 he was still recorded as a tailor and postman.

Plate 2
A private commission, as a Staithes couple pose for Morley in front of coble Mary Ann (WY175) on the beach

INTRODUCTION TO THE PHOTOGRAPHERS

Plate 3
Unknown Verrill of Staithes

Plate 4
A H.C. Morley private commission, depicting five circular vignettes, believed to be for the Cole family of Staithes

Plate 5. H.C. Morley c1906
A spectacular image from Morley, with coble 'Morning Light' (WY183) to the left and 'Star of Hope' (WY 174)) to the right and a lot going off inbetween. Taken on the day of the fish sale, the barrels are full on the Staith and the Carters wait in the wings to transport the fish, away from Staithes.
Children play, while the women with near perfect deportment, carry their baskets, galvanised buckets and wooden skeels, as they go about their duties, on this important day in their lives

 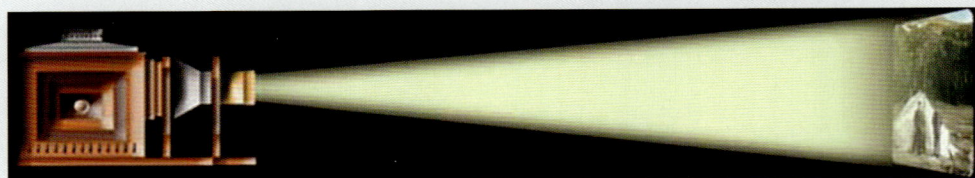

T. BUTTERWORTH

Little is known about this important and very talented photographer, who operated along the North Yorkshire coast, where he visited mainly Staithes, Runswick and Whitby between 1890 and 1908. His images were captured on glass 'positives', in the form of glass magic lantern slides, where he characteristically taped the edges in red, to hold the two pieces of glass together, with the 'positive' sandwiched between the two. His images provide an important insight into the day to day life of the fisher folk earning a living in the fishing villages of Staithes and Runswick.

Butterworth has captured some amazing heritage images and he deserves every credit as his work has recorded a bygone era, never to be seen again.

T. Butterworth photographs have never been published and hence the images in this book provide a rich source of new and previously unseen material, that allows the reader an insight into an unrecorded social and topographical history of Staithes.

Incidently a T.Walter Butterworth accompanied Staithes Group Artist Fredrick Jackson, on his development trip to Russia and he may just have also been the photographer of several images in this book.

Plate 7. T. Butterworth c1897
The cottages at the far end of Seaton Garth close to Penny Nab were very basic and always looked in need of care and attention. The large white painted cottage was at one time the oldest cottage in Staithes and a crude name sign above the door appears to say 'Sandside', and you had to step down to enter this old house. It has since been re-built with a new front elevation and is now called 'Anchor Cove'. The far cottage closest to Penny Nab is 'Mizpah', now fully restored as a holiday cottage.
The old barking copper can be seen on the high left, above 'Mizpah'.

FRANK MEADOW SUTCLIFFE (1853 to 1941)

Much has been written about this famous photographer, who is synonymous with Whitby and the social history of the fisher folk there. He devoted his whole life to photography and throughout his life he won many medals for his exemplary works, where his style and composition, was second to none. He was born in Far Headingly near Leeds and his father Thomas Sutcliffe was an accomplished artist. In 1870 they set up home at Ewe Cote Hall near Whitby. After a short but disastrous period trying to make a living in Tunbridge Wells, Frank returned to Whitby in 1875 and set up his studio in Waterloo Old Yard, near Flowergate.

He became an accomplished portrait photographer, producing hundreds of carte-de-visite, lantern slides and cabinet photographs, as shown at the top of page 7. In 1894 he opened his new studio on Skinner Street and the rest is history. Although his fame was assured through his Whitby photographs, he also photographed some important scenes at Sandsend, Runswick and Staithes.

INTRODUCTION TO THE PHOTOGRAPHERS

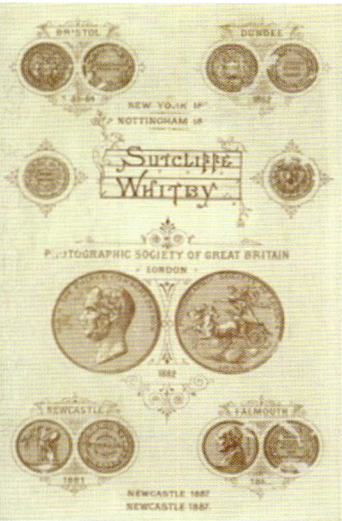

Plate 8a/b
A Sutcliffe portrait from his Waterloo Old Yard studio of the Winterburn and Oldroyd families from Leeds who were friends of the Sutcliffe's, the reverse side shows the various medals won by Sutcliffe (image supplied by good friend Anthony Mellor).

Plate 9
Suttcliffe always gave his photographs titles, this being no exception and was initially titled 'After Forty Years' and later changed to 'Life's Evening' and shows George Longster(1852-1901) sitting on an old fish barrel near the sea front with his wife Elizabeth Longster. They lived on Seaton Square/SeatonGarth. The fishermans knitted smock jacket carries the traditional pattern synonomous with Staithes.

JOHN THOMAS ROSS (1862 to 1929)

J.T. Ross, a former shipbuilder, commenced his photography business around 1902, with a studio on Flowergate, Whitby and until his death in 1929, he produced a wealth of real photographic studio carte-de-visit's and postcards that captured social history, events, disasters and local architecture. Much of the history of his life and the postcards he published, have been captured in a fine recent publication titled 'Ross, Photographer, Whitby,The Life and Work of a Yorkshire Artist' by Colin Bullamore. He was mainly responsible for real photographic post cards which he published himself, as well as being involved in a coloured series, the 'JTR Series' and many more printed types including an artistic series featuring the artists of the day.

Plate10. J.T.Ross c1908
Ross titled his photograph 'Off for the Herring Ground Staithes' and he has captured four traditional three man cobles, passing through the Beckmouth on their way to the German Ocean. The rearmost coble on the right ,is sailing coble 'Mizpah' (WY84) and the middle coble is 'Confidence' (WY87). The cobles would row out of the Beckmouth during the early evening in order to net shoals of herrings.

Several local fishermen sit at the end of the slipway and ladies in their fine summer coats, holding parasols, all watch the cobles proceeding on their journey. Coble 'Dawn of Hope' (WY254) is on dry ground, alongside the Lifeboat House. This view card was sold at Matthew Trattles Drug Store on the High Street (later the Post Office)

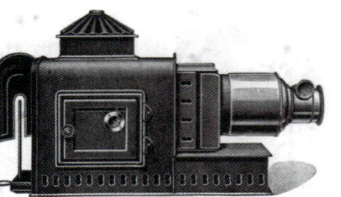

WILLIAM GILBERT FOSTER R.B.A. (1855 to 1906)

Gilbert Foster was the founding father of the Staithes Group of Artists and he commenced visiting Runswick during the 1880's, eventually buying a cottage high up on the south side of Runswick village, which he named 'Ileene Cottage' after his second daughter. He was responsible for many fine canvases and for mentoring and teaching many young aspiring artists. His paintings were accepted at the Royal Society of British Artists and at the Royal Academy, where his first work was accepted in 1876. Apart from his artistic talent he was also a very accomplished photographer and we have been lucky enough to acquire over 70 of his glass magic lantern slides, that he took of the fisher folk and artists in and around Runswick Bay in the 1890s. Prior to this important find he was completely unknown as a photographer.

The bulk of this collection, together with another Runswick private collection will appear in a future book, planned for 2014/15.

Plate 11. c1898
Foster was responsible for this family photograph on Runswick Bay beach, of his wife, himself, four daughters, his fellow artist & father, young fisher girl artists model and friends, possibly artists too. His father was already an established artist and ran a successful portrait studio in Leeds.

Plate 12. c1899
Foster produced this superb image of his youngest daughter Hermione, into a fine magic lantern slide ('positive')

TOM WATSON (1863 to 1957)

In 1863 William Watson, Toms father was the head joiner at Mulgrave Castle, working for the Marquis of Normanby and he initially lived in the Lodge House, at the entrance to the estate in Lythe. Tom was apprenticed to his father and remained as a joiner on the Mulgrave estate until 1892, leaving due to the demise of the economy on the estate. Tom commenced his photographic business almost straight away and had darkroom facilities within the Lodge.

He was kept busy by many commissions for photographs of family and events by the Marquis, who encouraged Tom in his changed working life from joiner to photographer.

His studio was based in Lythe, opposite the 'Stiddy' public house, built by himself using his obvious joinery skills. However this once neat little wooden structure was for many years almost in a state of complete collapse, which is a disgrace to this eminent mans work and the legacy he has left for us all to enjoy.

Plate 13. c 2005
Watson's studio (now demolished) had a small glazed window (8½" x 6½") in order to take a full plate negative in a printing frame when producing a print by daylight as he did not use electricity at all. It is a shame that his studio has not been restored and utilised as a museum of his important work.

Tom Watson's photography is rated very highly.

INTRODUCTION TO THE PHOTOGRAPHERS

GEORGE WASHINGTON WILSON (1823 to 1893)

Lantern slides were his forte and most bore his initials 'GWW.' He recorded events, topographical scenes and also produced several educational series of lantern slides. He was both an artist and a photographer, but unlike William Gilbert Foster, photography was his main passion. He produced hundreds of Victorian carte-de-visite's, cabinet photographs, magic lantern slides and also stereo cards.

Plate 14. G.W.W. c1900
This lantern slide was titled 'Waves and Marine Erosion, (E) Coast Erosion, Headlands & Coast. It was numbered 292 and his appended notes read; "A River Valley with sloping slides, Debouching into the Sea, Staithes, Yorkshire".This photograph shows Thomas Rodham's old boatyard and joinery business, adjacent to Cowbar View house and the old curing and salting buildings that lined the Beckside. The old buildings shown here were thought to be once owned by fish curer William Thompson (1866 Coble Race Fame), who offered them for sale in 1864.

There appears to be a small well on the beck side of Cowbar Bank, possibly on the site where the alligator-pond and spoof "Cowbar Diamond Mine" is situated today opposite No7 Cowbar Bank.

FRANCIS GRAY SMART M.A. J.P. (1844 to 1913)

He was an enthusiastic botanist and President of the Tunbridge Wells Photographic Association, since the founding of the Association in 1887.He was also a qualified Doctor, as was his father, physician John Cass Smart M.D. and also his grandfather Dr George Smart. The life and photography of this eminent man are well described in Bob Charnley's excellent book, 'The Summer of 89', which describes his Grand Tour of Scotland in 1889 and contains some fantastic heritage images of fishermen, tinkers, crofters and washerwomen, taken from Francis's bound leather volume, recording the tour.

The author of this Staithes book has been lucky enough to find Francis's other leather bound tour album of 1890 when he made his way to Whitby. Just one image out of nearly 200 has been included in this book, that of the Staithes mule 'Star of Hope' (WY 257) in Whitby waters. However the cream of this unpublished album will be released as a separate book in the near future and will include some incredible heritage images of the Whitby fisherfolk, coastguards and sailing ships that are as good if not better than the master, Frank Meadow Sutcliffe!

NATIONAL PHOTOGRAPHERS

The large companies such as Francis Frith, John Valentine, J.Salmon, Brittain & Wright, Rotary Photographic, Lilywhite Ltd, E.T.W. Dennis and Judges Ltd etc also came to the North Yorkshire coastal villages and they too captured some very important bygone scenes, which have been included in this book. Valentines in particular produced some excellent large format sepia photographs, that were eventually published as postcards and Brittain & Wright from Stockton-on-Tees, were prolific photographers in the North East, both in coastal towns and many inland villages.

It is also known that some of these larger companies, engaged certain local photographers such as the eminent Frank Meadow Sutcliffe, to carry out several assignments on their behalf. Just to give some idea of how large these National photographers could be, the Francis Frith collection archive, consists of 300,000 views of towns and villages in Britain between 1860 and 1970.

Local photographers like H.C. Morley of Staithes, possibly only produced around 150 different, photographic viewcards and probably printed no more than say 50-100 off of each. Morley's photographic viewcards were on sale during the Edwardian period in both Joseph Verril's general store, Seymour's general store/post office and in James W. Legg's Newsagent shop near his studio.

Thus you can see how important they are, as only handfuls survive today. In the case of the magic lantern slides, at most possibly 10 images may have been produced off each and in many cases they would be 'one-offs' as they were often not produced for commercial purposes at all.

Plate 15a. R A Series c1960
Typical examples of mass produced multi-viewcards, produced in large quantities for the many visitors to send home to show where they had been for their day out or their 'big holiday'.

Plate 15b
Valentine's

Plate 16. 1904
An excellent image from The 'Dainty' Series (E.T.W. Dennis) of their photographic view cards and titled by their photographer, 'Good Fortune Guide Thee'. The traditional small coble has been launched bow first from the open beach. The fisherman in his over the knee waders, smock jacket and so'wester, is pushing the coble from the stern out to sea. In Staithes dialect terms, those helping to launch a coble are known as 'laggers'.

As you can see this coble has the long, main mast and short mast, which would eventually be erected, when ready to set sail. Masts would often equal the inside length of the boat and the oars would be twice the cobles breadth, at the widest amidships.

 INTRODUCTION TO THE PHOTOGRAPHERS

— An Amateur Photographer —

MODERN DAY PHOTOGRAPHERS

THE UNKNOWN AND AMATEUR PHOTOGRAPHERS

It is almost impossible to trace those responsible for some of the excellent photographs in this book, however we must thank all the unknown/amateur photographers for the archive material that they have provided.

TERRY LAWSON

The tradition carries on and Staithes has Terry Lawson to thank for the production of his series of coloured photographic postcards and prints which he sells from the family Gift Shop on Staithes High Street. Terry has been producing some excellent photography for many years now and he has been dubbed 'The Modern Morley' for his devotion in producing 120 plus, different local postcard views, several of which have become collectors items now. Terry works entirely with film in his camera and has yet to try digital photography. Always keen to capture something special, Terry often gets up at all hours and in all weathers, in order to further his excellent range of photography. Terry is completely self taught and has to combine his photography with working seven days a week in the family business on the High Street in Staithes.

Plate 17. c1937 Margaret Burgess

An amateur 'snapshot' taken by Margaret Burgess in 1937 on the far end of the Staith nearest to Penny Nab. She has captured fisherman Francis Verrill and his wife Margaret Ann (nee Harrison) with bonnet and a Mrs Gunning sitting on a rudimentary seat made from an old ship's beam, directly in front of 'Mizpah' cottage.

Margaret used to visit Staithes and stay with the Verrill family, where the Verrill's gave her the knickname of 'Gretchen', which is a female given name of German origin, but became used in many countries and was a pet name for Greta or Margaret and also associated with her blond hair.

Margaret Burgess, however always referred to Frank and Margaret Ann as Mr & Mrs Verrill respectively.

Plate 19

A fine photograph from Terry Lawson from a lofty vantage point on Aukness looking towards the houses on Granary Yard, Beckside, Bob Bell's Bank, through to the houses high up in the Mount Pleasant area of Staithes, with Prospect House uppermost.

Twenty or so cobles are moored on the Beckside just up from the bridge.

The Wesleyan Chapel is prominent on Beckside.

Plate 18. c1926

The cobles are launched up, stern first on the shaled beach and lined up between the left hand 'Ocean View cottage' and the right hand 'Harbourside' house, situated behind the lengthy wooden staith. An unknown female artist on the beach is working on her latest canvas, whilst her husband plays with their child.

Cobles on view include: 'Lizzie Robinson' (WY188), 'Addison' (WY244), 'Ethel & Aida' (WY258) & coble WY343. A lone cow is silhouetted on the field behind Rolling Cross.

This scene was captured by an unknown photographer on a glass negative.

Plate 20. T. Lawson

The restored 4-storey Smokehouse in the foreground and 'Back Road' behind leading to 'First & Last' house.

Plate 21. T.Lawson

A young Sean Baxter, long before he ran the now very successful 'Real Staithes' business with wife Tricia and sons Luke & Thomas. This family offer the Staithes experience of exploration of the foreshore, fishing/cooking what you catch and more.

11

TONY MURPHY L.R.P.S.

Tony grew up in Ireland and borrowed his mother's box brownie camera, to capture on film the boats and activity on the Shannon river at Banagher. He studied Fine Art in Dublin and later trained as an art teacher in Manchester. He worked as a photographer in the North East and studied photography in Newcastle, where he was awarded a distinction in Exhibition Printing.

Plate 22. Tony on Location

Tony has lived in Staithes for eighteen years now and much of his work reflects the incredibly stimulating environment of Staithes and his love of the Staithes cobles. He is both an artist and a photographer, Licentiate Member of the Royal Photographic Society (2004) and also a tutor, offering short courses in Beginning Digital Photography.

Working entirely with digital photography, Tony has produced and exhibited his excellent works in solo and joint exhibitions over several years. In 2006 he and Terry Lawson had their joint 'Eye to Eye' exhibition at the Pannet Park Museum & Gallery in Whitby.

Plate 23. T. Murphy
Tony titled this photograph 'Willie's Boat (Mizpah belonging to local character Willie Wright)

Plate 24. Tony Murphy
Tony has produced a superb image of this line up of various boats in Staithes harbour, including; Pilot Me B (WY216) & Flora Jane (WY251);the light and reflections captured by Tony make this an award winning photograph.

SECTION 2.0 – 'A HUDDLE OF RED TILES AND CHIMNEYS'

T.Bulmer & Co in their Directory of 1890, described Staithes as "A large fishing village at the north-eastern extremity of Hinderwell Parish and partly in the adjoining parish of Easington. It is romantically situated in a deep narrow creek, between Colburn Nab (Cowbar Nab) and Old Nab (Penny Nab), which completely conceal it from the view of the approaching traveller, until he reaches the summit of the cliff above. A stream formed by the junction of the Roxby and Easington Becks, flows through the deep narrow glen, between the cliffs and contributes not a little to its 'picturesqueness'. The inhabitants are chiefly engaged in fishing in which an extensive business is carried on.

The houses are built in terraces one above another on the slope of the cliffs, the floor of one row being on a level with the chimneys of that in front".

Plate 25a. G.W.W. c1900
Taken from an early glass magic lantern slide, this view shows the many red tiled roofs of the houses built haphazardly along the beckside and either side of the High Street. To the right of centre the defunct old Rodham's Boatyard is visible on the site to later house Staithes Co-Operative store. Compare this view with the modern photographs on page 14 to see how the roofs and houses have changed in the hundred or so years.

**Plate 25b.
Rod Jewell**

Plate 26a. Rod Jewell
A hazy huddle of Red Tiles and chimneys.

Plate 26b. Rod Jewell

An early extract on Staithes dwellings, reads as follows:"The red roofs, which give so much character to Staithes, are modern innovations. In the beginning of the 19th Century, every house was thatched. The first red-tiled one was built of good freestone by a man for his own residence ; but its roof was such a novelty that he was ever after called "Red-roof Dick." He kept this name much longer than he kept his house, for it was one of the thirteen swept away at one fell swoop (the time of the great storm that washed away Sanderson's grocery store, early home of the young Captain Cook to be). A gaunt old house on the hill-side, which is built of ironstone and mortar hard as stone, and is full of what one of our sailor friends called Amoritee and Bedlamites (better known to fossil- collectors as ammonites and belemnite), would surely have braved the elements better than Red-Roof Dick's".

Plate 27. H.C. Morley c1914

Staithes has often been described as an interesting huddle of red tiles, and smoking chimneys.
Laura Knight likened the houses of Staithes 'as a giant child's box of bricks thrown from the top'. This interesting photograph shows that the Staithes village houses were built just about where anyone wanted and that planning permissions were not a requirement at the time (unlike now!). In the centre lies Friendship Cottage and you can clearly trace the path towards High Barrass, York House and up to Burtons Cottage. Behind Kirkhill House in the foreground, stands the old sea captains abode of Balmoral House on Church Street and behind here lies Gun Gutter. The pathway on the left, lines the area known as 'Old Stubble', where James Crystal, one of Staithes early coopers lived.

'A HUDDLE OF RED TILES AND CHIMNEYS'

Plate 28. c1956
This wide angled photograph shows the shape of the village from Seaton Garth on the left, Church Street, New Landing, Garth Ends and the huddle of housing either side of the High Street. The old army huts at trig Point are just visible high above the village, with the huge iron viaduct behind.

In 1538 there were approximately only 38 cottages in Staithes, rising to 305 by 1861.

The table below reflects the population figures for the Parish of Hinderwell and indicates the rise and fall, with a near 50% increase in the 10 year period 1851-61, mainly due to newcomers entering the parish to work in the new iron-stone mines in the district:

1851	1861	1871	1881	1891	1901	1911	1921	1931
1756	2571	2599	2467	2021	1957	2491	2608	2146
					Hinderwell Ward		1058	1205	1050
					Staithes Ward		1455	1405	1116

When the Grinkle Iron-stone mines opened, many Staithes local fishermen, switched from fishing to mining and the following ironstone miners are recorded as living in Staithes and working in the mines: James, Thomas & William Marshall, Richard Dix, John Day, Thomas Unthank, Thomas Crooks, Joseph Cook, George Roe, William Porrit, Joseph Cummings, Richard Longster, John D Laverick and many more. Whilst others came from further afield such as John Atkins (Lincs), William Hymen (Cumb), Jonathan Wiseman (Lanark), Albert Yeomandale (Scot), George Burns (Durham) etc.

Further known population figures for Staithes only are as follows:

1851	1861	1871	1881	1891
1211	1414	1412	1417	1282

The fall in population between 1881-1891 was due to the decline in the number of miners.

Plate 29
Grinkle Mine was an inland drift mine, opened in 1875 to supersede coastal mining at Port Mulgrave. All the output was taken by a 3feet gauge, loco worked line over the 2 ½ miles to the Port for shipping to Jarrow on the Tyne.

So remote was the location, that a passenger service was introduced for the miners. In 1916 an incline was built to provide access to the standard gauge rail system. The mine closed in 1930.

Plate 30
The tiered houses are clear in this view, looking south to north, taken from a lofty point on Penny Nab and shows the arched window of the large Kirk Hill house in the foreground. The Staithes photographer has captured the High Street, climbing to the right, starting with Tom Englands cottage ('Cocked Hat' house) and the many pantiled cottages leading towards the high ground of High Barras and Darlington Terrace on the left hand side.

The old miners cottages, sit high on top of Cowbar.

The message on the back of this postcard of 1908 read "Went here by train with mother, a very curious little town with two openings to the sea, one made by the river. The inhabitants look very poor and the place generally not very clean, but extremely picturesque."

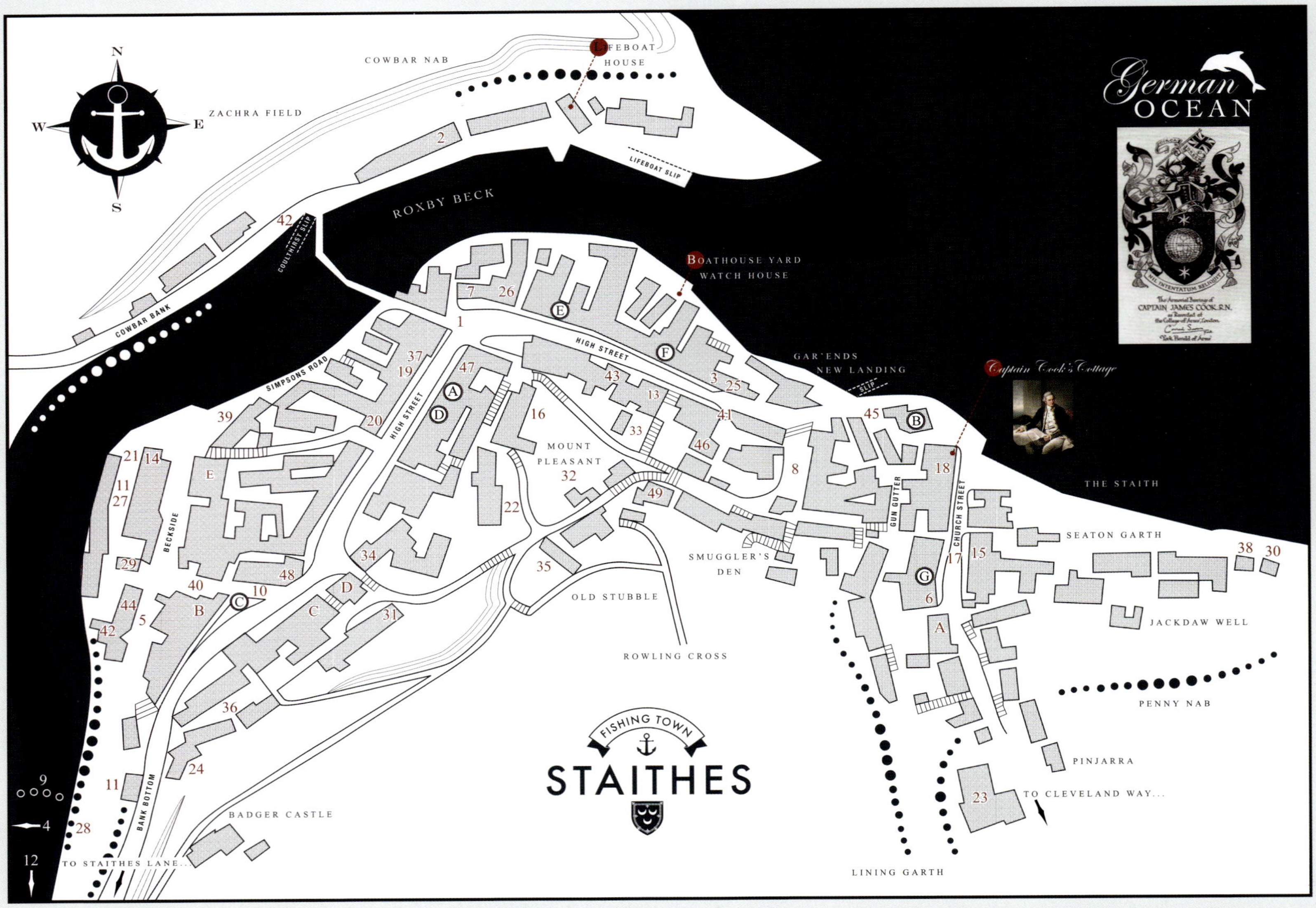

STAITHES 'BETWEEN TWO NABS'

1. Abraham Lane
2. Alum House
3. Ash Cottage
4. Aukness
5. Back Road
6. Balmoral House
7. Bank House
8. Barris Square
9. Battlestones
10. Bell's Bank (Bob Bell's Bank)
11. Blacksmith
12. Black Watter Stream
13. Blue Jacket House
14. Boiling House
15. British Legion
16. Broom Hill
17. Church Street
18. Captain Cook's cottage
19. Co-op 1st store
20. Co-op 2nd store
21. Cole's Boat Yard
22. Darlington Terrace
23. Felicity House
24. First & Last house(Inn)
25. Fishermans Institute
26. Gallery
27. Granary
28. Kiln
29. Long House
30. Mizpah cottage
31. Morley's Studio
32. Mount Pleasant
33. New Hall
34. Poplar House
35. Prospect House
36. Ropery (Browns Terrace)
37. Ruby House
38. Sandside house
39. Simpson Road
40. Silver Street
41. Slippery Hill
42. Smokehouse
43. St Martins Lodge
44. Stables
45. Tinker Hill
46. True Love house
47. Victoria House
48. Westgate House
49. York House

'7 Deadly Sins'

- Ⓐ Black Lion
- Ⓑ Cod & Lobster
- Ⓒ Freemason's Arms
- Ⓓ Golden Lion
- Ⓔ Royal George
- Ⓕ Shoulder of Mutton
- Ⓖ White Horse

'5 Virtues'

- A. Anglican Church
- B. Congregational
- C. Primitive Methodist
- D. Methodist School
- E. Weslyan

In the 1840's the North West part of Staithes as far as Abraham Lane was stated to be; Main Street, Back Lane, Broom Hill, Barrass, Church Street and Seaton Garth. The 1841 census shows that none of the houses were numbered, but guess John Lawson who was the 'Letter Carrier' knew all, not that the average person had any mail to receive or send in those days. By 1851 the census shows that a numbering system had commenced, but you need to be a psychic to interpret the system! Generally villagers lived on; Front Street, the High Street or the Main Street, whilst others were listed as living on Back Street or Back Road or Back Lane. Initial thoughts were that Front St. was the main street leading to the sea front and the High St. was the higher portion of the main street above Abrahams Lane, but this is only true some of the time! Front Street was the name used from Abrahams Lane to the Royal George and above Abraham Lane was generally referred to as the Main Street. Also intial thoughts were that odd numbers were on the left, even numbers on the right as you travel down the Main Street from Bob Bell's Bank, again this was true some of the time!

At this time Back Street was anywhere that could be accessed off the Main Street and in 1861 residents on the Barris were recorded as being on (Back Street or Barris).

Back Road was where William Mitchell, the Independent Minister (Bethel Chapel) lived with his wife Jane in the Manse provided by the chapel, thus confirming that Back Road ran from Bob Bells Bank, to the rear of the Bethel, towards the steep bank out of Staithes, by Valley View cottage. In 1851, thirteen dwellings were listed on Back Road, including that of Robert Bell, blacksmith and Indiana Trufitt (39) who ran her millinery and dressmaking business here, with assistance from one of her two daughters Diana (19), who was also an experienced dress maker. Back road was the abode of joiners, blacksmiths, washer-women, char-women, pedlers, carriers and the odd pauper and Backroad also included Beckside.

Staithes has always been a Postman's nightmare! – even as late as 1901, the census forms listed such addresses as; 'near sea', 'near Beck', 'off High Street' and 'near Wesleyan Chapel', however the people of Staithes were generally not in favour of a house numbering system. Some numbering does exist today but makes no sense at all! This has led to some important and pertinent names being given to the houses and this gives a sense of uniqueness to the village.

THE VILLAGE

The main residential areas of the village are as follows:

Staithes Lane/Lane End	Tinker Hill
Old Stubble (Bank Top/The Hill)	Slip Top
Browns Terrace (The Ropery)	Gun Gutter
High St. (Main St. or Front St.)	Church Street
Back St/Back Lane/ Back Road	Seaton Garth (Seaton Square)
Granary Yard	Cowbar Cottages
Chapel Yard/Wesley Square	Cowbar Bank
Elliots Yard(Ward's Yard)	
Abraham's Lane	
Post Office Yard/ Barbers Yard	
Royal George Yd/ Boat House Yd	
Gar' End/Ryders Yard	
Various small Yards/Nicks	
Slippery Hill	
Webster's Steps	
Darlington Terrace	
Broom Hill	
Mount Pleasant	
Barris/Barrass/ Barrass Square	
High Barris (or Top Barris)	

Plate 31. F.M.S aerial view

A JOURNEY ROUND STAITHES WITH THE POSTMAN IN 1861

The following table gives an insight into the layout of the village of Staithes and the deviations away from the main street that the postman had to endure, as he went into the various nicks and yards and back onto the main street, delivering his post:

Interestingly the term Front Street was only used for dwellings situated on the South side of the main street, whilst those on the North side were said to be on Main Street.

Brown's Yard was on the North side, yet Brown's Buildings were on the South side.

The term Back Road was reserved for those houses off the North side of the main street and Back Street for those off the South side. Hence this census does make some sort of logical sense and is easier to follow than most.

1861 – North Side of the Main Street & East Side of Church Street	
Street/Place	No. of Dwellings
High Street	27
Abraham Lane	2
Back Road	15
Back Buildings	10
Granary Yard	3
Back Road	6
High Street	4
Alley Toner Nick	5
High Street	2
Mary Crispin Nick	6
High Street	2
Boat House Yard	7
High Street	8
Browns Yard	2
High Street	2
Tinker Hill	2
Church Street	15
Seaton Square	29
TOTAL	**147**

1861 – South Side of the Main Street & West Side of Church Street	
Street/Place	No. of Dwellings
Front Street	1
Back Street	5
Front Street	12
Lane Yard	5
Front Street	14
Brown's Buildings	2
Front Street	19
Barris or Back Street	11
Barras	2
Harburn Yard	1
Front Street	3
Tinker Hill	3
Church Street	19
Gun Gutter	17
Broom Hill	33
TOTAL	**147**

Remarkably the total dwellings on the North side, match exactly the totals on the South side of the village, giving a grand total of 294 dwellings. The term 'Seaton Square' was applicable to the North side figures and was in use during 1861-1871, but was eventually dropped in favour of Seaton Garth. Lane's Buildings were between the Golden Lion and the Primitive Methodist chapel.

There is no doubt that during the period from the early part of the 18th Century, up to around the 1930's, that Staithes had been no more than a fishing village, where the inhabitants concentrated on fishing and surviving, with little money to improve housing or appearances.

However beauty is in the eye of the beholder and Staithes for most people will always be a special magical place, with interesting cottages & houses, with even more interesting interiors and of course the people. As you turn towards the village from the top car park and the old Station Hotel (now Captain Cook Inn) and pass the 'Tea Shop' cabin opposite, where the old railway viaduct once existed, the fine Sea Captains houses on the right, beginning with Roraima and the beautiful Gully where Roxby Beck flows on the left; you can sense you are about to enter a special place.

'Staithes Head' as graphic artist Paul Wheat, depicted author Rod Jewell on the back of a torn dish washer tablets packet, in February 2008 on his first visit from Australia to stay at the author's house, 'The Granary', Granary Yard, Beckside, Staithes. This will now form the author's business logo for his prints and other local memorabilia.

The steep descent down Staithes Bank, towards the old cobbled High Street and the winding route past the old Bethel Chapel (now Arc House), Bob Bell's Bank off to the left leading to Beckside, Staithes Heritage Centre & Museum in the old chapel, the Emporium Gift shop, Chapel Yard entrance, the Gift Shop, the old Post Office, Cleveland Corner Bistro, Art Gallery, Royal George, Kessen Bowl gift shop, the red painted Butchers shop, The famous Cod & Lobster Inn and down to the scenic sea-front, sheltered between the two Nabs, will always hold a fascination.

The village can never be spoilt, only improved, as more and more properties become cared for, by people who love the place. The High Street in 2013 is especially looking good, with many properties restored and freshly painted.

Thankfully the village has a soul and a good community spirit exists between true 'Staithers' and those who have chosen to live there but were born elsewhere. Now that the heady days of full-time employment for all within the village, has long gone, the Staithes economy and future now relies on it's many visitors and 'outsiders' who are now 'within'. The Staithes fisher folk were a proud community and outsiders had to earn respect (they still do).

Where else in the world will you find a Gun Gutter, Dog Loup, Slippery Hill, Gar' Ends, Barbers Yard, Slip Top, Sky Shitings, Low & High Coble Gardens, Pot A Boiling, Old Stubble, Penny Nab, The Battle-stones, Badger Castle, Sea Drift café & its unique Coble Cake and The Cod and Lobster Inn - the only pub in the world with this name. There is no doubt that the author of this book has his 'Staithes Head' well and truly on with his passion and interest in everything in and around Staithes.

SECTION 3.0 – 'COBLES, CAPS & CLAY PIPES'

At its height in 1817, through to 1847, Staithes was the largest fishing station on the Yorkshire coast and boasted in the order of 80 plus fishing vessels, from large yawls (14) and sailing cobles (70). By 1840 the year of the Penny Black, the worlds first adhesive postage stamp, bearing Queen Victoria's head, there were in the order of 300 men employed in fishing around Staithes, and by 1861 there were 120 boats employed in the fishing trade.

Plate 32. 1925/6
An unknown photographer in the mid 1920's has recorded four cobles, 'Breadwinner' **(WY 109)**, 'True Love' (WY 7), 'WE Gladstone' (WY15), and 'Love Divine' (WY149), all beached up at the Penny Nab end of the foreshore. The silhouettes of two hayricks and sheds appear on the horizon of the opposite cliff, Cowbar Nab. This was taken off a glass negative. Note the two old slipways.

A letter to the Times newspaper in 1803, recorded that Staithes fishermen had played their part in taking a massive haul of 20-25 lasts of herrings - (a last = 10,000!)

There were many varieties of sailing vessels on the Yorkshire Coast, as listed below (not exhaustive) :
- Yawls (normally 8, occasionally 10 men boats, generally including 2 or 3 boys), typically 56 ft long and 16 ft wide, often painted black.
- Large Coble or 'Plosher' or Herring Coble (5 man boat or 4men+boy) usually 30-35 ft in length.
- Small flat bottomed Sailing Coble (2 or 3-man coble), early cobles were 21 ft long & only 2 ft wide, later increased to typically 28 ft long & 5 ft 5ins wide.
- Mule, Double-ended coble or Herring Mule, 35-40 ft long, usually half decked.

Coble size varied and some known examples are as follows:
- Lizzie Robinson (WY 188) was a small two man coble with sail lug & jib for crabbing and measured 19.1 ft x 5.5 ft, weighing 2.02 tons.
- Breadwinner (WY 109), pictured here, was a 3 man motorised coble, measuring 24.3 ft x 6.1 ft, weighing 2.65 tons.
- Both of the above two cobles were owned by William Henry ('Enny') Verrill (1867-1937)
- Star of Hope (WY 257) was a mule (large coble), measuring 42 ft in overall length, weighing 11 tons.

THE YAWLS

There were several large Yawls (early one's had 3 masts, later reduced to two), operating from Staithes during the 19th Century and they often carried a coble on board, sometimes two for independent fishing. The Yawls had white painted, lute sterns and were used for long lining and herringing. They were built on stocks, similar to those for boat building, without moulds or frames of any kind. They were built of oak wainscot, with narrow planking about 1½ inches thick, with a deep overlap. For c150 years (1730-1880) there were between 14-20 yawls operating from Staithes and some noteable names were: Richard & Sarah, Good Intent, William Clowes, Felicity, Truelove, Nancy, Bluejacket, Ann, Ruby, Venus, Princess Royal, Prosperity, to name just a few. By 1883 despite articulate protests from James Fell (William Clowes yawl) and other eminent boat owners in Staithes the sailing trawlers (Smacks) and finally the iron, steam trawlers gradually sapped the fishing grounds and the fishermen of Staithes, until by 1914 't'ard yalls' were finished in Staithes, leaving but a few cobles to carry on with the tradition. Herring fishing was a staple industry at one time, but only line and pot fishing exist today.

Plate 33a

Plate 33b. Comic Edwardian PC

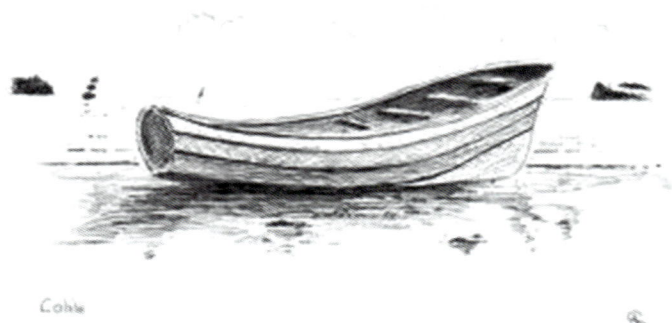

THE COBLES

Spelt coble but pronounced 'cobble', the name is thought to be rooted in the Celtic 'Ceubal' or the Breton 'Caubal', both which simply meant boat. The name has been used for more than a thousand years, and was mentioned in the 'Lindisfarne Gospels'

Early cobles were propelled by sails (jib sail in good weather & reefed main sail, with short mast vertical in bad) and had large ash oars for rowing. The coble was designed to be launched bow first from an open beach, thus suiting Staithes very well. They were flat bottomed, high prowed and square sterned and were mainly used for line fishing, but herring fishing with nets was not uncommon. The flat bottoms allowed launching from and landing upon shallow, sandy beaches, which was advantageous at Staithes.

From 1923 the traditional sailing cobles were gradually replaced by motor cobles. The motorised coble had only a main sail for when the engine failed and today's oars are for emergencies or when taking cobles to their moorings.

The cobles were essentially an inshore boat returning daily and each fisherman treated his coble as the most important possession in his life. They were lovingly cared for and painted each year, and there was no shortage of skills to carry out essential repairs; with several joiners and boat builders operating in the village.

An amusing local advert in one of the cottage windows read:" Woman wanted, must be good looking, of clean appearance, good cook, thrifty and own boat – please send photo of boat!"

Fishing was a dangerous business and over the years there were many, many tragedies.

> ### "AT STAITHES"
>
> Hid in their tawny cleft, the fisher clan,
> Untravelled, seldom climbing to the moor,
> With the wild ocean knocking at their door,
> Wage the same war their forefathers began;
> Build the same boats; the same nets weave and tan;
> Eat the same bread, salt savoured, and are poor;
> Content in hopeless labour to endure, till death shall find for them a nobler plan.
> But some there are, adventurous souls, who feel
> Fresh inspiration from their prison bars;
> And stirred by narrow confines such as these,
> Go forth to plant beneath their roving keel
> This solid earth, this canopy of stars,
> And bring back word of the Antipodes.
>
> From "Sonnetts around the Coast"
> By the Rev. H.D. Rawnsley

Thankfully the following photographs record some of the cobles and the hardworking fisher folk from the late 1890's through to the mid 1930's when just six full time cobles were still fishing out of Staithes

Plate 34. T.Butterworth C1897

With the imposing Penny Nab in the background, the photographer has captured the original stone jetty, Breakwater, with large coble (thought to be 288 WY) in full sail. Three men and a lad are onboard, close to the jetty, where the fisherman aft is just dropping the jib and starting to take the sail down. The smart young boy in plus fours and boater appears to be impressing the bonneted girl with his 'man-skills' of throwing stones into the sea. Butterworth titled his slide 'Port Oho' Staithes.

The coble sails were often 'cocoa' coloured or venetian red, rather than black and this relatively close-up image of a coble in sail, so close to the beach, is extremely rare.

Plate 35b. WY257

Large coble 'Star of Hope' was a double ender, herring fishing vessel and when photographer Francis Grey Smart took the left hand photograph in 1890, the coble was registered as WY25. Some years later the registration has changed to WY257, and in 1897 Ralph Cole was recorded as her Master.

Both photographs were taken when Staithes mule, Star of Hope was in Whitby waters.

WY25 has four men and a lad (tratter or trat lad) on board, whilst WY257 has just the four men.

Plate 35a. WY25. Francis Gray Smart 1890

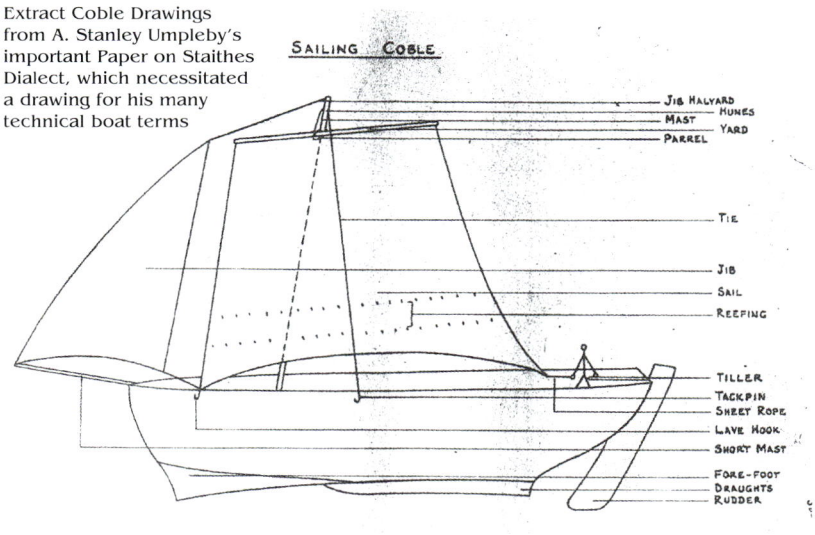

Extract Coble Drawings from A. Stanley Umpleby's important Paper on Staithes Dialect, which necessitated a drawing for his many technical boat terms

/ˈtɪm@z/ "timbers", (the vertical frame-bars of coble from rim to keel, see diagram) (OE. timber).
/ˈtɒnil/ /ˈtʊnil/ "tunnel" (wooden casing of propeller-shaft in motor-coble). (OFr. tonel).
/ˈwi@lin/ "waling", "wale" (top rim of coble) (OE. walu).

Plate 36a

Plate 36b

The construction of the 'Coble' is remarkably similar to the ancient Viking 'Long Ships'. Many of the features on these boats, have Scandanavian names. A peculiar feature of the 'Coble' is that the planking is constructed first, and the frames 'joggled' in, to fit afterwards. This is the reverse of normal boat construction methods. Also, instead of a 'keel' being laid, a flat, horizontal central plank called the 'Ram', forms the first stage of the build. Three generations of Thomas Rodham's were recorded (1787-1895) as Joiner/Boat Builders, in Staithes. The second boat builders in Staithes were John Trattles Cole & his brother William and an advert in 1924, stated that they were established in 1878 and they were recorded as still active in 1928. Other joiner/boat builders were John Hicks on Back Road and James Hansell in Gun Gutter, both in 1871. Staithes cobles were clinker built, where the normal seven strakes or planks overlapped one another and clenched together using copper nails, they were flat bottomed, without a keel. During the early 1900's and for several years there after, cobles were built at the going rate of £1-0s-0d per foot.

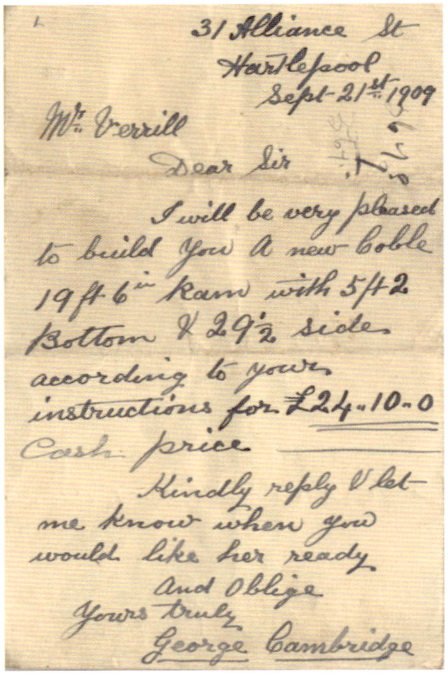

George Cambridge, the Boat Builder from Hartlepool, offered to build a new coble for Francis Verrill in 1909 to the following specifications: 19ft 6 inches Ram with 5ft 2 inch Bottom and 29½ inch sides. George specified a cash price of £24 10s 0d, however as you can see from the final bill, he knocked off the 10s and added an extra £1 for 2 masts & 1 sail yard and a further 8s for loading to Docks, giving a total of £25- 8s- 0d.

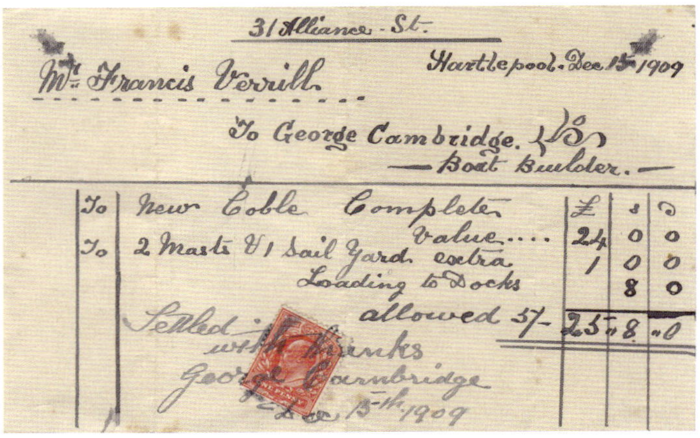

After his intial quote on 21st September 1909, the build was swift, with the new coble ready for dispatch by train on 15th December 1909, in just under three months.

Francis Verrill named his coble 'Bretheren.'

Plate 37a

Plate 37b

Plate 38. HC Morley c1907

The three man coble leads the way alongside the old Lifeboat slipway and one of the fishermen appears to be manouvering the course of 'Success' (WY12), as he holds onto the main mast. A larger than normal gathering is evident outside the Cod & Lobster and unaware of any dangers, several local children are on the slipway, to watch their voyage. The 'Success' was at one time owned by James Grimes.

Plate 39. HC Morley c1907

'Charity' (WY 282), was a 13 planked 'Mule', a double ender, 35foot sailing coble, built for herring fishing.

Morley captured this fine view, whilst in The Beck, looking towards the Lifeboat House through the newly built metal girder style bridge, replacing the old wooden trestle bridge in mid 1905. The initials 'AH' can be seen amongst the litter of large bladder floats, cork floats and barrels, strewn on the Beckside.

Plate 40. George Washington Wilson c1900

G.W.W. simply titled this glass magic lantern slide, 'Fishing Boats at Staithes'. Several traditional small cobles including 459 WY and 'Providence', out of Whitby, on the extreme right can be seen on the scaurs, where they have just arrived back from fishing in the German Ocean. They meet the typical Staithes description of being flat bottomed, high prowed and square sterned (scudguard).

The scaurs are large platforms of rock stretching from the foot of the cliffs down to and beyond the waters edge and are millions of years old.

Plate 41. T. Butterworth c1897

An unusual view from the seabed looking towards the pent roofed Cod and Lobster Inn. Fishermen lean on the fine looking coble 'Endeavour' (WY166) and stare towards the Slip Top, whilst young lads play in the rock pools. The small whitewashed cottage on Seaton Garth was thatched at this time and this was one of only 3 or 4 thatched cottages remaining in Staithes during the 1890's.

Plate 42. HC Morley c1909

The chimney smoke, creates a haze over the rooftops, in this fine photograph of the quayside at Staithes. The wooden Staith (landing stage) and old slipway can be seen, along with several fishermen tending to their cobles, including 'Anchor of Hope' (WY267), 'Friendship' (WY 284), 'Safeguard' (WY68) & 'Richard' (WY67), where their sails are hung out to dry. Several shacks are evident on the skyline on the high ground behind.

Plate 43. HC Morley c 1906

In this busy scene, twenty local Staithes men can be seen preparing their nets and cobles ready to catch the tide.

'Thomas Elizabeth' (WY281) and 'Confidence' (WY251) are carrying a large quantity of bladder floats for the nets and both were known as 'Bulwark Ploshers', as they had an extra piece of planking on top of the whaleings (gunnals). John Trattles Cole (master) is aboard the coble Prosperity (WY151), assessing some damage sustained to the vessel. Cobles, Success (WY12) & Mizpah (254 WY) are but three of the eleven or so cobles on view, below the old salting and curing sheds lining the Beckside..

Granary Yard, the old crab Boiling House and the old Boathouse belonging to John Trattles Cole are to the top right of the picture.

Plate 44. HC Morley c1909

Coble W.E.Gladstone (WY15), heads the line up of a dozen or so traditional Staithes cobles, launched up on the beach, including 'Four Sisters' (WY264) & 'Good Tidings' (WY80). The Coble WY15 was named in honour of this great man following his visit to Staithes on 22nd October 1871.

Nine men and just one woman are pulling coble 'Mars Hill'(WY235) from the sea to the beach, which was made up of rough shingle rather than today's sandy surface.

The cobles masts lean on the wooden planked Staith in readiness for their next sea outing.

'COBLES, CAPS & CLAY PIPES'

Plate 45. HC Morley c1906

The local fishermen, have amazingly managed to store twenty cobles, including 'Mary Ann' (175 WY) and 'Richard' (67 WY) into the confined area in the vicinity of the old bridge and the Beck Mouth. The old 'smoke-house' belonging to the Ward family, to the left of the wooden bridge looks to be in fine condition, in this view titled by Morley,' The Beck'.

Fish and washing hang together, having been left out to dry on the railings to the right hand side of the bridge, close to Abrahams Lane.

Plate 46. HC Morley 1903

Sailing coble (plosher) 'Brotherly Love' (228 WY), manned by Francis & William Verrill, has just passed underneath the old wooden trestle bridge. The bridge is draped with several nets drying, 'Brotherly Love' is being rowed on its way to the Beck Mouth and out to sea. This untitled photograph, is attributed to H.C.Morley.The date of this photograph and thus the date that Morley commenced his valuable work in Staithes, is assumed to be late 1903, (This is supported by an identical view in the authors collection, with a literary overprint from Dickens – "Keep a Bright Look Out For'ard and Good Luck to You" and is signed on the back Howard Westwood, September 1903, who was staying at 'The Cliffs' in Staithes).

The unusual narrow planked vessel moored to the right of the picture is 'Daisy' and appears different to the traditional coble; this was a yacht type sailing boat and likely used for pleasure, rather than fishing.

The message on the back reads: "Walter and I were at the sale of herrings by auction this morning. We can buy them cheap here for you if you are fond of them, 2/9d for 132 herrings, which they call 100, I shall be returning back with a cart hawking herrings etc and doing Mr Moore out of a job"

Plate 47. HC Morley c1909

Coble 'Safeguard' (WY 68), spelt with a mixture of both lower & upper case letters, dominates this Edwardian photograph from Morley.

This boat belonged to one of the Theaker family, as his name is clearly written to the inside of the coble scudguard.

Other cobles in view are 'Mary's' (WY253) and 'Thomas & Elizabeth'(WY 181).

The 'writer' of this postcard was a Mr Parks who was being 'put up' by Mrs Thompson in Staithes.

He wrote to a Mr Tykes in Sheffield stating that Mr Hopwood left Staithes last year, a possible reference to H.S. Hopwood a member of the Staithes Group of Artists.

Plate 48

An unusual place to carry out net and boat maintenance on the lifeboat slipway, unless of course the lifeboat station was closed as it was 1922-1928 and again during the period 1938-1978.

Plate 49. Butterworth c1900

Children play on the shaley beach, in front of the large coble 'Three Brothers' (259WY). Other cobles in view are 'W.E.Gladstone' (WY15) and 'Leading Star', where several fishermen are active with repairs and fettling. The wooden planking of the staith is clear to see and is amok with masts & large ash oars (wars, which is the Staithes name for oars or 'warwash' blade, with the 'war clog' being the thickest part of the oar). Note on the left, the two curved tillers stuck up in the cobles gantries, where the mast is stepted (put up). The fine hand hewn stonework on Sea View and Spray cottages is evident as is the barking tank, top left where the nets and lines were tanned or barked for protection from the North Sea.

Between 1869 and 1893 there were 70 cobles and 14 yawls registered in the area of Staithes, but by the 1930's the Staithes 'Fishing Fleet' was reduced to just six cobles as shown below:

COBLE NAME	COBLE NUMBER	COBLE OWNER
Flora	WY 186	Richard Verrill
Freda	WY 117	Francis Verrill
Minnie	WY 170	Thomas Harrison
Rose of England	WY 3	R Theaker & J Horne
Silver Line	WY 184	Addison Verrill
Star of Hope	WY 174	Matthew Verrill

The last two cobles to be built in Staithes were 'Star of Hope and 'Minnie', both from John Trattles Cole's, boatyard, Granary Yard, Beckside. Star of Hope was first launched in 1928 and was destroyed in the great storm of 1953. The coble 'Golden Crown' was built for Richard (Titch), Matt & Frank (Tange) Verrill to replace her. Other new cobles soon followed: 'Coronation Queen' built for Bill/George Harrison and Richard (Dickie Bott) Verrill and 'Sea Lover' (WY 199), for George Hanson, Howard Theaker & John Verrill. It was during the period that the above cobles were operating in the 1930's that the Thompson brothers recorded the largest crab ever caught at that time' when on 18th June 1937 a large crab of 5½ lb and measuring 14inches in length was landed by these Staithes fishermen.

Plate 50. Margaret Burgess, Amateur c1937
Two of the last six cobles built in Staithes are moored below the old bridge towards the Beck Mouth, motor coble, Freda (WY117) in the centre was Frank Verrill's coble with Silver Line (WY184) belonging to Addison Verrill, behind it.

Aboard 'Freda' are from left to right: Bill Verrill, & Willy Verrill, with Richard Verrill (Dickie Bott) on Silver Line. The boat in the foreground was named 'City of Leeds'.

Plate 51. Margaret Burgess, Amateur c1937
Two of the last six cobles built in Staithes can be seen, with Matthew Verrill's, Star of Hope (WY174) to the right and Addison Verrills coble, Silver Line (WY184), loaded with many 'pots' to the left.

By 1965, Matthew Verrill senior, his son Matthew Verrill junior and his cousin Leonard Cole, were fishing in motorised coble WY 223, also named 'Star of Hope.' This coble was 31ft 6 inches in length and powered by a 34 horse power engine. They would be line fishing from November until Easter, when they would start potting for crabs and lobsters. They would haul in, up to 256 pots each morning, six days every week. The pots would then be cleared, re-baited, using fresh whiting and put back into the sea, in the grounds that generations of Verrills have used.

BILLIE BLACKWELL AND THE LAST FULL TIME WORKING COBLE

Billie was not born in Staithes, but he comes from a family with a fishing background, where his father fished on the Tees. When he first entered the village, he fished part-time in his first coble 'Pilot Me' (HL161), whilst working in the Ship Yard at Smiths Dock, South Bank and in c1969 he 'shipped' up with John Cole

His second coble was 'Pilot Me B' (WY 216), built by Jack Lowther of Whitby and with John Cole he went full-time fishing from c1975, through until c1991.

John 'retired' momentarily, around this time and Billie carried on until he sold his beloved coble in c2008, thus Staithes lost their last full time working coble WY216 at this time.

Plate 52a/b
Billy was never one to be idle, he could never give up boats completely and he is pictured here lending a hand to re-furbish 'Seaton Rose'.
Bill not only had fishing skills but he could also carry out a complete strip down, re-paint and the sign writing too.

Plate 52c
Billy Blackwell's coble, WY216- 'Pilot Me B', lies in the beck alongside Flora Jane (WY 251)

SECTION 4.0 – 'WHATS IN A NAME' (Part 1)

To the fishermen of Staithes, cobles were their greatest possession and their entire life depended on this Yorkshire craft.

The Staithes fishermen new every coble registration number of every coble to enter and leave Staithes and could recite number and owner and crew simultaneously.

The following is a list of Coble/Mule Registrations from 1903 – Present Day and most of these cobles, feature, somewhere in this book (vessels changed hands at various times and in some cases the boats were renamed/re-numbered and those with the same registrations represent different years of registration):

Coble Number	Coble Name
WY 3	Rose of England
WY 4	True Vine(Runswick)
WY 7	True Love
WY 12	Success
WY 14	Sunbeam
WY 15	W.E. Gladstone
WY 19	Crab Catcher
WY 22	Ellen
WY 23	Bretheren
WY 23	Lilian
WY 24	Thankful
WY 28	Brighter Hope
WY 30	Susannah
WY 32	Sanderson & William
WY 32	Bon Esperance
WY 34	Provider
WY 36	Margaret & Rose
WY 38	Honour
WY 52	Silver Jubilee
WY 58	Galilee
WY 60	Kittiwake
WY 63	Toiler of the Sea
WY 66	Gratitude
WY 67	Richard
WY 68	Safeguard
WY 72	Guide Me
WY 74	Nildesperandum
WY 76	Elizabeth Suzanna
WY 80	Good Tidings
WY 83	Polly
WY 83	Launch Out
WY 84	Mizpah
WY 87	Confidence
WY 88	Good Intent
WY 89	Endurance
WY 93	Osprey
WY 97	Venus
WY 99	Knight Commander
WY 101	Guiding Star
WY 108	Lizzie Robinson
WY 109	Breadwinner (boat)
WY 117	Freda
WY 123	Louise Becket
WY 123	Lillian
WY 125	Success
WY 130	Felicity
WY 133	Helena
WY 138	William
WY 138	Golden Hope
WY140	Love Devine
WY 142	Sarah
WY 146	Mizpah
WY 146	Mary & Jane
WY 147	Rebecca
WY 149	Love Divine
WY 151	Prosperity
WY 152	Amey Robinson
WY 155	Brothers
WY 162	Margaret & Elizabeth
WY 166	Endeavour
WY 168	Wavelet
WY 170	Minnie
WY 170	Frank & Elizabeth
173 WY	Sarah Margaret
WY 174	Star of Hope
175 WY	Mary Ann
WY 177	Star of Hope
WY 181	Thomas & Elizabeth
WY181	Edward Campbell
WY 183	Morning Light
WY184	Silver Line
WY185	Margarets
WY 185	Flora
WY 188	Lizzie Robinson
WY 190	Ocean View
WY 195	Faith
WY 197	Mary Anne
WY 198	Success
WY 200	June & Eileen
WY 206	Lizzie Robinson
WY 207	Embrace
WY 208	Jane
WY 209	Olive Branch
WY 211	Three Sisters
WY 212	Faith Hope & Charity
WY 216	Isobel
WY 216	Pilot Me-B
WY 218	Hugh Gilmour
WY 220	Phylis
WY 221	Ralph Thomas
WY 222	Two Sisters
WY 223	Annie Elizabeth
WY 223	Star of Hope(1965-1975)
227 WY	Lizzie
WY 227	Bold Robin Hood
WY228	Brotherly Love
WY 231	Thomas & Edward
WY 233	Confidence
WY 234	George
WY 235	Mars Hill
WY 237	Florrie
WY 242	Johns
WY 244	Ethel & Ada
WY 244	Providence
WY 244	Addison
WY 249	Johns
WY 250	Perseverance
WY 251	Confidence
WY 251	Flora Jane(boat)
WY 253	Mary's
WY 254	Dawn of Hope
WY 254	Mizpah
WY 257	Star of Hope
WY 258	Ethel-Aida
259 WY	Three Brothers
WY 261	Hannah Dawson
262 WY	Margaret Elizabeth
WY 264	Four Sisters
WY 267	Anchor of Hope
WY 274	Unity
WY 281	Thomas & Elizabeth
WY 282	Charity
WY 283	Chrysanthemum
WY 284	Friendship
WY 291	Peba
WY 310	Sea
WY 432	Brotherly Love
WY 479	William Clowes
WY 545	Primitive
WY 548	Penguin

What's in a name you might say, well in the case of Staithes yawls & cobles quite a lot actually, as they can reflect important information from the past regarding Staithes fishermen, Master Mariners, their family/loved one's or important events.

Boat Number	Boat Name	Owner/Master	House Name
WY 1	William Ash(yawl) #1	John Richard Verrill	Ash Cottage, High St
WY 3	Rose of England (yawl)	R. Theaker & J Horne	Rose of England Yard & Cottage, Gun Gutter
WY 35	The Felicity (yawl)	James Theaker	Felicity House, Church St
WY 146	Mizpah (coble)	E. Verrill	Mizpah Cottage, the Staith
WY 174	Star of Hope(coble)	Matthew Verrill	Star of Hope Cottage, Beckside to rear of Post Office (where Titch Verril & his sister Mary lived.
190 WY	Ocean View	-	Ocean View, the Staith
WY 216	Pilot Me (coble)	Billy Blackwell	Pilot Me Cottage, Granary Yard, Beckside
WY 251	Confidence(coble)	-	Confidence cottage, near Mann's Yard
WY 553	Truelove (yawl)	Richard Thompson	True Love Cottage, Slippery Hill
-	The Blue Jacket (yawl)	Joseph, then John Richard Verrill	Blue Jacket House, High St
-	The Ruby (yawl)	Richard Verrill	Ruby House, High St
-	Venus (yawl)	George Cole	Venus, High Street
WY 284	Friendship(coble)	Isaac Verrill	Friendship Cottage, Gun Gutter

#1 Eventually, sadly sold in Scarborough where it became SH 210

Plate 53. Rod Jewell, 2011
Local character Willie Wright, with his 'lines crossed', stood up, in his coble 'Mizpah', moored up on the Beckside. Willie reached 12.5 of a Millennium (80 years) during August, 2013 and a small family gathering was held in the Royal George Inn on the High Street, to mark this splendid occasion.

Plate 54

Mizpah is a type of emotional bond between two people separated, either physically or by the death of one of the persons.

Mizpah means - the Lord watch between me and thee when we are absent from one another.

Mizpah was first mentioned in the Bible in Genesis 31 to refer to one of several places in ancient Israel.

Plate 55a. T. Murphy
Willie and 'Mizpah'

Plate 55b. T. Murphy
Willie fettling with his favourite coble 'Mizpah'

Many of the house names give an obvious insight to their former use or position such as: Surgery House, Coast Guard House, Boiling House, The Granary, Primitive House, Alum Cottage, Harbourside, Harbour View, the Stables, High House, Coastguard Cottage, The Old Watch House, Captain Cook's cottage, Slip Top Cottage, etc

BOATS NAMED AFTER SPECIAL EVENTS OR PEOPLE

Boat Number	Boat Name	Owner/ Master	History behind the Name
WY 4	The Good Samaritan	George Longster	Biblical association
WY 15	William Ewart Gladstone	-	In honour of Gladstones visit to Staithes in 1871
WY 140	The Grand Old Man	-	In honour of Gladstones visit to Staithes in 1871
WY 78	Golden Crown	-	1953 QEII Coronation
WY 75	Coronation Queen	-	1953 QEII Coronation
WY 181	Edward Campbell	James Ward	Named after PM Minister coming to Staithes in 1887
WY 186	The Star of Bethlehem	J.W. Harrison	Associated with the Hymn
WY 224	Indian Prince	-	In honour of Maharajah Duleep Singh of Mulgrave Castle
WY 228	Brotherley Love	William Francis Verrill	Possibly associated with The Loyal Brotherley Love Lodge No.3781 of Oddfellows (Manchester Unity) formed in 1859 for Hinderwell & Staithes, but more likely just associated with the brothers Verrill
WY 242	William Mitchell	-	In honour of Rev William Mitchell (Congregationalist Minister)

Plate 56. FMS c1894

The famous Frank Meadow Sutcliffe photograph was in fact formally titled by Sutcliffe 'The Young Orthographer and his Grandfather'.

It was often referred to as 'The Spelling Lesson' where the sign writer got it wrong by missing out the 'p' in Campbell. Isaac Verrill('Lodney') in his trademark three quarter jacket, keeps a watchful eye on the young lad, son of William Francis Verrill (Billy Fanny) who points to the error. The coble WY181 was named after Edward Campbell the Primitive Methodist Minister who came to Staithes in 1887and lived on the High Street until c1891.

Whilst other boat names are related to family and loved one's or some other significance as follows:

Boat Number	Boat Name	Owner/Master	Name
-	Rachel(coble)	John Dawson, senior	After his wife Rachel (nee Ward)
WY 261	Hannah Dawson	John Dawson, junior (1858-1938)	After his sister
-	Thomas & Margaret	William Cole	After his son & mother
-	Cynthia (boat)	Alfred James	After his daughter
WY 200	June & Eileen	Matthew Verrill & Leonard Cole	After their respective daughters
WY 249	Johns	John Carling Cole	This was John's potting coble!
-	All My Sons	Sean Baxter	After the Arthur Miller play of 1947 & Sean's business involves his 2 sons.

Plate 57

The coble Louise Becket, arrived aboard the first Goods train, to stop at Staithes on the 26th December 1887.

George Verrill (Master) is pictured left, sitting on the coble Louise Becket (WY 123), with coble Sarah Margaret (173WY) behind, both cobles await the evening tide. Over the knee waders are evident and the centre fisherman, Richard 'West' Verrill, carries his 'Tommy Tin'(or Wow Tin), a purpose made tin to carry his 'pack-up', with Robert Longster (Bobby Hopper) (1869-1902) to his right, hence this photograph must pre-date 1902.

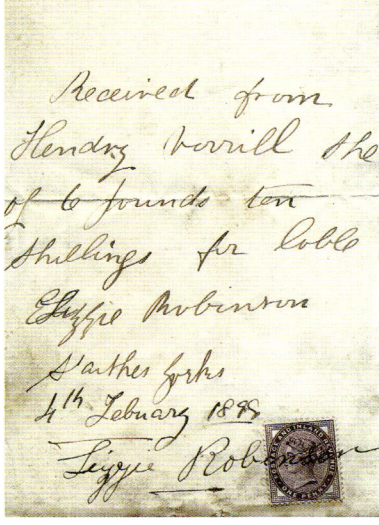

Plate 58

On the 4th February1899, Elizabeth (Lizzie) Robinson received the sum of six pounds ten shillings, from Hendry ('Enny') Verrill (1867-1937), for the sale of her coble Lizzie Robinson (WY188,) as shown in the signed receipt. This coble was one of three cobles, built from monies provided by Captain John Robinson of Balmoral House and Deacon of the Congregational Chapel. All three were named after his family members: Joseph Robinson, Amy Robinson (WY152, with Robert Longster as Master) & Lizzie Robinson (WY108). This philanthropic act was to assist Staithes fishermen, who found themselves on hard times.

'LOST' STAITHES STREET AND HOUSE NAMES

 Because house and street names can reflect important information, associated with Staithes history, it is important that these names are not changed (it should be made illegal!).

Some names already lost are as follows:

Back Road, ran from Bell's Bank at the back of the Bethel and 'The Stables' on Granary Yard, through to Staithes Bank emerging at 'Valley View' house. **Back Buildings** were here.

Beck Meetings & Keepers Cottage -

Taken in 1966 this is the meeting point of the two Becks and hidden in the trees, lies the old Keepers Cottage. This is the meeting point of Roxby and Easington Becks and flows through the deep narrow glen between the cliffs and eventually into the sea at the Beckmouth Staithes. James Cheetham was recorded as the gamekeeper at Beckmeetings in 1891, where he lived with his wife Hannah, fours sons and daughter

Coulthirst Slip – Fish Dealer, John Coulthirst in 1891 resided at No.11 Cowbar Bank, next door to Joe Ben Verrill, Staithes first coxswain and close to the lifeboat slipway. The slipway near Jane Wards Kipper House, at this time was referred to as Coulthirst Slip

Custom House, next to the old Post office and now called Lyn House, was a former Coastguard house..

Dawnas Row, Cowbar – was listed in the 1901 census immediately after the 24 Cowbar Cottages for the iron-stone miners and before the fourteen dwellings of Cowbar Bank. Tom Crake a fish seller lived at No.1 Dawnas Row, No.2 was uninhabited, with iron-stone miner James Armstrong, residing at No.3. Dawnas Row is believed to have been demolished to make way for the stone building where 'Crow's Nest' exists today.

Front Street was the former name for the south side of the High Street.

Glenhow Cottages, Church Street, early home to Vera Marsay

Golden Hill was an early crude sea defence, being the name given to the mound on the Staith near where the public toilets are today.

Gosforth House – was two doors up from the Bethel Chapel on the High Street and was the former six roomed home of Sarah Ann Nelson in 1911. Matthew Webster was a boarder here and he was recorded as a general dealer in the Rag Bone Industry. This is now named 'Meldene'.

Lavinia House, Bake House Top, home of Mary Jane Verrill, married to John Verrill (Fish Shop), they had a daughter called Lavinia.

New Houses – were situated on Church Stree and in 1911, Boulby iron-stone miner, Richard Porritt & family resided in this five roomed house and thought to possibly be Lyne Garth house (Lining Garth)

Seaton Square had 34 dwellings listed here in 1861 and eighteen in 1871 and the area would appear to cover Seaton Garth and also Gun Gutter, but the name has now been lost.

Silver Street – allegedly this was the name given to Granary Yard, but it is also thought to be the name for the lower bank off Bell's Bank leading down to Granary Yard.

Simpson's Road, ran from the base of Chapel Steps on Beckside to the nick leading to Simpson's Yard or Ruby House Yard.

Smugglers Den is accessed from Gun Gutter, up Waller's Steps adjacent to Friendship Cottage, towards High Barris, turning left at Barris View House and the steps there lead directly to Smugglers Den.

Sotherby's Passage – Mrs Sotherby was the fish frier down the nick close to Ruby House.

Tavistock House, So called as Richard Burn and Sarah Jane first brought their five daughters from Tavistock in Devon to Port Mulgrave in the late 1870's. By 1891 Sarah Jane was a widower with seven daughters and she set up her grocery & shopkeeper business on the south side of Staithes High Street at their new home Tavistock House (thought to now be either East View or East Lea).

The Studio – In 1911, Mary Ann Johnson resided at 'The Studio', which appears to have been a four roomed house, adjacent to the Royal George PH.

Tinker Hill, is the area near the Cod & Lobster and opens into Gun Gutter.

Wallers Steps also known as Gun Gutter Steps or Gutter Stairs, close to Friendship cottage in Gun Gutter..

White Horse former inn has been re-named 'The Whitehouse'!

It would be a great Heritage project if certain of the above were to receive a grant for the provision of some cast-iron style signs in order to 'mark the spot' to provide a future record of these important names.

SECTION 5.0 – FISHERMEN OF STAITHES:

A century or more ago there were in the region of 300 men in Staithes engaged in fishing, declining to around 100 by 1905. Some of the real old fishermen were: Thomas Brown, John Brown, Richard Pinder, Zachariah Trattles, Richard Unthank, William Truefit, Robert Verrill, John Trattles, Jacob Storm, Dick Thompson, James Fell and many more, too many to mention all.

Although not all fishermen were listed in the Directory's of the time, Staithes contained many eminent fishermen, to name but a few:

FISHERMEN			
Isaac/Luke Abraham	William Brown Harrison	Mason/Thomas Shippey	Edward/Henry Verrill
Mark/Ralph/Robert Brown	Francis Harrison	Francis Theaker	Isaac Verrill
Richard/William Brown	Charles Horne	George Thomas Theaker	John Richard Verrill
Joseph Brown	Joseph Jefferson	Isaac/James Theaker	John Verrill
Thomas/Zaccariah Burton	James/William Jefferson	James Abraham Theaker	Joseph Verrill
Burton Verrill Cole	George Gill	John Richard Theaker	Richard 'West' Verrill
Abraham/Daniel Cole	James Grimes	Mark/Matthew Theaker	Robert Verrill
John/George Cole	John Lawson	Ralph/Richard Theaker	Thomas Verrill
Richard/Thomas Cole	George/John Longster	Roger/Stephen Theaker	William Francis Verrill
Philip/William Cole	Richard/Robert Longster	Thomas Theaker	William Henry Verrill
Matthew Corner	John Manship	William Theaker	James/John Ward
Joseph Crispin	Nelson/Richard Porritt	Coates Thompson	George Ward
Isaac/John Crooks	Thomas/William Porrit	Joseph B Thompson	Richard/Robert Ward
Thomas Verrill Crooks	John/Matthew Robinson	George C Thompson	Thomas Ward
Robert/William Cummings	Simeon Robinson	William Thompson	William Ward
George Dawson	Ralph Sanderson	John Thurbeck	George Webster
John Dawson	William B Sanderson	Isaac/John/David Tose	John Webster
Isaac Ellis	James Sanderson	Joseph Tose	Edward Wise
John Fell	Edward Shippey	Richard Unthank	
James Grimes	Burton/George Shippey	Francis/William Unthank	
Isaac/John Harrison	John/Richard Shippey	Addison/Burton Verrill	

The 1891 records show that 14 year old boys were registered as fishermen and there were many instances of 12 year old's at sea with their fathers and grandfathers.

Several women are recorded as the 'head of the household' due to their husbands being absent at sea.

Mr George Pyman JP(1822-1900) was the founder of the steam shipping trade of the Hartlepools. He owned the first steamer built there and became one of the first Mayor's of Hartlepool and the Pyman Institute at Sandsend is a tribute to him. However it is little known that he started his working life as a simple fisherman in Staithes.

Many Staithes fishermen worked away from Staithes and their address was recorded as that of their vessel's name and their family members would be the crew e.g. Joseph Verrill, born c1856, was recorded in the 1881 census as an A B Seaman, residing at 'Good Intent', with a Civil Parish of 'vessels', with 47 others in the same 'household', including eight other Verrill's.

Mark Charles Palmer, opened the Fishermen's Institute in 1888 and in his opening speech he declared that "he knew of no more precarious life than that of the Staithes fishermen, there was not a more courageous or daring class of men. They exceed Seamen and they give the country cheap food".

These very pertinent writings of Richard of Raindale (Richard Addison), the Moorish bard, give an insight into the hardships of the Fishermen of Staithes.

An article published in 'The Times' on the 18th October 1881 gave news of a great tragedy in Staithes when 12 out of 16 fishing cobles, belonging to Staithes, were out between Middlesbrough and Whitby, during a late gale and all were believed to have been lost, with all hands. Thankfully this proved to be not the case as the cobles eventually all returned.

TITLED: A PEEP INTO STAITHES (1807)

"Nature, which nothing form'd in vain,
Has rous'd the sleeping muse again
To tell her works of curious art
Display'd at Staithes in every part.
Enclos'd by hills on every side,
Save where 'tis washed by the tide:
And there old Neptune's fiercest power
Threatens the natives to devour.
His waves, which terribly rebound,
Off tumble houses to the ground.

Here fishermen, a hardy race,
The greatest danger boldly face,
Early and late attention keep
To snare the wanderers of the deep,
And after toiling all the night,
Return again to land the freight;
While middle aged, old and young
Hail their approach with thankful tongue.
And soon as e'er they reach the land
Each freely lends a hand
To pull the cobles to the shore.

Of all who plough the raging sea
None venture for humanity
More than this race of hardy men,
In dangerous enterprises, when
Seas running high, like mountains roll,
Undaunted they the waves control,
And, double-mann'd, the coble push
Into the waves, and boldly rush
At hazard great, by strength of oar,
To bring the sufferers to the shore;
May heaven protect them evermore."

Plate 59. T. Butterworth Aug 1890
Photography does not get any better than this incredibly rare 1890 close up of four 'fisher' characters, sat at 'Slipway Top', adjacent to the Cod and Lobster Inn at Staithes. Undoubtedly there will be Verrills (top right certainly resembles Tom 'Parr' Verrill), Theakers, Coles, Porritts or Unthanks here and each man has a different pattern to their gansey's, but each is synonymous with Staithes. The large split fish are hung out to dry, on both railings and cast iron winch, used for hauling the cobles up the slipway.

Other photographs exist, when this old slipway was used in earnest, showing over 25 women and children watching the Staithes fishermen rowing out to sea.

Behind the railings lies the area known as New Landing and the high sea wall, protecting the area known as Gar'Ends (Garth Ends) and close inspection shows a hoist existed here to lift up the cobles from the beach area.

Plate 60. George Washington Wilson c1900

'Oilslops' or Oilskins and Southwesters, are the order of the day on this wet and windy day. Where approximately 10 or so cobles including , 'Ellen' (22 WY) and 'Providence' of Whitby, with its name inscribed on the scudguard, can be seen on the scaurs; when the fleet returned safely into Staithes. The soaking wet boots and the lone fisherwoman, top right, re-inforce that the cobles have just returned into Staithes scaurs. The coble 'Providence' was approximately nine years away from a disaster. As on a Thursday morning in November 1909, it sailed out of Whitby harbour to haul it's lines, which were shot off Sandsend Ness. In the coble were Thomas (Tommy) Hutchinson, his 17 year old son Joseph and David Forden also 17. A fierce gale sprang up and they headed for Runswick, being unable to make it back to Whitby, however the winds were too strong and they were blown towards Skinningrove and were spotted off Staithes the next morning. Tommy, son and friend were in the storm for 25 hours without food or water. Joseph unfortunately died of exhaustion and lack of nourishment.

Plate 61. c1904

Titled 'Three Generations', this view was produced by Raphael Tuck & Sons and sold as part of their 'Picturesque Yorkshire', Oillette, N.E.Coast series No. 7557 of coloured postcards and offered for sale during 1904. The scene is taken from 'Yorkshire, Coast & Moorland Scenes by Gordon Home'.

The message printed on the back states: "This is a typical group of Staithes fishermen:- grandfather, father and t' youngest bairn, sitting in their boat the coble, which, differing only in size and colour, is used by every fisherman along the Yorkshire coast. The Staithes men are known up and down the east coast of Great Britain, as some of the very finest fishermen that sail the seas"

Boys had to grow up quickly and James Cole (1895-1975) went to sea at the age of 12, sailing with his father and grandfather on the 'Venus'.

Plate 62. Britain & Wright c1906

Three local fishermen are overhauling their nets, at the Beckside (south) opposite the cottages near to the foot of Cowbar Bank.

All three are wearing the typical Staithes fisherman's smock jacket, the man on the left, smoking from his pipe is Tom 'Parr' Verrill. The cottages in the background were eventually rendered, covering up the fine hand hewn stonework. Francis (Frank) Unthank lived in the right hand cottage prior to the coble 'Knight Commander' disaster of 1899 when he and his two sons, Billy and Frank were drowned.

Plate 63. T. Butterworth, 1890

Local characters were plentiful and this sea hardened veteran, leaning on his flat sterned boat at Beckmouth, looks as if he would have plenty of stories to tell about the hard life as a working fisherman in Staithes. He is wearing a pair of 'warnie britches'(oilskin trousers).

Plate 64. Margaret Burgess, Amateur 1937

Willie Verrill returning across the shaley beach, from a fishing trip in motorised coble 'Freda' (WY 117), can be seen carrying one of his four bowed pots and fuel can, alongside him is Richard Dewsbury Verrill (known as Dickie Bott) complete with second fuel can.

Plate 65. Butterworth c1896

This is one of the finest social history photographs of Staithes, where it is all 'hands to the pump,' as women, children and the fishermen all busy themselves with a variety of tasks, as they unload the days catch from several cobles including WY450. All but a small boy out of 25 people, are wearing some sort of hat, including deerstalker, school style cap, Russian style seal skin cap (hairy hat), Sou'wester, Staithes bonnet to a tall style bowler hat, in this busy seafront scene, taken from an 1890's magic lantern slide. Some of the nine or so lads are barely 9 years old!

The fisherman in the seal skin cap was painted by Laura Knight, in her canvas titled 'The Old Bridge' and is thought to be Richard Verrill.

The portly fisherman in the right hand coble, complete with tall bowler hat, looks to be a character, as he draws on his pipe.

Plate 66. Margaret Burgess, Amateur 1937

Four Verrill's for the price of one! in this photograph of the 'more recent' Verrill fishermen, gathered together outside 'Ocean View,' on Seaton Garth, where James Clemence James, Clerk to the NE Fisheries and Staithes Harbour Committee lived.

Visitors are fascinated by the four fishermen and especially the fish . The fishermen in their signature smock jackets, from left to right are: Francis Verrill (Frankie Titty), his son Willie Verrill, Bill Verrill & Jake Verrill.

Plate 67. Hartman c1907

The photographer has captured 17 fishermen & boys together with two fisher women and a lass in this photograph titled 'Preparing for the Fishing Grounds', Staithes. Each of the fishermen gathered round the coble has their own unique identity, through their different style of cap/hat. Several guide posts are evident behind the coble. The rudder and tiller, along with nets are strewn upon the beach, whilst some sort of emergency repair work is undertaken by the joiner in the shirt and braces.

Note the woman left, heavily draped in fishing nets, as she waits for the repair to be completed.

Plate 68. Credited to H.C.Morley

This is a large crab table in the cramped yard within Gun Gutter, to the rear of Captain Cooks cottage, close to Bramla Cottage. The message penned in 1906, to the reverse side, reads;'Fetch cap George,similar to the other. Coble launch today(Mon). Two painters on at Hopwoods Store, plans passed but not out for tender as yet. Willis plans passed, not commenced operations yet. A.F. off today Monday, sail Tues. Fetch your bike lamp if you will need it. Pleased to see you, Hope you are well, John W.' This was addressed to George Ward in North Ormesby.

The young fisher couple and their delightful son present a great picture of life at the beginning of the 20thC.

The initials 'GP' on the fish barrels are thought to be a reference to George Porritt

There was considerable status in receiving the title of fisherman and initial years meant young boys had to spend time in an unofficial 'style apprenticeship', learning their trade, from fathers, grandfathers and other family members. Many of the Staithes fishermen spent their fishing years on a variety of vessels, doing a variety of jobs and it is worthy that the fishing years of Francis Verrill are recorded, as they give a great insight into the role and life of a Staithes Fisherman, as follows:

FRANCIS VERRILL - HIS LIFE AT SEA:

Boat Name	Boat No.	Type	Owner	Job	Years
William Clowes	WY89	Yawl	J.Fell	Cabin Boy	1868-1869
Princess Royal	WY90	Yawl	I.Verrill	Warp Coiler	1870-1876
Prosperity	WY91	Yawl	J.Cole	Fisherman	1876-1892
Confidence	WY87	Yawl	R.Cole	Fisherman	1893-1896
Anns	WY93	Yawl	R.Shippey	Fisherman	1897-1899
Penguin	WY548	Sailing coble	JR Theaker	Fisherman	1900-1901
Guiding Star	WY101	Sailing coble	G.Webster	Fisherman	1902-1903
Brotherly Love	WY432	Sailing coble	WF Verrill	Fisherman	1904-1905
Brotherly Love	WY228	Sailing coble	WF Verrill	Fisherman	1906-1912
Brothers	WY155	Sailing coble	WF Verrill	Fisherman	1913-1914
Bretheren	WY23	Sailing coble	F.Verrill	Fisherman	1915-1918
Girl Rhoda	WY78	Steam Drifter	Rawcliffe	Fishing Co.	Fisherman
Lilian	WY23	Motor coble	T Spencer	Fisherman	1923-1930
Freda	WY117	Motor coble	F Judge	Fisherman	1931-1936

Fisherman Francis was born c1857, the son of fisherman Francis senior and Jane Verrill and he was one of 3 sons and he had 3 sisters, one of whom was Kittawer Verrill.

'Frankie Titty' as he was widely known, was recorded as single in 1881, but by 1891 he was a widower with a four year old daughter Sarah Jane. He later married again, to Margaret Ann (nee Harrison) and they had a further 3 daughters, Esther, Margaret Ann (Meggie) & Lily plus two sons Francis & William Verrill.

It was 8 years after he first started as a cabin boy, before Francis Verrill was able to use the title 'Fisherman' and he spent 10 years fishing with his brother 'Billie Fanny' Verrill, from 1904-1914.

It was 47 years after he started as a Cabin Boy, before Frank Verrill stopped working for others and used his own boat 'Bretheren'in his own right.

All in all, his fishing career spanned 68 years man and boy.

STAITHES LAST REMAINING 'HOME GROWN' FISHERMAN

Plate 69. Tony Murphy

Dave Hanson has the honour of being the only person born in Staithes, who is classed as a full time fisherman. Both David's father and grandfather were full time fishermen too.

Dave Hanson (above) is pictured at work with his regular mate John Cole, all set to go 'potting' for crabs and lobsters.

Between the two of them they know everything there is to know about 'potting' and they are both passing their skills and knowledge onto Dave's son Darren.

Plate 70. Tony Murphy
An excellent close up of Dave Hanson onboard his boat 'Semira' (Hebrew girls name meaning 'From Heaven')

SECTION 6.0 – WHATS IN A NAME (PART 2) – ORIGIN OF STAITHES FAMILIES SURNAME

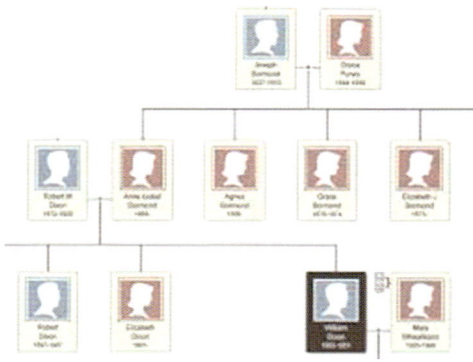

The lineage of the Staithes Fishermen families, such as the Coles, Porritts, Longsters, Theakers, Trattles, Unthanks and Verrills etc is extremely difficult to substantiate, because so many sons had the same forename as their fathers and due to inter-marriages, they often contained two second names

Cole – generally accepted as having English and Irish origins and possibly derived from 'cola' meaning black or from the Old English 'col' meaning coal, and once used to describe people of a swarthy appearance.

Porritt – has French origins, with variant spellings and derived from the French male Pierre a cognate of Peter, from the Greek Petros, the masculine form of petra meaning 'rock'. Porritts date back to 1626. The Porritt's stronghold in Staithes, was in Gun Gutter and Weatherill Street.

Theaker – has Norse origins – name for a Thatcher and the old village of Staithes had many thatched houses prior to 1890. (In the 1891 census, at least 77 Theakers were recorded and in the 1901 census 81 Theakers were listed as residing in Staithes & most of the men if not all were recorded as fishermen). During the 100 years between 1800-1900 the Theakers resided in dwellings all over Staithes including: Barris/BarrisTop (this was their stronghold, with at least 7 dwellings), Slip Top, Webster's Steps, Gun Gutter, Church Street, Main Street and 'The Village' – all of the Theakers recorded in 1881 were born in Staithes.

Trattles – at one time the Trattles dominated the trade in Staithes, it is alleged that this name may have come to the shores of England from Denmark and the Trattles families were predominantly in the NE of England, specifically in the parish of Hinderwell during the 1600's. The name has alleged links with bowmen and woodworkers. John Trattles (c1794-1887) was a ship owner & founder trustee of Staithes new Wesleyan Chapel in 1865. Whilst John Trattles(c1815-1883) was a renowned Master Mariner, as was his son also John Trattles (c1850-1923) and his son Matthew Trattles was the Staithes chemist/druggist on the High Street.

John Trattles Cole was a renowned Staithes joiner/boat builder.

Unthank – This unusual name originates from Cumbria where two villages exist with this name, there is a third in Northumberland. The Unthank's held a family seat in Cumberland during ancient times before and after the Norman Conquest in 1066. The Unthank's of Staithes were predominantly fishermen.

Verrill – Thought to be of French origins, possibly from ship wrecked French sailors from the Napoleonic period. The name is linked with French baby boys names and has alleged links with being true, loyal and masculine.

However according to the scholar Elsdon C. Smith, the English surname Verrill and its varients Verrall, Verrell(e) and Ferrall, are predominantly found in East Sussex. It is derived from the first name of the father of the initial bearer, indicating 'son of verrill', an ancient personal name of uncertain origin; possibly derived from the latin 'vere', meaning 'true'

In 1651 the first recorded member of the Verrill family Anna Verrill is captured in an early baptism register. Dinah the daughter of John Verrill is recorded in baptism records for Whitby in 1798 and Harrison Verrill, son of William and Esther, was christened in Hinderwell in 1828. The marriage of Francis Verrill and Jane Kirby is recorded in the same church for November 1839. The Verrill families provided the backbone of the fishing trade within Staithes and also during the 1860's/1870's many Verrill's were ironstone miners.

There were of course several other well established fisher folk families in Staithes such as the Crooks, Harrisons, Browns, Lavericks, Wards, Longsters, Thompsons, Jeffersons, Shippey's, Truefits, etc

THE STAITHES BOAT BUILDER'S THOMAS RODHAM (1st. 2nd & 3rd)

The initial Staithes Boat Builder was Michael Rodham (c1770-1817) born in Staithes. He married three times and the 1st boat builder with the infamous name of Thomas Rodham (1787-1817) came from his 3rd marriage to Adilinah Adamson.

The 1st, Thomas Rodham (1787-1866), married to Hannah Trattles lived on Main Street, Staithes, adjacent to his first son also Thomas Rodham (1815-1895), where in 1841 they were both recorded as joiners. Thomas/Hannah were recorded as having a daughter Jane and another son George and they also had a 74 year old joiners apprentice named John Hicks living with them (I wonder when he came out of his time!) By 1861 both Thomas's were recorded as boat builders.

The 2nd Thomas Rodham (c1815-1895), was recorded as a boat builder from 1861, through to his retirement in c1891 at the age of 76. He initially married Eleanor Laverick and they had a daughter Mary Hannah Rodham, born in 1839. They went on to have a son also Thomas who was born in 1847, the year of Eleanor's unfortunate death. Thomas went on to marry Jane Crossley and they produced a further daughter Mary Jane Rodham.

The 3rd boat builder, Thomas Rodham (1847-1890) was married initially to Sarah Ann Sanderson and they had two children; Thomas Rodham and Ralph Sanderson Rodham. Several years after Sarah's untimely death at the age of only 28, Thomas was re-married to Ann Elizabeth (nee Robinson) and they had three further children; Eleanor Rodham, Mary Jane Rodham and Sibbel Smales Rodham.

From an early age he worked in wood and was first recorded as a joiner in Staithes, at the age of 23 and Thomas soon branched out to be a boat builder of some repute, akin to his father. Thomas's life was short lived and he died in October 1890 at the age of 44 years.

His son Thomas (the 4th born c1867) obtained his 2nd & 1st Mate certificates in 1890 & 1892 respectively and his Master Mariner certificate in 1894. Sibbel Smales Rodham went on to marry Albert Bell from Dalehouse and they lived together initially at Dalehouse in Fern Cottage and later at 'Belmont' on Bell's Bank. After Thomas (the 2nd) death in 1895, the old Rodham's boat building yard off Chapel Yard, gradually fell into disrepute, with the buildings becoming derelict. All was cleared when the Co-operative society bought the land for their new store.

The cabinet photographs, below, were taken by Henry.C.Morley of Staithes and John T. Ross of Whitby The photograph of Eleanor was taken on November 3rd 1902, when she was 23 years old.

Plate 71. JT Ross 1906
Ross has recorded the new Co-operative store buildings, under construction in 1906, utilising the site of the former Rodham's Boatyard as pictured right.

Plate 72a
Ann Elizabeth Rodham, (Thomas's widow) Born c1846

Plate 72b
Sibbel Smailes Rodham, (3rd daughter) Born 14th December 1883

Plate 72c
Mary Jane Rodham, Born 29th January 1881 (2nd daughter)

Plate 72d
Eleanor Rodham, Born 9th August 1879 (1st daughter)

STAITHES NAMES & NICKNAMES

For well over 130 years now, Staithes fishermen have used nicknames, often to differentiate between family members with the same forename. It was commonplace for boys to receive their fathers name and the Verrill families of Staithes were the most prolific family to apportion nicknames.

Some nicknames were given in order to shorten the number of words used, whilst other nicknames were merely a corruption of first & second names or based on their chosen profession e.g. John Henry Roe was nicknamed 'Jack ta' Barber' on account of cutting hair as well as running a General Mason's shop, whilst his wife was known as 'Marthan', a corruption of Martha Ann.

The Verrill family are allegedly descended from Frenchmen, fleeing from persecution and marrying Staithes brides. The Verrill family have a long established tradition of nicknames, some of them quite risque' at the time! Today there are very few Verrill's left in Staithes, but the French-Yorkshire seed has been set far and wide.

The 1881 census records four Thomas Verrill's, the 1891 census shows us that there were five Edward Verrill's in Staithes at that time, whilst the 1911 census records five Richard Verrill's and ten John Verrill's residing in Staithes! A few of these nicknames are listed right.

The list is not exhaustive, but suffices to show how necessary nicknames were for the Verrills of Staithes. Kitling means young kitten or whelp, hence name probably given to show that John Verrill was the youngest

Real Name	Nickname
Isaac Verrill	'Lodney'
Isaac Brown Verrill	'Argy'
Joseph Verrill	Joe 'Ben'
John Richard Verrill	'Podgy'
John Richard Verrill	'Kebbin'
William Francis Verrill	'Billie Fanny'
Richard Dewsbury Verrill	'Dickie Bott'
Thomas Verrill	Tom 'Parr'
Frank Verrill	'Tange'
Jack Verrill	'Caggy'
John Verrill	'Kitling'
Matthew Verrill	'Matty Barney' or 'Loiny'
Tommy Verrill	'Talking Tommy'
Thomas Verrill	'Tom Captain'
Thomas Verrill	'Tommy Winner'
John Verrill	'Nagg'
Richard Verrill	'West'
Richard Verrill	'Boorly Dick'
Richard Verrill	'Titch' or 'Cabbish'
Richard Verrill	'Ranter Dickie'
Richard Verrill	'Leaholm'
Robert Verrill	'Little Bob'
William H. Verrill	'Billie'
William Henry Verrill	'Enny'
William Verrill	'Bushy'
Francis Verrill	'Frankie Titty'
Edward (Ned) Verrill	'Chicken'
Edward Verrill	'Ikers Ted'
Edward Verrill	'Fishy' or 'Teddy' or 'Neddy'
Jimmy Verrill	'Dutch'
Isaac Verrill	'Spink'
Lavinia Verrill	'Luvvy'
Mary Ann Verrill	'Polly Spink'
Margaret Ward Verrill	'Margit'
Patience Ward	'Paashy'
Ken Verrill	'Kenny Boy'

in the pack! The meaning of some of the others, are possibly best left out of this book!

Many Christian names within Staithes have completely died out (not surprising!): Sabena, Indiana (there were x3 within Staithes & Hinderwell), Zipporah, Zebedee, Zaccariah, Lavinia, Octavia, Poppy, Fanny, Valentine, Mercy, Beatrice, Burton, Newark etc.

There was a Russian connection in Staithes when Master Mariner Thomas Spink married his Russian bride Natalia in 1873, when she was 22 years of age. They went on to have six children together, where one daughter carried on a Staithes tradition of also being named Natalia. By 1901 they moved to Saltburn. Other nicknames, known to exist or to have existed are as follows: Robert Longster (Bobby

Hopper), Richard Cole (Crampton), Richard Porritt (Nelse Dick), Alice Harrison (Auld Aunt Ailsie), Alan Fawcett (Snapper), Andrew Manship (Munch), John Hudson (Bam Bam), Alan Young (Big Al) and many more.

At one time the local inhabitants of Staithes were nicknamed 'Ringers', on account of the lack of water closets, they had to squat on buckets and over the years this left it's mark! The contents of which were tipped into the sea at Scar Shootings, the polite name for 'Sky Shitings'.

A century or so ago it was unthinkable for Staithes people to marry outside the village and the close knit intermarriages often led to the bride and groom carrying the same family name. It is now considered 'posh' to have a double barrelled name, not so in Staithes, as this became a necessity!

The following are just a few early examples: Trattles-Cole, Cole-Theaker, Coates-Crooks, Cole-Harrison, Cole-Thompson, Brown-Verrill, Brown-Cole, Verrill-Beswick, Verrill-Manship, Verrill-Dunn, Weatherill-Verrill, Cole-Featherstone, Harrison-Featherstone, Fell-Verrill, Marker-Verrill, Ward-Verrill, Brown-Weatherill, Theaker-Weatherill, Rodham-Laverick, Rodham-Murdin, Trattles-Smales, Rodham-Smales, Longster-Porritt, Hansell-Bennison, Grimes-Dawson, Laverick-Hugill, Harrison-Stonehouse, Spink-Dix, Bennison-Conn, Hansell-Bennison, etc

The tradition has carried on more recently leading to: Verrill-Armstrong, Sanderson-Verrill, Longster-Laverick, Crispin-Cole, Weatherill-Cole, thus keeping some of the really early and important names from Staithes from dying out completely (thankfully there were no Verrill-Verrill's!).

William Francis Verrill (1847-1935)

Plate 73
Complete with cork life jacket, this was William Francis Verrill aka 'Billie Fanny,' when he was a lifeboat man in the late 1870's. He was Great Grandfather to well known and loved, Staithes lady, Eileen Huby (of Family History fame). Billie found fame many times during his life and none more so than the incident of 13th July 1916. Billie and his crew (Francis & Jacob Verrill) were fishing in coble 'Success', when a German U-Boat surfaced. They were ordered to stop fishing and their nets were cut away on the orders of Oberleutenant Werner Furbringer. Other cobles involved were the 'Mary Anne' which was sunk by German sailors, smashing her with heavy hammers and the 'Richard' which escaped unscathed. The crew of these two latter cobles were ordered onto the 'Success'. The U-Boat (UB39) then struck a purposeful glancing blow to the 'Success' and Billie Fanny sustained a substantial injury. To know the fate of Billie, his crew & the crew of the other two cobles and the role of the 'Venus', you will have to read John Howard's excellent book, William Francis Verrill of Staithes and the German U-Boat, published in 2006, shortly before John sadly died.

Plate 74
Isaac Verril (1811-1895) married Susannah Verril on 2nd October 1836, at Hinderwell Church (Susannah's maiden name was Verrill, so we nearly had a Verrill-Verrill!)
Isaac's parents were Richard Verrill (1779-1859) and Ann Smales (1783-1851).
This photograph of Isaac 'Lodney' with his trademark long clay pipe is credited to Frank Meadow Sutcliffe.

SECTION 7.0 – SMOCK JACKETS

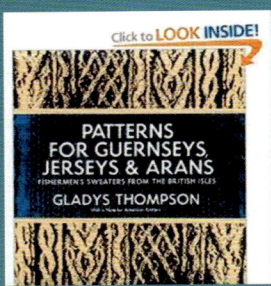  

The traditional Staithes smock jacket, was a blue knitted jersey (unlike now a days, it was never referred to as a gansey!), this was a work garment for fishermen to wear at sea and was often the only top garment they wore, apart from oilskins ('langslops & shurtslops, with warnie britches & westers'). The wool used was often a four ply worsted for strength, durability and to withstand a certain amount of water. They were usually knitted in the round, casting on evenly over three needles and using a forth needle to work with, however it is stated that the real traditional Staithes method was to use five steel needles. The smock jacket was made from a single strand of yarn, without seams. For years the pattern of the smock jackets were synonomous and often unique to each village. Thus enabling identification of a fisherman's origin, however this was not perpetuated as the modern knitter adopted the easier two needle method and patterns and techniques became diffused along the coast.

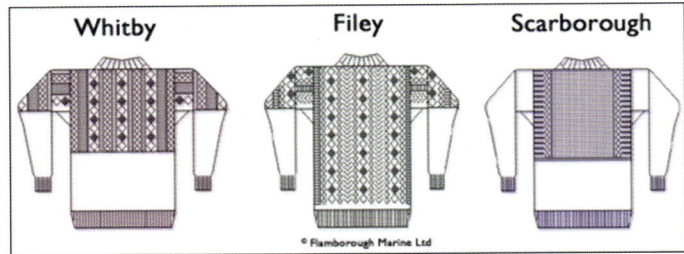

It takes around six weeks to knit a gansey by hand. They were usually made by mothers, wives and sweethearts and the patterns were passed down the generations via word of mouth - they weren't written down. The ganseys are knitted without seams, all in one piece on five or more small needles using very fine, hardwearing four or five ply wool. They are knitted very tightly to make them weatherpoof. The tighter the knitting, the more water and weatherproof it is. The pattern is concentrated round the upper body for extra warmth and thickness.

Gansies were worn next to the skin with nothing underneath. A pure silk scarf was often worn around the neck to stop the wet wool chaffing the skin. Fishermen wore their gansies all the time and even had a 'Sunday best' specially for chapel. Young women often knitted their intended husband a 'wedding shirt' gansey to get married in.

Plate 75. H.C. Morley

The old Staithes design, was mostly plain with two, three or four cables at the arm edge to hold the smock jacket in shape.

Patterns were developed by Gladys Thompson, Mrs Manship, Mrs Verrill and Mrs Dix but there must have been so many more.

Certain patterns were not only appertaining to the village of Staithes but also to families, such as the Coles, Verrills etc who adapted patterns that were synonomous with their family, with small variations to the standard patterns. Tragically many Staithes fishermen were lost at sea during severe storms and it is alleged that they could be returned to their village of origin, through the recognition of the village pattern. This will have been true, some of the time!

It was actually, common practice to sew in some form of identification, in case the fishermen were lost at sea.

Plate 76. T. Butterworth

Two very basic traditional Staithes smock jackets are portrayed right, from the 1890's, where ribbed shoulder straps and further ribbing each side of the armholes and cuffs are evident. However all three are different in several ways, possibly due to family traditions, where the patterns are handed down from previous generations, or maybe they just liked to be different. Photographs support this to be the staple pattern within Staithes from 1880-1930's, but as stated previously there were several variations on the theme.

Plate 77

Vertical panels of double moss and cable, not dissimilar to the pattern known as Mrs Manship's pattern, can be seen left where the fisherman Tom 'Parr' Verrill, repairs his pots, outside his home 'Mizpah' on Seaton Garth close to the foot of Penny Nab. This pattern stops halfway across the chest and arms. The fisherwomen of Staithes were prolific knitters, their hands were never idle.

Plate 78. Margaret Burgess, Amateur c1937

This group from left to right are: Francis Verril, with his fedora, Jake Verrill, Willy Verrill & George Willie (Bill) Verrill.

Willy Verrill, the fisherman second from the right wears a smock jacket with a vertical pattern, similar to that of the previous photograph e.g. Mrs Manship pattern, with vertical panels of double moss and cable, but with the pattern only half way down the chest and arms, with a higher neck. This group are standing on the Staith close to Clem James house, 'Ocean View'.

Plate 79a   **Plate 79b**   **Plate 79c**

Staithes fisherman, William Henry 'Enny Verrill (1867-1937) had at least three different smock jackets. In the left hand studio portrait, his smock jacket has much thicker vertical cabling, again the pattern finishes half way down the chest and arms. Whilst in the centre photograph, he wears his 'working gansey', which has the horizontal bands of pattern, representing the pattern known as the ridge and furrow, along with a different neckline. It has been suggested that the gansey had a horizontal pattern which represents birds eyes, separated by narrow bands of knit two rows, purl two rows. The ridge and furrow representing a ploughed field. However this was not the common pattern found in Staithes. Pictured later in life 'Enny wears a more traditional smock jacket along with his trademark fedora.

A lot of 'poppycock' is spoken about smock jacket (gansey) patterns and some of the information has to be taken with a pinch of salt. Many different patterns actually existed, as can be seen right on the fisherman sitting left, near the Cod & Lobster. The wide cabling comes from the top of the shoulder to halfway down the back, but in the main early Staithes patterns were simple with little decorative pattern, as shown on the young Staithes lads centre and to the right; this was considered to be the staple pattern for Staithes.

Nowadays there are many yarns spun about fisherman's smock jackets and the myth that every man in Staithes wore a 'gansey' synonomous with Staithes is probably untrue, as individual's demanded an individual pattern.

Plate 80a **Plate 80b** **Plate 80c**

Plate 81

There is always an exception to every rule! – This early photograph of Edward Verrill ('Ikers Ted'), son of Jake Verrill shows a very strong cabling in 4 rows to the shoulders and arm holes, very different to anything seen so far.

Plate 82. Butterworth 1897

This weather beaten veteran, who's eyes appear almost shut, sports a knitted jersey with several 'darn holes' and no doubt this would have to last a little longer before it was replaced!.

Plate 83 **Plate 84**

Traditional Staithes smock jacket, with thicker ribbing in 6 rows as worn by Francis Verrill (bottom left) in c1937.

Fishermen often had at least two smock jackets, one for work and one for Sunday best, where they would add a fine touch by wearing a white silk scarf inside the neck of the smock jacket.

Isaac Brown ('Argy') Verrill (bottom right), married Sarah Ann Theaker and was the father of 'Enny' Verrill who married Patience Ward and 'Argy' again wears the typical Staithes pattern, similar to those, seen previously, but the decorative ribbing is finer in 12 rows. 'Argy' Verrill (1840-1909), befriended Laura Knight during her early years in Staithes and she often visited his house in Gun Gutter.

SECTION 8.0 – MASTER MARINERS

From the mid19th Century to the early 20th Century Staithes could boast 130 Master Mariners.

By an order of 1845, the Board of Trade authorised a system of voluntary examinations of competency, for men intending to become masters or mates of foreign going British merchant ships. The system was made compulsory, by the Mercantile Marine Act of 1850 and extended to masters and mates of home trade vessels, by the Merchant Shipping Act of 1854. A masters or mates certificate of competency, was issued to each man who passed the examination. Men who were considered by examiners, to have sufficient experience as a master or mate were eligible, without formal examination, for certificates of service. Lloyd's Captains Registers give details of the careers of captains and mates of merchant ships between 1869 and 1947.

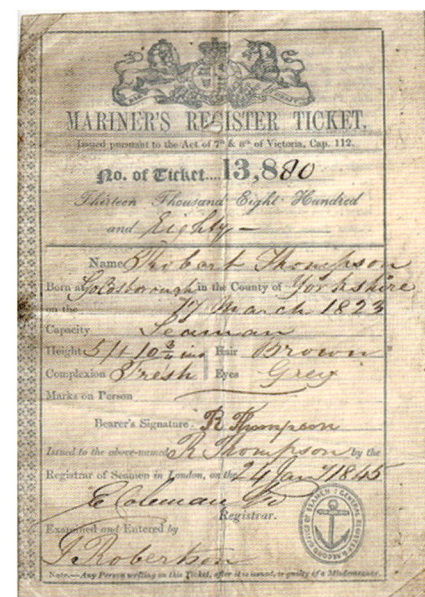

Plate 85a. 1845

Plate 85b

Each of the Master Mariner's had to gain their 'Ticket,' after thorough training & examination or experience and peer mentorship from father's/grandfather's/other Mariner's. The ticket's were issued from the Central Register & Record Office of Seamen, in London. The one (left) is for Seaman Robert Thompson of Goldsborough, where he was registered as Number 13,880 on 24th January 1845.

'Any person writing on this ticket after it is served is guilty of a Misdemeanour'

Thomas Spink of Staithes gained the following certificates;
1870 at the age of 19 – Second Mate certificate
1871 at the age of 20 - 'Only Mate' certificate
1874 at the age of 23 - 'Master' certificate

You only have to visit Hinderwell Cemetry to see the gravestones of past Master Mariners and many of the Master Mariners grave stones bear the 'Anchor' symbol

Various Staithes men are recorded as seamen or mariners, neither of which are compatible with the competency of Master Mariner.

Captain George Delaval of York House was a Sea Apprentice at 16 and gained his masters certificate in 1872. George was the son of John Laverick a shipowner and postmaster at the Postal & Telegraph Office on the High Street (now the Gallery)

There was also another George Delaval Laverick (c1825-1903) who was a Master Mariner and he had a son also called George Delaval Laverick, who was a joiner, born in 1861

Shown right is a list of known Staithes Master Mariner's:

John Richard Verrill (45) was the Master of the 'William Ash' and his crew of able seamen on board on the night of 3rd April 1881, consisted of: Francis Verrill (51), John Verrill (25), Thomas Ward (33), Robert Douglas (32), John G Verrill (25), William J Verrill (22) and Ralph T Verrill (18), all but Douglas were from Staithes.

Thomas Rodham (1847-1890), gained the following certificates:
1890, 2nd mate Certificate
1892, 1st mate Certificate
1894 Master Mariner's Certificate

EARLY MASTER MARINER's	LATER MASTER MARINER's
Thomas Adamson	Simon Clark
William Adamson	Isaac Cooper
William Armstrong	George Delaval Laverick (1845-1924) – York House
John Verrill Beswick	James Pinder (1841-1913) – Prospect House
Joseph Brown (1),	John Joseph. Robinson (1846-1892), Balmoral House
Joseph Brown (2)	Joseph Robinson (1875-1939)
Matthew Brown	Thomas Rodham Laverick
William Burton	Richard Seymour (buried in Easington)
John Campion	George Shippey
John Cole	Thomas Spink (1851-1899)
Thomas Cole	Edward Theaker – Felicity House
William Galilee	James Theaker
Tom Hall	Richard Thompson (1845-1880), Fern Dale House
Joseph Hodgson	William George Thompson – (1852-1927)
George Daleval Laverick(b1825)	Frederick William Thompson
Thomas Rodham Laverick	George Thurbeck
George Longster	John Trattles jnr. (1851-1923) – Roraima House
George Mann	John Trattles Sanderson (1854-1907)
Ralph Sanderson	Matthew Trattles
John Seymour	William Trattles
Richard Seymour	Addison Verrill (1870-1948)
Francis Unthank Taylor	Edward Verrill (1907-1978)
George Thompson	John Richard Verrill (born1896)-
Richard Thompson	Richard Verrill (1839-1890)
John Trattles snr.(c1815-1883)	William Brown Verrill (1891-
Matthew Trattles	John Waller (1849-1912)) – Glen View House
William Truefitt	
Robert Unthank	
Addison Verrill	
Richard Verrill	
Zebedee Verrill	
John Welford	

SECTION 9.0 – THE 'STAITHES PARLIAMENT'

The local Staithes fishermen have made the Cod & Lobster Inn a focal point for many years, gathering here, to share tales of their time at sea, the dangers, the tragedies, problems with their boats, the size of their catches and of course the weather!

Taken from the 1891 book, 'Yorkshire by the Sea' by George Radford, the following observations by Walter Beasant are relevant:

'The men lounged on the Staith, talking all day, if it was fine and not too cold –no Neopolitans could seem lazier, but they are not lazy, they are resting. An hour after midnight, they will be on board their craft, outward bound for the German Ocean. They are not lazy, but ashore, they love to sit and stand together all day long, exchanging few words, where the waves wash the beach and where they scent the fragrance of the fish lying on the shingle and where they can keep an eye upon the open and watch ships'.

There are but a few locals left to form the 'Staithes Parliament', but those who used to fish and those that still do fish, often meet on one of the benches, near the Cod & Lobster or on the Staith to discuss their boats, sea-trips from the past, lost friends, the weather and of course their current ailments! Two such stalwarts are Billy Blackwell (Pilot Me B) and Willie Wright (Mizpah).

Plate 86
A dozen or so fishermen along with a young fisher lad stare out to sea, probably wondering what the weather and sea will be like that night. Richard Verrill is believed to be standing left with sealskin hat (hairy hat), smoking his pipe. Note all the smock jackets are of a relative plain pattern

Plate 87. Britain & Wright c1905
This could have been titled 'The Style Council' or 'The Gansey Boys,' with all twenty three fishermen gathered outside the replacement Cod & Lobster Inn, wearing a vast array of different styled headgear. Including bowler, sealskin, flat cap to floppy trilby with ten smoking clay pipes. All the fishermen wear their Staithes gansey's (smock jackets), the only two without, being the suited Captain Pinder the retired Master Mariner from Prospect House and the landlord of the Cod & Lobster Isaac Cooke, in white shirt and waistcoat. The four fishermen seated show us that at the time of this publication, the area in front of 'The Cod' had split levels. Verrills, Coles, Porritt's, Unthanks and Theakers will be here for sure.

Plate 88. Judges Ltd. C1931

The ten 'flat caps,' tell us that this was taken 25 years later and shows the split level ,of where the cobbles from the High Street and Church Street finish in front of the Inn. Standing or seating, this excellent photograph was titled 'Idle Moments' and shows 15 or so, hatted local Staithes fishermen enjoying the afternoon sun, outside the Cod & Lobster Inn. Although this postcard was posted in July 1945, the view is believed to date from the early 1930's.

From left to right the names are: standing, Jake Verrill, Jimmy Cole, Isaac Cook landlord of the Cod & Lobster, Isaac Harrison, Willy Verrill, unknown,

Sitting, Willy Dowson, Nelse Cole, Isaac Verrill (Spink), Jimmy Verrill (Dutch), standing Isaac Ward, Dick Cole and Tom Harrison. The man bending down is Willy Smales and he is at this time resetting the cobble stones. The man carrying the fish-box on his shoulder is Tom Crake.

Plate 89. R. Johnston & Sons c 1923

Ten or so fishermen, mainly with flat caps, gather in their usual spot at the wooden bench, just a few feet from the Cod & Lobster public house, in this photograph titled 'Seaton Garth'. This is the early name for The Staith and derived from the early settlement of Seaton (Sea-Town. The Garth extends from the foot of Penny Nab to Garth Ends (near Ryders Yard, behind the old 'Shoulder of Mutton' public house and Beckfoot Cottage.)

Generations of Staithes men have gathered here, staring out to sea, commenting on the weather, and of good & bad times past. Francis Verrill is the fisherman in smock jacket and trilby, with one foot on the bench.

Plate 90. Margaret Burgess, Amateur c1940

This group have formed a 'breakaway' group, from the normal Cod & Lobster assembly and are sat on the old stone reinforcements outside of the Chandlery, next to Captain Cooks cottage at the base of Church Street. This group of fishermen are as follows; Johnny Verrill, Willy Verrill, Tom Harrison, Isaac Cook, Ted(Titch) Theaker, Frank Verrill, and Richard Porritt (Nelse Dick)

The sign above is inscribed 'Pictures, Studio Door at the Back' – this was not a reference to the Staithes early cinema! But the studio of an artist where pictures (paintings) could be viewed and purchased. Gloria Wilson the daughter of famous Staithes artist Lilian Colburn, once lived here and she is believed to have exhibited here

SECTION 10.0 – THE FISH SALES

 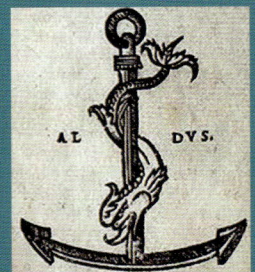 

The Fish Sales were almost always held on Seaton Garth (the Staith) and an auctioneer/Fish salesman controlled the proceedings.

Early Fishmongers/Fish Merchants in Staithes were: William Thompson, George Trattles, George Webster, Thomas Hick, James Ellerby, Richard, George & John Humphrey, Johnson Ridley, Coates Crooks, Zachariah Hick, Jacob Marshall, George Porritt, Richard, Robert & Thomas Shippey, Jacob Marshall, James Sanders, Isaac Porritt, Richard & John Verrill, Robert Turnbull & his two sons Miles & Edward, Thomas Waller, Robert Cowburn, James Longster and John James etc. Thomas Humphrey and John Porritt were recorded as Fish Hawkers.

Some of the Fish merchants were also Fish Curers and some early Curers were: Daniel Cole, Thomas Trattles, Christopher Moore, John, Robert & Thomas Hick, Mary Cowburn, John & George Laverick, Matthew Trattles and the not so famous Elizabeth Taylor, who was also recorded as a baker!

Fish Auctioneers recorded around 1895 were: Richard Humphries and Robert Atkinson when fish were selling for 2s per 100 (actually 120), rising to 3s 9d. Fish Auctioneer James Clemance James, arrived with his wife and three children from Newlyn, Cornwall in c1901. J.C.J. was known to all as 'Jimmie.'

Benjamin Ridge was listed as a fish salesman c1904-08 and by 1925 William James son of James Clemance James senior, became a salesman and his other son John James was a fish merchant in the early 1930's.

Plate 91. Brittain & Wright 1904

The gentleman with the bowler hat in the centre of the picture, holding his notebook and pencil, is the auctioneer Mr James Clemance James (senior). He had the task of selling a relatively poor catch displayed on the wooden Staith. To his right stands Jim Turnbull, CWS Manager, complete with fob-watch & flat cap.

According to Elsie Humphrey Taylor, her grandfather Richard Humphrey, is sixth from the left in the soft trilby, who purchased fish and sold in various markets throughout Cleveland, however Hannah Theaker has claimed this to be her father, Thomas Frank Harrison! He also meets the description of George Longster, who was famed for always wearing a waistcoat over his gansey! From other photographs seen, (Hannah Theaker is believed to be correct).

It is notoriously difficult to ensure all the names are correct as this was over 100 years ago, but others within the group are thought to be (L-R): Unknown, Frank Verrill, Joe or Matt Thompson, Tom 'Parr' Verrill, Tom Francis Harrison, Mr J.C. James, Jim Turnbull, Mr Unthank (probably William), Ned Verrill, Unknown, Arge Unthank & Mr Cole.

Plate 92. H C Morley c1909

A large crowd and at least six carters, are gathered on the Staith for the Fish Sale. A young man complete with drop handle cycle can be observed on the distant left, no doubt a visitor who came to view this busy affair. Herrings were often sold on the Staith at 8 o'clock in the morning and the agents from Whitby & Teeside with their flat carts would wait to buy quantities, counted out in warps (33 to 100) for the various markets or for hawking around the localities.

Plate 93. H.C. Morley c1905

The man to the right in the striped linen shirt, enjoys a glass of ale to seal his deal with the 'Captain' believed to be Benjamin Ridge, Fish Salesman, based in Staithes, who is checking his notebook regarding the fish sale. Benjamin Ridge senior also had a son called Benjamin and they were both Fish Salesmen in Newlyn, Cornwall; thus following in the footsteps of James Clemance James, who hailed from the same area. (However written on the back of this viewcard is 'Mr Watson', without any explanation as to who he was. There was a William Watson in Staithes during 1901 and he was a Chief Petty Officer and Coastguard at that time.) The Staithes bonneted women, can be seen carrying out their everyday task of Herring packing and salting. The 1851 census listed 46 women and girls working in the fish trade, ranging from 81 year old Ann Ward to 8 year old Ann Theaker.. The fisherwoman centre, smiling, holding the skeel is believed to be part of the Hick family of renowned fish merchants.

Plate 94. H. C. Morley c1908

Herring Packing Staithes, was the title of this Morley photographic postcard, posted in August 1914, but the view is earlier, c 1908. Two ladies with their summer clothes and boaters, have wandered down to Seaton Garth in order to observe the fishermen and fisher lad activities.

The left hand image shows a relatively large catch of fish, displayed on the Staith during the 1920's, whilst the right hand image shows a similar fish sale 10 years later. The 'wrangem', small piles of haddock/whiting are evident in three distinct piles, these would have been much cheaper to purchase.

Plate 95a. 1920's   Plate 95b. 1930's

Plate 96

Only two carts are evident (one distant) in April 1930, showing the decline from the heady fish sales of the Victorian and Edwardian period. Over 40 men and less than 10 women are present though, in this photograph of the Fish Sale at the end of the Staith, close to the far slipway and not a single one without hat or bonnet. The quayside on the Cowbar/Lifeboat side is obviously being strengthened, as can be seen with the derricks and huge concrete blocks in situ there.

Vera Marsay the well known fishmonger can be seen left of centre and the young Joey Horne the grandson of Staithes 2nd Lifeboat Coxswain is close to the skeels of fish. If you look closely a small boat appears to be sat outside the Cod & Lobster and it would be interesting to know why?

Plate 97. Judges c1920's

Fish sales rarely occurred anywhere else but on the foreshore or Staith of Seaton Garth, however this photograph, has captured a small sale taking place in the Beck bottom, close to the steps from Abrahams Lane. Several onlookers have gathered on the bridge, to oversee the proceedings. Cobles 'Felicity' (WY130) and 'Safeguard' (WY68) are close by.

Plate 98

A small sale is evident at the far end of the Staith, close to Staithes oldest cottage 'Sandside' (now 'Anchor Cove').

Plate 99. Amateur, Margaret Burgess c1937

A serious faced Vera Marsay (1909-1975), sits behind the box of crabs, centre, along with helpers: Molly Hick (left), Ann Laverick (right) and Mary Hick to the extreme right almost hidden from view. They are under the steps of James Clemance James house, on the Staith, with the warehouse doorway behind them. A large box of crabs are for sale, and the hand bell was to attract attention to the fish hawkers sales pitch. By all accounts 'No Nonsense' Vera Marsay was a force to be reckoned with. No challenge was too big for Vera and she took on the mighty MacFisheries for the rights to sell her fish where she wanted.

Plate 100

Vera came from a well established Staithes family, spending her very early childhood at Glenhow Cottages, Church Street, Staithes and then Gun Gutter. She is recorded in the old telephone directories as residing at 'Greystones' on the High Street and then from 1956-1975 at 'The Coppins' which was next door. She was listed in some editions as Vera Fish Marsay, a reference to Vera being a fish dealer!

Not so much a shop sign, but a sign displayed wherever the Fish Hawker, Vera (No nonsense) Marsay and Son could find an alleyway or suitable opening on the High Street or Seaton Garth (the Staith) for selling their crabs and lobsters prepared on Granary Yard. On other occasions Vera would hawk her sales to Whitby & District, Redcar or even Middlesborough, when transportation was offered.

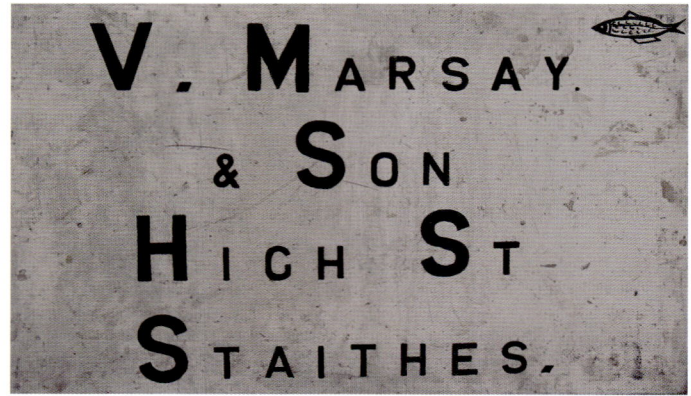

SECTION 11.0 – STAITHES WORKING WOMEN

Walter Beasant wrote in 1891: 'The bright eyed, clear skinned girls ran then as now, lightly along the steep and narrow lanes and courts of the town, carrying baskets of fish on their heads. The wives sit in their porches in their sun bonnets, talking and knitting'.

The Staithes fisherwomen were hardworking individuals, who ran the household, brought up their families, fetched the water, knitted the gansey's, cooked the meals, washed clothes, skaned the mussels/limpets /baited the lines and also assisted with beaching the cobles.

Plate 101. Judges mid 1920's

The photographer captured several sailing cobles, launched up on the beach front at Staithes and gave it the title 'Staithes and its Women'.

Eleven men and seven strong women, are attempting to pull and push a heavy sailing coble, into its allotted space next to 'Ethel & Aida' (WY 244), which in turn is along side 'Olive Branch' (WY 209). They were always beached stern first, other cobles in view are 'Elizabeth & Suzanne' (WY 76) & coble 'George' (WY 234). The message penned to the rear of this view reads: "You would like Staithes with its tiny houses perched up the steep, narrow, cobbled streets and its hard working women folk in their cotton bonnets, hanging out the washing along the harbour wall – so different from Birmingham."

Plate 102

Taken from a glass lantern slide during c1890, we can see that the original pent roofed Cod & Lobster Inn, in the distant left, is still standing at this time.

The fish are being packed into the fish boxes with straw, ready to be carted away from the Staith.

Several young boys, busy themselves as was expected at the time.

I wonder if the cat caught anything!

Plate 103

A fresh faced young and beautiful, Staithes fisherwoman, stands outside her shuttered cottage, with arms bare to the elbow as was usual, where she appears to be repairing a dress. This small cottage is the last cottage on the Staith, nestled into the foot of Penny Nab, now called 'Mizpah', home to Tom 'Parr' Verrill, at this time.

53

Plate 104

Nellie Erichsen, the well known Victorian illustrator, sketched this picture of a Staithes fisherwoman, mending the nets. Several Staithes women were recorded as official Net Repairers.

Plate 105. W H Young c 1905

An Old Fishwife Staithes, Yorkshire, was the title of this artists impression, which went on sale during 1905 right through to 1911. The artist was Walter Hayward Young, better known by his 'pen-name' of "Jotter".

This artists impression, gives an insight, as to how the fisher women of Staithes would carry on working to a ripe old age and it was not uncommon for women to be carrying heavy baskets of nets on their heads into their early eighties.

Plate 106. Friths c1909

Everybody looks happy in this photograph, including Tom Francis Harrison, in his well worn gansey & floppy trilby, which were his trademark. Pictured here along with his wife Mary Ann (nee Verrill), known as Polly Spink to the left and other family members. Tom's three sons Isaac, John & Ralph were all ironstone miners.

This view was titled: "Baiting the Lines at Staithes". The Staithes womenfolk, played a big part in this tedious task, which is taking place on a rudimentary table top, twixt barrel and drum, outside the family home, the first house on The Barris.

This was very much a posed photograph, as to do their baiting tasks, would have involved working from the front of the table!

Plate 107

Simply titled: ' Drying Ground of Old Houses', this pre 1st World War photograph, proves that not all the Staithes women laid their washing out to dry along the hedgerows or Beckside!

Taken from a magic lantern slide, the photographer has captured a rare scene, initially thought to be in the upper area of Gun Gutter, towards Lining Garth, but now confirmed to be behind Harbour View and Spray cottages on Seaton Garth, in an area known locally as 'The Shales'. In their day, young Staithes lads, including Bill Hinchley would get their fun by sliding down the shales. The days washing is hanging on a make-shift line between ramshackle wooden sheds/pigeon lofts.

Plate 108. T. Butterworth 1890

No washing machines, no washing powder, just woman power!

This much earlier lantern slide was titled,' Staithes Women Washing'. Here four bonneted fisher women, are busy washing clothes and possibly carpet mats in the freshwater, flowing from Roxby Beck into the sea; note the wooden skeel and 'paddle' shaped poss. A quote from the past stated,"Why they kneel and deal resounding blows to garments, with their wooden bats, they energetically exchange a running fire of chaff and very personal remarks, in loud fearless tones"

Plate 109. Butterworth c1900

T. Butterworth was again responsible for this photograph, taken in August 1890, where a woman stoops to carry out her washing task opposite the old lifeboat slipway. This was at least two years away from, the provision of piped water from Ellerby Reservoir and provision of the fifteen fresh water taps placed strategically around the village. Hence this woman would also have to carry a skeel of water back from the beck to her home. Cobles in 'dry-dock' are : 'Primitive'(545 WY) & 229 WY, amongst several other cobles around the slipway and the old ironstone store, now 'Alum Cottage.'

Plate 110. T. Butterworth 1890

This excellent close up, is an extremely rare lantern slide taken on the top of the original slipway close to the Cod & Lobster Inn where the alignment is different from today's slipway.

Both Staithes fisher women are carrying heavy wooden skeels on their heads, which would normally contain crabs or herrings and were also often used for carrying water. These skeels were made from oak with iron hoops by local coopers and were wider at the bottom than the top and painted white on the inside and often green on the outside. To ease the weight on their heads the women wore a circular 'bun' shaped cushion under their bonnets, known locally as a 'rowler, pronounced roller.'

The 'cheeky' smile for the photographer, has softened this rare close up and they can be seen wearing traditional lilac bonnets and heavy boots, showing beneath their petticoats. Their arms were always bare to the elbow and they often wore red petticoats, covered by a blue linen apron.

The building behind at Slip Top, with shutters and upper bay window, was believed to be an early shop selling bread and cakes, the elevation of this building has since changed dramatically.

Plate 111. Valentines c 1904

Having climbed up the best part of Church Street, this poor image of the two hard working Staithes women, shows the huge burden of nets, across their shoulders, to be carried up Kirkhill Bank. No doubt that these nets were to be "Barked" in the large copper just a few yards further up the bank, where they would be coated in a tannin solution ('cutch') in order to proof the nets against the harsh treatment from the North Sea or possibly just simply laid out to dry on the grassy banks..

The sloping pathway leads to the large cottage now named 'Pinjarra', which no doubt has connections with Western Australia.

Plate 112. c1928

Taken 21 years later this amateur photograph shows a local Staithes woman with a large basket of washing, being carried as usual on her head, in the upper reaches of Kirkhill Bank above 'Felicity House'.

No doubt she would be looking to hang the washing, on the many hedgerows located in this area as shown just to the top right.

Plate 113. Frith's Series 1930's

Two out of the four fisher wives wear the traditional bonnets, whilst they carry between them a large box of crabs, ready for washing and dressing. The ladies are from left to right: Joan Cuthbert, Lizzie Theaker, Edith Marsay and Eva Hanson. This photograph was taken near the slipway into the Beck at Granary Yard, Beckside, close to the crab boiling houses, the stone wall existing today is yet to be built. The author can well remember Edith in the Royal George in the late 1990's, having her usual tot of whiskey and a bag of crisps for her faithful dog 'Murphy'

Plate 114. Hartmann's 1905

This atmospheric picture is the real Staithes, just as it was at the turn of the century and before. The old cottages, house the hard working fishermen and women, who have gathered a whole host of 'fisher' materials, including a sturdy mangle at the end of the Staith outside their cottages 'Mizpah' and 'Sandside' (now Anchor Cove) The masts for sailing cobles can be seen strewn around the rough path leading to the old 'Barking' well. The narrow path disappearing off to the left enabled nimble folk to gain access to the upper reaches of Penny Nab and the ironstone mine that existed here.

The fisherwoman in the foreground is carrying several painted bladder floats for the fishing nets' which would often be colourfully painted and bore the boat owners initials. Such floats were made from pigs bladders or sheep stomachs.

This was the cottage where Thomas(Parr) and Margaret Verrill lived.

The message on this view card posted on 12th April 1906 reads; "Dear Miss Hurst, Father 'as sent a box of crabs off today, hope you will get them alright for Good Friday, you must excuse the short letter inside the box, His eyes keep very nice now. Kind regards to all, Grace Shippey".

SECTION 12.0 – 'BONNETS and BUNS (ROWLERS)'

  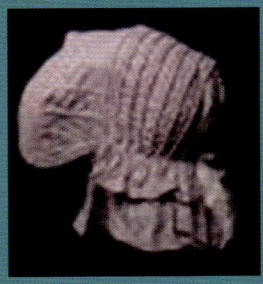 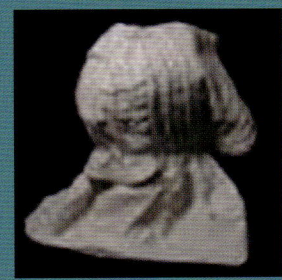 

The Staithes bonnet was traditionally a working hat for fishermen's wives, made out of a yard of cotton material, but was worn by young women and children alike. The women often carried skeels of herrings, crabs or water on their heads, so the bonnet had a double crown for support. The frill at the back stopped drips from running down their necks and the poke at the front kept the sun out of their eyes. They would place a bun shaped coil, on top of the bonnet in order to relieve the weight on their heads and to improve balance, this often took the form of a sand filled sock or a rolled up apron or duster, tied at both ends to form a quoit and known in Staithes as a 'rowler' or roller. The bonnet is gathered inside with pull tapes and adjusts to fit any size, whilst the bow at the back is for decoration. The poke at the front was quilted to stiffen it and dishcloth material was used for this purpose, because it washed and wore well. The ties to hold the bonnet on the head were called strings and could be tied under the chin or round the back of the neck.

Bonnets were formerly available from Seymours shop at the end of the High Street, from the late 1880's towards the 1st World war period and from Joseph Verrill's shop higher up the High Street. The bonnets were always made in the village and were never 'bought in'.

Traditionally white bonnets were worn and exchanged for black when they were widowed, which they were expected to wear for at least one year, but many just carried on wearing the black. After the first year of widowhood, they could wear a lilac bonnet, again for a year and then they could wear whatever colour they wished.

Prior to WW1 it would be fair to say that every single woman and girl in Staithes wore a bonnet with little exception, every day of their lives, it was nothing to do with fashion, it was simply a practical tradition and it was expected. By the end of the 2nd World War in 1945/6 there were still many bonnet wearers in Staithes and many carried on into the 1950's. The following postcard message from a Channel Islander, who was lodging with Mrs Harrison on Church Street and written in September 1949 supports this; "Everything here is quaint, all the women wear bonnets, like the Jersey folk back home, so it's really nice. We are staying right below the cliffs".

Plate 115
Traditional Staithes bonnet as worn by Martha Ann Roe ('Marthan'), daughter of John Henry Roe, General Mason & Barber, who had his shop on the High Street adjacent to the Royal George public house for many years.

Plate 116. 1979
This is Miss Teresa Clark, wearing the Staithes bonnet as late as 1979.

Plate 117. Harvey Barton & Son c 1908

The distinguished lady complete with hand woven cardigan and Staithes bonnet, is Mrs Elizabeth Anne Sanders, who was Grandmother to today's local character Willie Wright. This portrait was titled: 'Fisherwoman Staithes'. However the publisher has used a great deal of poetic licence by superimposing both colour and pattern to the traditional Staithes bonnet. Much to the annoyance of Mrs. Sanders and family as it was done without their consent.

All the villages along the east Coast had similar bonnets, but the Staithes bonnet, was different in various ways and thus unique.

Elizabeth Ann's father John Sanders was the local blacksmith as was her brother Richard Sanders

Plate 118. Margaret Burgess, Amateur c1937

Two fishmongers, complete with bonnets, pictured near the steps up to Clem James house, 'Ocean View' on the Staith.

On the left is Elizabeth Ann Sanders, born in 1851 and to the right Rachel Longster, born in 1879, both in typical pose with their arms folded.

Rachel's grandson Jim Longster has over the past few years put considerable effort into rebuilding the four storey, old Smokehouse on Granary Yard.

Plate 119. Friths mid 1950's

Hands on hips, is a young Eva Hanson, who went on to be the last bonnet wearer in Staithes with Mary Ann Dawson to the right.

Plate 120. HC Morley c1908

This Morley photograph is interesting on a number of fronts, but especially for the 'Rollers' to go on top of the bonnets. The fleet have just landed and a hive of activity is apparent, in this view as women unload the days catch. One of the standing women has a 'roller' on her wrist and the woman in the bottom right hand corner has the 'roller' on top of her bonnet. The women would carry the baskets of fish and crabs onto the Staith, ready for packing into the various barrels. It is very rare to see the 'roller' uncovered as shown here.

Plate 121. c1924

An unknown photographer produced this photograph, from a glass negative, of a bonneted lady, carrying her child past the Cod & Lobster Inn and Slip Top. The white bonnet and bare armed child tell us that this is summer in Staithes. The building facing, was known as 'Meal House' as this is where grain and animal feeds were stored and usually had an array of lobster pots stacked here. This has since been demolished, following severe storm damage in 1925 and provides a useful turning area for motor vehicles today.

Plate 122. H C Morley c1908

Henry Charles Morley took this 'Studio' portrait of two Staithes lasses, they are probably Verrill's as the message on the back was addressed to Mr Francis Verrill, 'Barris', Staithes.

Both women are dressed 'to the nines' in their finery and ankle length heavy skirts, complete with a freshly washed and ironed Staithes bonnet.

Plate 123a/b
Some fine and ornate bonnets.

LAST BONNET WEARER

By the late 1960's, the tradition was fading fast, with only about 20 ladies keeping the tradition alive.

The last two ladies to wear the bonnet as part of their everyday clothes were Eva Hanson and Olive Cole. Eva was still carrying on the tradition until 1991 and she is credited as being the last bonnet wearer in Staithes. Eva was the grandmother of well known and respected local fisherman Dave Hanson who lives at 'Lindisfarne' on Church Street. Today the bonnets are worn only for special occasions and by little girls at christenings.

Plate 124

Ann Lawson's mother was born in Staithes and she presented Ann with her first bonnet at the age of four, made by Harriet Adamson.

Ann and Terry took over The Gift Shop in 1968 and a certain Patience Calvert, from Granary Yard came into the shop and gave her a bonnet and said 'that's how you make them'.

Ann still makes the Staithes bonnets today, always in cotton and to Patience Calvert's pattern and the advice she received from Harriet Adamson and one size will fit all ages from five to ninety with smaller one's for babies.

Ann makes most of her bonnets for children and for those having treatment for cancer and have lost their hair, as they are cool and keep the sun at bay.

Terry Lawson who produces excellent photographic postcards and prints of the village has adopted a personal logo 'Ann Maid' which appears on his merchandise and depicts Ann wearing her traditional Staithes bonnet.

Plate 125a/b

Compare the fashions and the era's!

The inset depicts a relatively modern card produced in 1985, which celebrates the working women of Staithes. This artist drawn postcard, was designed by American Margi Cochran and was originally a 9 x 8 inch oil & verine painting. It was an imaginary portrait, of what the Staithes bonnet might look like on a modern lass, with her forbears sketched in the background and inspired from her first visit to Staithes in 1981.

Whilst the main picture depicts the height of fashion in 1905 where 'Pop' Porritt displays a magnificent dress, with laced neckline and sleeves and a very well made bonnet.

SECTION 13.0 – "THE SEVEN DEADLY SINS"

The various chapels within Staithes, were referred to as the 'Five Virtues', whereas the public houses were known as 'The Seven Deadly Sins'. This reference by the older generation within Staithes is more or less true, as generally speaking there were seven public houses in the lower village of Staithes, for long periods of time. Little if any records of the 'First & Last' public house exist after 1823 or before for that matter! The former Station Hotel (Now the Captain Cook PH), situated on Staithes Lane was not in this count, as it was not previously classed as a public house, but as a hotel.

No.	PUBLIC HOUSE	POSITION	DATES IN USE
1	First and Last	Staithes Bank'	1856
2	Free Masons Arms	Staithes Bank'	1872-1937
3	Golden Lion	High Street	1823-1925
4	Black Lion	High Street	1840-2004
5	Royal George	High Street	1834-present day
6	Shoulder of Mutton	High Street	1823-1937
7	Cod & Lobster Inn	Seaton Garth	1823-present day
8	White Horse Inn	Church Street	1840-1925

The least known public house is the 'First and Last' formerly situated at the bottom of the steep bank, as the last house on the left when you leave Staithes. Little is known about this public house and it was not recorded in any of the Directories from 1823-1937 and it may just have been a small beer retailers establishment.

In 1823 there were just the three pubs in Staithes, rising to four in 1834, six in 1840 and the seven by 1872. Hence without counting the Station Hotel or the First & Last, the 'Seven Deadly Sins' was applicable from 1872 to 1930's, as by 1933 the numbers had reduced to five.

Some what puzzling is the reference in Whitby Library for the Year of 1823, to joiner Will Hudson of Staithes being the licensed victualler of the 'Three Tuns' and ship owner Thomas Brown being the licensed victualler of the 'Red Lion' – no records appear to exist to collaborate this.

The 1901 census refers to a Joseph Cuthbert being the innkeeper of the Red Lion, just one house away from the Black Lion i.e. where the Golden Lion should be. Joseph came from Newton Mulgrave and was a farm labourer in 1891 and by 1911 he was an iron-stone miner. So either the census form got it wrong or the Golden Lion was re-named for a short while.

It was usual practice for the proprietors to employ their own daughters as barmaids and Thomas Johnson of the Black Lion, went further, as in 1901 he employed daughters Dinah as a General Help, Martha as a barmaid and son Joseph as a Yeast Merchant and Spirit Bar Traveller!

RECORD OF PUBLIC HOUSE PROPRIETORS IN STAITHES FROM 1823-1937

Pub	1823	1834	1840	1872	1893	1905	1909	1925	1933	1937
Cod & Lobster	Matthew Trattles	Matthew Trattles	Matthew Trattles	Lavinia Lane	Lavinia Lane	Mary Bell	Isaac Cooke	Isaac Cooke	Isaac Cooke	Miss Cooke
Golden Lion	Thomas Bowness	Thomas Bowness	Thomas Bowness	Thomas Spink	Thomas Spink	D. Will Smith	George R Dunn	Will Tose		
Shoulder of Mutton	C. Duel	Margaret Duel	C. Duel	Richard Seymour	George Loyd	George L.Hugill	George L.Hugill	George L.Hugill	George Pattison	George Pattison
Mulgrave Arms			John Crossley	Re-named Black Lion						
Black Lion				James Spink	James Spink	Thomas Johnson	Dinah Johnson	George Edward Thackray	George Edward Thackray	?
Royal George		John Breckon	Thomas Seymour	Elizabeth Seymour	Emma Askworth	John Hansell	John Hansell	Hannah Hodgson	Hannah Hodgson	?
White Horse			Margaret Cole	Thomas Featherstone	Robert Atkinson	Robert Atkinson	John Rob Scott	Thomas Roe		
Freemasons Arms				Addison Verrill	Ellen Verrill	John Legg/B Smith	John Legg/B Smith	Lydia Pierson	Thomas Clark	Thomas Clark
Station Hotel					George Dawson	Ann Spink	Will Mortimer	Levinia Faulkner	Weave Faulkner	Weave Faulkner
Beer Retailer		William Gibson		Indiana Truefit						

STAITHES PUBLIC HOUSES

Directories can be valid for a few years hence landlord's/landlady's can change within this period and the above list can be subject to minor changes as follows:

- John Carling was recorded as a publican in Staithes during 1841.

- At the Shoulder of Mutton evidence is available that Mary Lamplough was in charge during 1842.

- In 1851 a Gofton Wilson was the Inn keeper of the Shoulder of Mutton for a short time and Isaac Bell was listed as Inn keeper and shoe maker.

- In 1851 William Laverick and Nesswell Pennock were both recorded as innkeepers in Staithes.

- Indiana Trufit opened her Victoria Hotel on the High Street in 1868/9, which allegedly was a Temperance Hotel, she was recorded as an Innkeeper in 1871, but later in 1872 she is recorded as being a Beer Retailer!

- In 1861, Thomas Featherstone was in situ at the White Horse, with stone mason Thomas Lawson, replacing him by 1881.

- In 1861, Walter Case Mann and Richard Cowle were recorded as Innkeepers in Staithes.

- Samual Adams was recorded as a Beer Seller visiting Staithes in 1881 from Suffolk.

- A Beer retailer was also believed to be working from 'Friendship' cottage in Gun Gutter at one time.

- Thomas Spink was in charge at the Golden Lion and Thomas Spink at the Black Lion in 1891.

- Ann Spink took over from George Dawson at the Station Hotel shortly after George sadly took his own life on 2nd March 1896.

- The Black Lion, following closure, was for a short time re-named the 'Hawthorn Grove' (c1989) housing a restaurant and catering for Bed & Breakfast.

Plate 126. J T Ross c1909

The '**First and Last**' public house was the first building on the right, before you enter Staithes High Street at the bottom of the Bank and somewhat obviously, the last house on the left as you leave the High Street to climb the Bank. Very little is known about this former public house, as it was not listed in any of the directories 1823-1937. It is however recorded, on the extract of the Ordnance Survey map of 1856, currently on show in The Staithes Heritage and Captain Cook Museum The publication shown right was sold from Matthew Trattles High Street shop and it appears to show the remnants of a former outbuilding belonging to the 'First and Last' and local myth has it that a cave existed here with a tunnel down to the 'Smugglers'/Art Gallery on the High Street (it could just be true!)

The steps to 'Back Road' are to the left and the extension to what is today 'New York' house, is yet to be built.

Plate 127. c1909

Blacksmith John Legg was the proprietor of the **Freemasons Arms** at the time of this mid 1909 photograph. The large wooden sign tells us that Scarborough and Whitby Breweries, sold their ales adjacent to the Bethel Chapel. This public house was in use during the 1870's, where retired Master Mariner, Addison Verrill, was the first landlord, he was a prominent Conservative and freemason and it was he who gave the pub its name. Other proprietors have been Ellen Verrill in the early 1890's, followed by Mrs Lydia Pierson in the mid 1920's. The front parlour bar was a pent roofed extension, on the front of what is now the garden of 'Chapel Garth' house, adjacent to the old chapel. Once the pub closed, this site has had various uses from sweet shop to a hairdressers. However all has long since been demolished. The adjacent white awning is where Ann Brewster ran her small general store ('Flither Cottage' today).Followed by 'Gosforth House', home to Sarah Ann Nelson (now 'Meldene'), then home of miner William Adamson (now 'Clevelyn') and last but not least, home of fishmerchant Robert Shippey (now 'New York House'), which now has a large extension towards Back Road/Valley View cottage and had a postal address of 'Bottom of Bank' at this time.

Plate 128. Brittain & Wright c1905

The large wooden sign of the **Golden Lion** public house dominates the front elevation, shown right of this photograph, where D.Will Smith was the licensed victualler, both wines and teas were advertised for sale here. This fine building is now 'Greystones', which is a 17th century Grade 2 listed, 3 storey, building, of sandstone with a smuggling history and can now be rented complete with 5 bedrooms.

The whole street appear to have turned out, while the photographer captures this busy scene with William Scarth standing outside his adjacent tailor and drapers shop. On top of the third bay window, right, the black statue of a lion belonging to the Black Lion public house is just visible.

The shop on the left (now 'Newholme') is believed to be Staithes 1st Co-op shop (1889-1906).

Plate 129. c1880's

There is no mistaking who the proprietor of the **Black Lion** was, as James Spink, pictured here with his family and staff, had his name on the large name-board above the left hand window. At this time in the late 1880's it was called the Black Lion Commercial Hotel and James Spink, also a farmer was here from the early 1870's, remaining here until the early 1890's. George Lloyd was employed as a groom/Ostler here in 1881.

The portico entrance, with the Black Lion figure above the porch looks quite grand in this late and somewhat grainy photograph and indeed it was the largest building in Staithes with 12 rooms. By 1897, Arthur P. Harrison held the licence here as James Spink went on to run the Station Hotel (later renamed the Captain Cook). During the early part of the 19th Century (1840's) it was named the Mulgrave Arms and was a place where locals paid their dues to the Marquis of Normanby. Indiana Truefitt had the Victoria Temperance Hotel built to the immediate left of the thatched house attached to the Black Lion in 1868/69. Sadly the 'Black' closed down in July 2004 and as yet does not have a re-opening date, despite several optimistic dates from the current owner.

Plate 131. c1931

Situated midway down the High Street, the **Shoulder of Mutton Inn** was indeed a very quaint local, with its parlour situated to the left of the passage; where a local bonneted lady is leaning on the wall of the passage, which eventually led to Garth Ends. The landlord at this time George William Pattison, can be seen standing in the bar doorway.

At the time of this c 1931 photograph, the Bass bitter sold for 3d per half pint and the Bar was situated at the front of the pub, with the 'port-hole' Club Room upstairs.

This photograph was at one time in the possession of Dan Hugill, an ironstone miner who lived at No.19. Cowbar Cottages and who's parents were one time landlords of this public house (1893-1928). The bonneted lady third from the left is local character Willie Wrights grandmother, Elizabeth Anne Sanders. This public house dates back to at least 1823 when Mary Duell was in charge. In 1842 Mary Lamplough was the recorded landlady and the ale at that time was 3d per pint (2½d if taken out in a jug), which means that it took 89 years for the price to eventually double!

This was the place chosen for the inquest into the 'Rachael' coble disaster of 1870, when Richard Seymour was the landlord followed later by George Lloyd in the 1890's.The dog in the photograph was 'Ben' who belonged to blacksmith George Laverick Hugill, who was the previous long time landlord here . This pub closed in 1937/8 and today it is 'The Mariners' a private house which has been restored to a very high standard.

Plate 130. Morley c1906

The Royal George, with the landlord's dog basking in the sun, is situated next to John Roe's shop, where the striped barber's pole is evident. Emma Ashworth had been the licensed victualler during the 1890's and succeeded to John Hansell by 1904, who remained here throughout the Edwardian period. The pub still flourishes today and just about everybody, locals and visitors alike enjoy suitable refreshments and good pub food and of course gossip here. John Seymour was an early shoemaker (1860's) in Staithes and owned the ship 'Isabella and Isaac' and his family were very early innkeepers of the Royal George Inn.

It was a shame that the council recovered the ornate, random cobble stones in the foreground of this photograph.

"THE SEVEN DEADLY SINS"

Plate 132. R.Johnson & Sons c1935
John Richard Verrill's Refreshent Rooms sign, has been replaced with a more modern Café sign, on Blue Jacket House on the High Street. **The Shoulder Of Mutton** sign is also different from the one shown on page 64, being narrower and configured differently. Such alterations appear to indicate that this view was taken in the mid 1930's. The woman with the pale is washing the windows and ledges of the Shoulder of Mutton as visitor's and locals stroll up the High Street together.

Plate 133. 1850

This is an extremely important and rare view, of the area between the Cod & Lobster old slipway and the Watch House in Boathouse Yard, when Staithes front was just a simple bay, with little or no sea defences. This is taken from an 1850 watercolour and shows Staithes to be very different from the photography of the 1890's, especially New landing and Gar' Ends.

The central white painted building bears the grey narrow painted strip sign, '**Shoulder of Mutton Inn**' and depicts the sea wall area of Ryders Yard. In those days the Shoulder of Mutton included the cottage known today as Garth End. The 'Watch House' flag pole is evident, within Boathouse Yard.

How the wooden structure fronting onto the beach area, survived the great storms of 1844 and 1849 is hard to tell. Almost certainly it cannot have survived the great storm of 1862 when the Cod & lobster was completely destroyed. The headgear of the two fishermen repairing their herring nets appear very different to the traditional Staithes fisherman's apparel.

The Staithes Lifeboat House is 25 years away at the time of this important image of Staithes Foreshore and the building on the extreme right, may have been the old Kelp house, which was sideways on.

Plate 139

Following the Great Storm of 1953 the Cod & Lobster again changed drastically on the main front elevation, with the introduction of a huge bay window construction, to the right of the new entrance (previously only had a side entrance).

A funky 'Cod & Lobster' poster style sign can be seen on the left of the building advertising Camerons Ales.

The usual small gathering of local fishermen is evident and the irregular shape of 'Five Bells' house stands to the right near Garth Ends

Plate 140. Judges c1955

The new Camerons sign can again be seen in this end elevation view of the Cod & Lobster, at the end of the High Street post the 1953 storm.

The two Staithes ladies Jennie Thompson and Meg Theaker, complete with their bonnets, have taken time out to have a chat close to the large bulwark off the end of the High Street, outside 'Sea Crest 'cottage. The heavy bulwark for protection from the sea is attached to Slip Top cottage which at this time was without windows on the front elevation. The street lamp left is mounted off 'Tom England's Slip Top Cottage.

The pub has undergone several changes in structure and also management over the past few years and has now completely departed from its origins as a fisherman's hostelry to a modern establishment, which due to its position will always do well.

Plate 141. JT Ross 1904

One of the lesser known public houses in Staithes was the **White Horse Inn** pictured here on the right, just below the St Peter's Church Mission Room, where a small oil lamp is positioned under the pub signboard.

Robert (Bobby) Atkinson was the licensee at this time, who was also both fisherman and fish auctioneer, the White Horse sold both 'Foreign and British Spirits'. John Robert Scott eventually became the licencee here for a short time.

The stationary horse and cart outside the White Horse belonged to Bobby who is sat on the steps leading to the grand Kirkhill House, just beyond the young girl sweeping outside her gate. He often offered the services of his luggage cart and it was recorded in Enid Lucy Pease Robinson's diary, that he took her mother and luggage to the station on 31st August 1901. The large house between the White Horse public house and St Peters Mission church is now 'Balmoral House' which at one time was home to Captain John Joseph Robinson, Master Mariner and Deacon of the Congregational Chapel. More recently this was the home for a short time of Nottingham actor Ace Bhatti of Bend it Like Beckham, Coronation St and East Enders fame.

Note the centre of the steep Church Street is well defined with longer cobbles. The former White Horse Inn, now a private house, belonging to Sean Baxter, who runs his successful 'The Real Staithes'business from here, has strangely renamed it, "The White House" and the upper door window depicts an image of the American Presidents house in Washington DC!

Plate 142. Valentines c1920's.

J W Legg sold this postcard from his High Street shop in Staithes, depicting the Station Hotel (now the Captain Cook), which as stated previously was not counted within Staithes 'Seven Deadly Sins', with its neat curtains and new palisaded fence. The pencil message to the rear clearly states that 'Hilda' bought the postcard on May 19th 1929 although the photograph would have been taken earlier. The outbuilding to the rear advertises that the hotel was fully licensed and had garage facilities. During 1897 James Spink left the Black Lion and succeeded Edward Henry Hutty at the Station Hotel. A William Mortimer was in charge here by 1908 and he was also listed as being a farmer and provider of fresh dairy produce and posting.

The message penned to the reverse side, tells us that Weave Faulkner was the landlord at the time of this view. The message was to Mrs R Wallace, The Heights, Rochdale and read;" Lunched at the Station Hotel, very nice Country Inn, good place to lodge at. Saw two old punch books with quaint verses, one was – Women make men love, love makes men sad, sadness makes men drink, drink makes men mad."(no change there then!)

The hotel was ideally situated for those travelling the coastline by train, until the staions untimely closure.

This fully licensed hotel came up for sale on Monday 6th October 1919 as lot No.10 in the Grinkle Estate Sale by auction, conducted by Messrs. Robert Gray & Sons. The lot included: 2 gardens, concrete yard with cart shed, coach house, saddle room, 6-stall stable, loose box with granary above, coal house and 2 sheds. The sale catalogue states that the hotel was in the occupation of Messrs. McPherson & Sons at the annual rent of £50 and lot 10a included 2.962 acres of Grass Land attached to the above.

SECTION 14.0 – "THE FIVE VIRTUE'S"

There had been no church in Staithes since the old Domesday Book Church of Seaton, that fell into disuse during the mid 15th Century.

John Wesley had been banned from the pulpits of the 'Established Church' and following the John Wesley tour in the late 1770's, his influence paved the way for early Wesleyan prayer meetings and classes being held in John Garbutt's old school room in Granary Yard and in another building on the Cowbar side of Staithes.

There is a record of Primitive Methodist preacher, J. Hutchinson having preached in the open-air at Hinderwell in 1821, when a notorious character called Sarah Smith was converted and of a society being formed in Staithes that year.

However the Congregationalists, were the first to have a formal presence in Staithes, opening their Bethel Chapel in 1822, at the bottom of Staithes Bank and remaining in use for almost 177 years. This was known as the High Chapel due to its elevated position within Staithes.

The Wesleyans were not too far behind the 'Congs' when they opened a small chapel on the Beckside near Granary Yard in 1824. This remained in use for 42 years before it was replaced by the larger chapel in Chapel Yard in 1866, which in turn remained in use for 123 years.

The third group to enter Staithes were the 'Ranters,' when they opened their first Primitive Methodist Chapel, on the opposite side of the road to the Bethel chapel in 1838. This remained in use for 42 years, before being replaced by an adjacent much larger adjacent edifice in 1880.

The fourth group here were the Anglican Christians, when the old National School in Church Street, became licensed as St Peter The Fisherman for Church Of England worshippers in 1849.

Last but not least were the Catholics, who opened in 1886 on Staithes Lane are still preaching the faith today.

There is no doubt that religion was a powerful force for the best part of 200 years in Staithes and with the ferocious storms, resulting disasters and loss of life over the years, religious belief was a comfort for those who shared in the tragedies. At one time up to 1500 worshippers went to chapel in one day in Staithes.

All the Staithes Chapels are now closed as places of worship.

The original Wesleyan Chapel in Staithes was built in 1824 and was a very small and rudimentary building by the Beckside. As 'Weslyanism' flourished the original chapel had to be replaced by a much larger building. The foundation stone laying ceremony was held on 16th February 1865 and was laid by The Marquis of Normanby and officially opened in 1866. A time capsule in the form of a sealed bottle, containing copies of the Methodist Recorder, Whitby Gazette, Leeds Mercury and names of the trustees, president & secretary of the Methodist Conference,was placed within the foundations, to ensure a record of the times was preserved. Local ship owner John Trattles (c1794-1887), who had been a seaman in the Napoleonic wars, became a founder trustee of the new Wesleyan chapel in 1865 and played a great part in its success until his death in 1887.

A certain worthy Quaker, George Fox visited Staithes in 1651 and describes at great length, his struggles and contentions with the priests and the ranters there.

The chapels in Staithes flourished, despite the observations of well known historian John Walker Ord, who in 1846 wrote; 'Although Staithes contains considerably more than a thousand inhabitants, no regular system of national religious instruction, has ever been afforded them and they are permitted to wallow in gross ignorance. Moreover to accommodate this mass of human beings, no means for spiritual instruction in the principles of the Establishment are provided; and whilst the Hindoos, Africans, Chinese and other distant lands, are liberally supplied with Christian ministers, twelve hundred of our own white bretheren, close at hand, in the centre of a wealthy diocese and in the midst of civilisation, are actually without a church. It is surely high time that the Archbishop, the Eclesiastical Commissioner's and the British public, should look at it.'

Methodist Chapels

WESLEYAN CHAPEL

Plate 143. Rear View of Wesleyan Chapel

In the right foreground stands the large edifice of Staithes Weslyan Chapel, situated at the Beckside, the Reverand W.Fern played no small part in organising working parties of local men, to prepare the site for this new chapel.

This c1908 photograph taken from the cliff path on the north side of the Beck, takes in the tiered village with Prospect House and Burton Cottage on high.

Plate 144a. Side View by Tony Murphy

The Wesleyan Chapel was once described as a handsome structure of brick and freestone, consisting of two stories. The upper story contained the chapel and was stated to seat up to 500 people including the gallery. On the lower story stood the vestry and a schoolroom with accommodation for 250.

Plate 144b. Front Entrance

The Marquis of Normanby during the opening ceremony stated that 'he trusted that the children might learn in the schoolroom, lessons of veneration and subordination'.

T. Bennison was a superintendent here along with Robert Featherstone the postmaster, who was a senior Superintendent. The Reverand Albert E Davison was here in 1905, Will Nicholson by 1909, Ralph Hughes by 1925 and FJ Bell by 1933.

The chapel recently closed for services during 2009.

The building has been bought by Staithes Art Gallery owners David and Allison Milnes, who are renovating the building, to further their popular Art classes and exhibitions, including accommodation for the would be artists. The lower Exhibition area opened in September 2013, for the Ian Burke/Tony Hutchinson 'Lost Archive', exhibition, forming part of the very successful, 2nd Staithes Arts & Heritage Festival on 14th/15th September 2013.

Plate 145. 1906

The people of Staithes were very proud of their Wesleyan Chapel, to such an extent that in 1897 they erected a very ornate cast iron sign, advertising its presence at the entrance leading to Chapel Yard, off the cobbled High Street. Hanging to the right above, this sign was hung between 'Rock Lea' and the former drapery & tailor's shop of William Sowerby Smales, later adapted by the Co-Operative Society as a butchery department. In high winds it used to rattle to the annoyance of those trying to sleep!

Plate 146. 1950's

Several years later this 1950's view, shows that the earlier ornate sign has now been replaced by a much simpler painted sign, 'Wesley Methodist Church,' with directional arrow affixed to the side wall of the Staithes Branch of the 'Loftus Co-operative Society' shop, now extended.

The chapel was fitted with a new organ in 1904 and modern lighting installed in 1926. A service of dedication was held on 23rd September 1959 for the Opening of a Reconstructed Organ, at a cost of £900 where a Mrs Betty Dixon unlocked the console and Arthur Jackson gave a Grand Organ Recital.

PRIMITIVE METHODIST CHAPELS

Staithes attained circuit rank in 1868, with William Bowe as first superintendent. It then had 185 members, one minister & twenty local preachers.

The following early extract regarding the Primitive Methodist Circuit is relevant:

'John Seymour, one of the early stalwarts, who toiled hard at camp meetings and in ordinary services ; Richard Verrill, better known as "Ranter Dicky"; Robert Verrill, generally called "Little Bob," quaint and good; Alice Harrison, known to all the village as "Auld Aunt Ailsie," with her sunny face; Helen Leng, afterwards Mrs. Richard Verrill, with many others whose names are written in the " Lambs Book of Life," had hold of God and men.'

"Was it any wonder," asks Mr. Gray, when recalling the fidelity and heroism of these chosen spirits" that in the winter of 1851-2 a powerful revival broke out, and a number of men (mostly fishermen) were soundly converted and added to the church.'

Adjoining the above early PM chapel is the somewhat grander replacement Chapel of 1880, (now the Staithes Heritage Centre/Captain Cook Museum, expertly run by Reg Firth and his wife Ann, who have created something special here). This centre contains a minefield of information and items of interest and is a 'must' for all people interested in Staithes and of course Captain Cook. Many items have been donated by the villagers, but in the main Reg has put his lifetime collections, into the museum and it is a privilege to enter this special museum. Correspondence dated 1st October 1879 tells us that the new Primitive Chapel was to be erected with a passage of at least five feet between the old and new chapels and that the old chimney abutting the old chapel should be pulled down.

The Primitive Methodist Circuit became well established in Staithes and the rousing choir choruses and demonstrative sermons earned them the nickname of the 'Ranters'. The Verrill family members and many of their descendants were worshippers here for many a year and during her time in Staithes Laura Knight (nee Johnson), the famous painter to be, attended the PM chapel every Sunday she could. The Reverand J.W. Felton was here in 1925 and Andrew Thornton in 1933.

Plate 147a

Towards the top left of the high street stands both the original Primitive Methodist Chapel of 1838, with canopy doorway (recently converted to the friendly 'Stonehaven' Café & now reverted to a private residence) and it's later 1880 replacement, now the Heritage Museum. The new' chapel contains a spectacular stained glass window to commemorate the fallen, in our two World Wars (1914-18 & 1939-45). This magnificent window was provided by contributions from the many village Methodist supporters. The window is inscribed 'Our Consolation Aboundeth In Christ' and 'Peace be Still' and contains pictures of the armed forces, together with maritime/navy, RAF and army badges, arranged in a spectacular artistic format.

Plate 147b

Plate 148. 1911

George Delavel Laverick, the Staithes local builder, carpenter and undertaker carried out improvements to the Primitive Methodist Chapel.

George was the son of Master Mariner George Delaval Laverick(1825-1903)

Details of the Chapel work, are depicted in the June 4th 1911 invoice from him with his unique engraved, coble logo, bill heading, to the chapel trustees Charles G Tetley, Matthew Trattles, Burton Verrill, Robert Frank and William Brown.

You will note that the cost of painting the interior of the Primitive Methodist Chapel, at this time was £16-10s-0d, doors were grained & varnished for 5 shillings each and the exterior was painted for 18 shillings. 'Butt inges and chaple' indicate that Mr Laverick was not so hot on spelling!

CATHOLIC CHURCH

Plate 149a. HC Morley c 1914

Early lectures and sermons on the Catholic doctrine were allegedly held in York House, off the High Barrass in Staithes during the late 1830's.

The Staithes Catholic Church was erected in 1885, at the expense of the Right Reverend Thomas Witham of Lartington Hall and dedicated to the Blessed Virgin, under the title of 'Our Lady Star of the Sea'. This neat stone Gothic building, consists of chancel and nave, with adjoining grand residence for the priest (recently converted to new apartments in 2013). The designer of this church, was a Mr M.Carr of Middlesbrough and the foundation stone was laid on 31st July 1884 and publicly opened on 2nd June 1886, catering for up to 600 people (optimistic). The alter was chastely carved from pitch pine and was highly polished. Above the west door a statue was placed of the Blessed Virgin holding up the hands of the Devine Child to bless, and a representation of a boat, rowed by two angels. A Father Sullivan initially took on the task of establishing this mission and by the early 1890's the Rev Patrick Joseph Leahy was a force to be reckoned with, followed by priest Patrick Gibsman and then the Reverand D. Charles Van Pouche by the late 1890's. Priest Lawrence Kempick came in 1901 then the Reverand Jas.Benvenutus Guy was here in 1905 & 1909, Thomas Noon 1911-1925 and Cecil Farrer in 1933.

Plate 149b

Plate 150

This rare photograph was taken shortly after the opening of Staithes new Catholic Church in June 1886.

Several monkey puzzle trees have been set within the grounds (I wonder what happened to them). The priests Manse was a very fine building.

BETHEL CHAPEL

The Bethel Chapel or Congregational Chapel was erected in 1822 and was previously referred to as The Independent Chapel (Independent Congregationalists) and was supported by the wealthy Boulby alum manufacturer George Dodds, who was both a landowner and ship owner.

The famous Reverend William Mitchell preached here from 1832-1869 and Staithes coble WY 242 was named in honour of this popular man.

In 1873 the Reverend J. Holroyd preached here and Reverend Henry Weale was recorded here in 1905.

Captain John Joseph Robinson of Balmoral House was at one time the Deacon of this Independent Chapel.

The chapel became very dilapidated following its closure in c 2000 but was refurbished during c 2006 when it was converted and put up for sale as a superior residence, 'Arc House' and eventually advertised as a holiday let. Some parts at the rear of the chapel were sold off as separate small character residences and includes the neat 'Buttress Cottage' and 'Bellebeck' cottage.

Plate 151
In this photograph 'The Congs' are dressed in their Sunday best, including fur coats and fur collars on this cold winters morning, when this group including the tall man wearing the 'dog collar' posed for the photographer, before attended chapel. It would be interesting to know if they were able to take the dog inside the chapel!

Plate 151a
How the chapel looks today

THE CHURCH OF ST PETER

Plate 152. c1926
The photographer in this early 1920's view has captured 3 small children and a lone hen, close to 'The Homestead' with wooden lean to and 'Brown Haven' with neat lace curtains.

The Church of St Peter, midway up Church Street to the right of picture was originally the old National School and cost £496.8s.8d to build, the money being raised through subscriptions.

The National School house was converted to a chapel of ease or mission room and dedicated to St Peter The Fisherman and licensed by the Archbishop of York as an Episcopal Chapel in 1849.

Churches and chapels were never far from a public house and St. Peter's was no exception, with the nearby 'White Horse Inn'.

SECTION 15.0 – 'SHOPPING ON THE HIGH STREET'

At the time that the young James Cook was in Staithes in 1745, as an apprentice in the shop belonging to William Sanderson (c1711-1773), at the base of Church Street, there was already an establishment of many houses, shops and public houses, as Staithes strived to be self sufficient.

As early as 1823 the following shops/businesses were recorded:

Business	Number	Business	Number
Bakers	4	Grocer/Draper	4
Blacksmiths	2	Fish Curer	4
Butchers	1	Joiner	5
Clockmaker	1	Mason	1
Cobbler	7	Victualler	5

In 1834 there were six Milliners & Dress Makers recorded in the Skelton in Cleveland directory and all were working in Staithes: Elizabeth Breckon, Elizabeth Cole, Mary Pindar, Mary Roddam, Mary Snowdon & Dinah Woods. By 1840 the following additional shops and trades were recorded: Barber (2), Cabinet Maker, Druggist, Plumber, Saddler & Surgeon. In the 1850's there were 30-40 shops within the village of Staithes and by 1861, 97 people were recorded working in Staithes shops and businesses.

By 1864 there were 53 recorded shops/businesses, including jet manufacturer (1), tinplate worker (1), vetinary (2), surgeons (2), druggists (2), clogmaker (1) & confectioner (1), with grocers/drapers (11).

The high number of Coopers and Joiners/Wheelwright/Cartwrights were reflections of the demands within the fishing trade in Staithes. The number of dressmakers and shoemakers does not mean that Staithes was the height of fashion! But rather associated with good honest working folk attire, plus of course Sunday best clothes.

Butchers increased to (3), victuallers (8) and it is easy to see why Staithes locals rarely needed to leave the village as they were virtually self sufficient for groceries, clothes, hardware, bread, shoes and of course fish.

Business	1890	1897	1908
Auctioneer/Fish Salesman	1	1	2
Baker	1	2	2
Bank	1	2	2
Barber	1	1	1
Blacksmith	3	2	1
Boat builder	1	1	1
Boot & Shoemaker	5	1	1
Builder	1	1	2
Butcher	5	4	4
Carter	2	1	0
Café/ Refreshments	0	1	1
Chemist/Druggist	1	1	1
Confectioner	1	1	2
Co-Operative	1	1	1
Cooper	1	0	0
Dressmaker	1	0	0
Farmer/cow keeper	2	4	3
Fish Merchant	3	3	7
General Dealer	2	2	1
Grocer	9	3	2
Grocer & Draper	4	4	2
Hotels	1	1	1
Joiner/Wheelwright	2	4	3
Librarian	1	1	1
Market Gardener	1	1	0
Mason	1	1	1
Pig Dealer	1	0	0
Photographer	0	0	1
Postal & Telegraph	1	1	1
Public Houses	8	8	8
Shopkeeper	1	6	7
Smoke House	2+	2+	1
Tailor & Clothier	7	6	3
Tobacconist	0	0	1
Veterinary Surgeon	1	1	0
Victualler	7	7	7

The number of shops/businesses in 1890 totalled 50, falling to 40 by 1897, not including victuallers or fish merchants.

The above statistics taken from various Directories of North Yorkshire, do not reflect the absolute true picture, but do give a pointer to the rise and fall of various trades/businesses and the trades that remained stable. For instance the opening of the Co-Operative first store in 1889 reduced the number of grocers by 50% (not unlike the current demise with Tesco, Sainsbury's, Morrisons etc Super Stores).

The coming of the railway in 1883 eventually led to Staithes people having a wider choice of where to do their shopping and where to sell their fish and this led to a drastic decline in the dress-making and boot/shoe-making trades.

There were of course many, many full time fishermen, all in their own way contributing to employment and to the self sufficiency of this unique village.

Most of the shops were situated on the High Street, the exceptions being a cobblers and a tobacconist/general dealer, which could be found on Church Street, also two small shops once existed within the Barrass Square.

It must have been quite a sight coming down Byron Bank, passing the Bethel and PM Chapels to then encounter a busy array of High Street shops, not unlike a busy town street of today. At its height there would have been 40 or so shops & businesses between the start of the High Street and it's end close to the Cod & Lobster. There would be horse and carts delivering, women buying their daily bread, children playing, dogs and hens straying across the cobbles all creating a very busy scene.

INTERESTING STAITHES PROFESSIONS/TRADES:

Year trading	Name	Trade or Profession
1823	Christopher Mason	Staithes Postman (pre postage stamps)
1834 -1872	Joseph Brown	Staithes Clock & watchmaker
1834 -1840	John Breckon	Surgeon & Victualler (Royal George)
1834	Jonathan Pindar	Clogmaker
1834	Thomas Laverick	Saddler
1841	John Lawson	Letter Carrier
1851	George Lawson	Hook Maker
1851	Thomas Finley	Hawker of Toys
1851	John Harrison	Ostler (hostelry/ inn to look after horses)
1851	Mary Marshall	Char-woman
1851	John Riley	Begger
1851	Margaret Weatherill	Proprietor of Houses
1851	Thomas Parkin	Scavenger
1861	John Ridley	Bell-man
1861	William Laws	Jet Miner
1861	Thomas Crakey	Jet Ornament manufacturer
1861	Dinah Theaker	Washer Woman
1861	John Cuthbert	Common Stage Carrier
1861	John Seymour	Letter Carrier Messenger & Grocer
1861	James Waite	Police Constable
1861	Richard Smales	Stage Carrier
1861	Thomas Laverick	Saddler & Gardener
1861	Elizabeth Taylor	Stay maker
1871	Elizabeth Laverick	Mantua maker (custom made dressmaker)
1871	George Gale	Timber merchant
1871	Mark Brown	Cordwainer (leather shoe-maker)
1871	Ann Unthank	Laundress
1871	John Hudson	Clogger
1871	Margaret Burton	Boot Binder
1871	John Foster	Stone Cutter
1871	Sarah Sanderson,	Net mender (also Hannah Shippy, Hannah Verrill & Betsy Shippy)
1881	Alfred Briggs	Brass Finisher
1881	Thomas Lawson	Stone Mason & Innkeeper
1890	Edward Steward	Market Gardener
1911	John Verrill	Shale Picker (miner)
1911	Margaret Verrill	Net Repairer at the age of 67

Joseph Brown the local Staithes Clockmaker was recorded as living on Front Street in 1861, his sister Mary Brown was a School Mistress, his son Mark Brown was a School Master and his youngest son Jonathan Brown was an apprentice Cartwright.

Joseph Verrill had the 'Old Established Shop' on the High Street and eventually John Richard Verrill had another just twenty yards away.

THE HIGH STREET SHOPS:

Plate 153. Valentine's, 1904

Posted at eight o'clock at night on 7th July 1904, the message on the reverse side reads, 'Wish you were here for the weekend, Staithes Fair this week, all very busy'.

Both the staff from the Postal Telegraphic Office and the Grocery and Confectioners shop, pose for the photographer in the mid-afternoon sun (twenty minutes to three to be precise), under the bare canopy frame.

The post-office is on the immediate left and Robert Featherstone (1849-1927) was both the sub-postmaster and shopkeeper, with help from his wife Mary (1851-1930), both standing left, this was a huge shop serving the Staithes inhabitants well. A 'Penny' Savings Bank was also situated within.

Letters would arrive here on week days at 7.57am & 5.51 & 6.18pm, being dispatched at 9.45am & 5.30 & as late as 8.30pm. The Staithes High Street cobble stones werebeautiful and unique, what a shame they were needlessly replaced.

These premises have had a variety of use since,such as the Central Café, Copper Kettle, Coffee House, Ian Croden's small factory designing/ producing Wind Surfing equipment and now the Staithes Art Gallery.

The barbers pole to the right denotes the premises of 'tonsorial artist' John Henry Roe.

Plate 154

Proof of the late posting is shown here, where this postcard was posted at 8.30pm, however an error has occurred where the postmaster has reversed the 07 on his rubber stamp.

Plate 155. Morley c1906

The original cobbled street was a beautiful work of art, it was a disgrace when the council dug them all up, replacing with uniform blocks. A dog lies patiently outside the doorway of the Royal George Inn, where the proprietor at this time was John Hansell. Mr Robert Featherstone the shopkeeper and sub-postmaster, is holding a chromo-litho framed advertising print for Cadbury's chocolate, next to the on looking army sergeant. The cellar trap door is open following a delivery of new stock. Further shops are situated between the Royal George and the distant Shoulder of Mutton as follows; Ellen Cole's grocers shop and Hannah Nesbit's drapers shop. In the distant left just beyond the Shoulder of Mutton, the white awning is that of John Codling the baker.

Plate 156. c1909

John Henry Roe, established his General Mason and Builders shop, on the High Street during the early 1890's and remained in business until at least the late 1930's. There were two halves to this shop, the right hand window displayed porcelain figures, clocks and miscellaneous pottery items, whilst the left hand side had paints, oil lamps, brushes, tools etc.

The striped pole, also denoted that stonemason, John Henry Roe, also cut hair for Staithes locals, his nickname being 'Barber Jack'. Hence why the adjacent alley leads to Barbers Yard. In the picture are John Henry's family: George William Roe, Martha Ann Roe ('Marthan'), second wife Hannah Roe (nee Laverick), holding John Thomas Laverick Roe.

John Henry Roe was the son of William Roe, a jet merchant of Blackburns Yard, Church St, Whitby and he was not the first Staithes barber as George Lawson (a Cooper by trade) & Thomas Lawson were recorded as such in 1872.

The fine wrought iron work above the shop balustrade was a quality feature, but all such features are now 'lost'.

This former prestigious property is now called the 'Anchorage' and is currently undergoing some much needed repairs to the frontage.

Plate 157. c1903

John Henry Roe is pictured outside his shop, with his wife and family members, where the hardware and giftware split window displays, are evident. John Henry Roe was recorded as a bricklayer and Contractor in the 1901 census and by 1911 he had seven children. His first wife Mary Ann Roe (nee Perison), bore him four children; John Thomas Roe, George William Roe, Martha Ann Roe and Mary Ann Roe. His second wife Hannah Roe (nee Laverick) bore him three more children; John Thomas Laverick Roe, Beatrice Mary Roe and Hilda Francis Roe.

Plate 158. C1931

Various fruits adorn the makeshift display stand, outside Herbert Mason's fruit shop, next to the Shoulder of Mutton Inn on the High Street; when prices were very different from today.

Bananas were only 1d each, new onions 1½ d per lb and good potatoes were an incredible 1½ d per stone at the time of this view in c 1931.

This old shop became Walker's Electrical shop in the 1970's, but has been closed for many years and the building has remained in a 'dormant 'state for sometime now. At the time of writing Masons old shop front is being refurbished as a private residence. The adjacent building was the old Shoulder of Mutton public house, which in the 1970's had a brief life as the Mariner's Antique shop.

Most of the grocers shops in Staithes from the 1890's through to late Edwardian times, were also drapers (Masons was one of the exceptions).

Plate 159. 1905

This photograph confirms that the roof line of the buildings close to Websters steps, was all on one level in 1905.

The shop closest to the large stone bink was the bakery, where Maggie Cole presided.

The ecclesiastical shaped plaque and the clock (which was double sided) on the right denote the position of Staithes Fishermen's & Seamen's Institute ('Clock House'), now Beckfoot Cottage. Initially this was for Men Only, who had attained 21 years of age and subscriptions were 3/- per year and it was open 9am-10pm. Gambling and swearing were not allowed.

This institute was converted out of two fishermans cottages and was opened by Sir Charles Mark Palmer and Lady Palmer on 15th August 1888. It contained a lecture hall, reading room, recreation room and a good library; it was stated as "further contributes to the interlectual pabulum (nourishment) of the members". Mr George Hodgson was the librarian during these early days and the various early secretaries were: D.Tough, H.S. Moore and Coates Crooks.

The Yorkshire Penny Bank (branch) was held here on Saturday evenings, where Captain James Pinder was the actuary and the Reverend A.C. Corner was the honoury Chaplain & Secretary.

Plate 160. JT Ross c1912

The shop on the immediate left appears to be a fruit shop with a tray of gooseberries placed on the high raised bink. This photographic postcard by Ross of Whitby was posted in August 1918, but the photograph dates earlier around c1912. The woman with hands on hips is standing outside her bakery shop, 3 doors down from Websters Steps. Deep grooves exist in the large bink to the front of this business.

The large flag pole immediate right, denotes the site of the Fishermen's & Seamen's Institute and the man with pipe carrying a metal pale is leaning on the wall with the Institute 'double sided' clock overhead.

To the right lies Gar' Ends and Daniel Cole had his bakery business here.

Plate 161

'Welfords' bread delivery vehicle is just visible at the top end of this high street view, parked opposite to the Royal George public house.

The bonneted lady walking down towards the seafront, is about level with John Richard Verrill's General Store (now Blue Jacket House) and the narrow passageway, leading to Webster's Steps. Adjacent is today's red fronted popular butchers shop, belonging to Richard Lyth, where fine meats and other essential products can be purchased.

Just beyond the leaning large stone of 'Kirsty's Cottage and passage to Slippery Hill, lies the old bakers shop of Maggie Cole (now Salmon Cottage), which had an extensive 'bink' in front of the shop.

'SHOPPING ON THE HIGH STREET'

Plate 162. c1914

Seymour's general dealers shop (now 'Singing Waters'), lies to the bottom left and the upper bay window displays a public telephone sign in this circa 1914 photograph. Initially run by Francis (Frankie) Seymour, who was born in Staithes and the son of master mariner Richard Seymour. He retired c1907 to live in Saltburn until his death in 1914. You could allegedly buy anything from this shop from a wedding dress to paraffin, so said Laura Johnson in her autobiography. In 1878 he was listed as a grocer and draper and the newly nominated Trustee of the Independent Chapel. Garth Ends (Gar'ends) separates Seymours shop from the old Fishermans Institute (now Beckfoot Cottage) on the immediate left and Slippery Hill lies to the right.

Plate 163. Pictorial Stationary Co 1905

The shop on the immediate right is today 'The Emporium,' selling good quality clothing and giftware and run by Kathie Cortese and Jim Hanwell.

At the time of this coloured publication, the shop belonged to James W. Legg who ran a successful Confectionery and Newsagents business here, where he sold local postcards, several of which are featured in this book.

Access to Mann's Yard, lies to the right and the bay window left does not form part of 'The Nook' today.

Emily Hanson had her fruiterer and confectioners business ('The Right Shop for Sweets & Fruit') on the left near to 'Coastguard Cottage'.

Plate 164. Francis Frith c1928

By the 1920's J.W. Legg's shop sign, below the shop lintel, advertises, 'Newsagent and Patent Medicines'.

Packets of Woodbine cigarettes were available, from a dispensing machine outside, to the right of the entrance door.

Sandwiched between the Golden Lion and Legg's shop, with the white awning is Gladstones old shop selling as always a variety of ices and sweets.

Plate 165. c1960

Taken about 30 years later, motorised transport is more evident and the Woodbine dispensing machine has gone, as James Legg's shop has now become the Newsagent & Tobacconist of E.Brooke. The Ices sign is that of Gladstones adjacent shop.

The message penned to the reverse of this view reads;"Uncle Harry knows a lot of the local people, to whom he introduced us. We spent a short while with an old lady, who lives in one of the old cottages near the beach and had afternoon tea with another old lady in Staithes, it was all very nice"

Plate 166. c1917

Joseph Verrill's shop window, is well stocked with all manner of bottles of alcohol, in the right hand window and he was recorded from the 1890's as being an agent for W. & A. Gilbey Limited, Wine & Spirit Merchants.

This shop was later to become that of W & H Dean (included a chemist's) and eventually the Endeavour Tea Shoppe. Followed by the charismatic, special fish restaurant, 'The Endeavour' run by celebrity chef Lisa Chapman of 'To Dine For' fame. To the right of here used to be the 'Spar' shop, which later became the Antique Shop (now used for exhibitions and to display artisans works).

Plate 167. Valentine's 1930's

Note the neat and tidy steps to each house on the left of the High Street, a Mrs Ann Brooks who now lives at Boulby, recalls the trouble that they would cause if they stepped on a freshly 'donkied' step. Several shops are evident on the right, the first shop belonging to Joseph Verrill junior (1855-1937), who always wore a white pinefore, was built with seven rooms. It originally sold ship chandlery, oilskins, sou'westers and everything else associated with the fishing trade. Three generations of shopkeepers were here and his father also Joseph Verrill (1821-1896), previously ran this shop. At this time, a new market has been established and he has woollen jumpers hanging high, boxes of lemons, nets, towels, Staithes bonnets and local view cards. Wooden toy boats and spades for the beach, denote the age of plastic is still to come. Joseph's daughters Lavinia and Lizzie often worked in the shop.

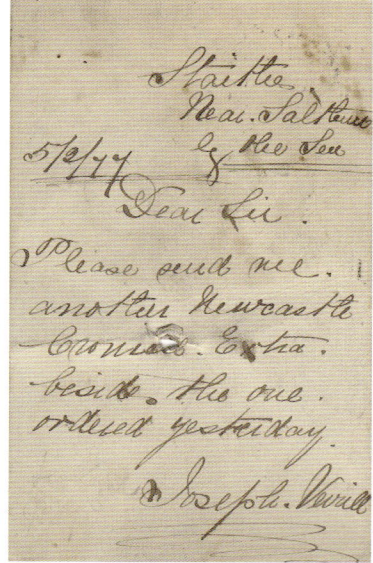

Plate 168. 1877

This is an early correspondence card as sent by Joseph Verrill in 1877, ordering an additional copy of the Newcastle Chronicle from A.B. Moss, Printers & Stationers in Saltburn.

Plate 169. taken from an original painting by Sue Brearley

The tall building on the right used to belong to Fish Merchant G.Trattles, who advertised in his window: 'Fried Fish & Fried Potatoes Everynight'. It then became P.T (Tom).Crake's (1860-1921) confectionary shop in the early 1900's and Fry's Chocolate was advertised on the window until c1933.Tom Crake allegedly was not too trusting of Banks and hid his money all over the house! It eventually became 'The Pork Shop' for several years as shown above, run by Joe Parkinson, who specialised in cooked meats and pies. It was advertised as 'The Tasty Shop'.

Plate 170

The Pork Shop is in the background of the Staithes Carnival parade during c1966.

Later it became a hairdresser's shop, 'Debon Hair/ Clipper Hair Salon'. It remained empty for around 15 years and in 2000 the popular 'Kessen Bowl' opened. Where all manner of gifts and beach ware could be purchased from entrepreneur Maurice Selby and wife Maureen.

Kessen Bowl means bladder or buoy, used for marking the location of broken long lines.

Maurice's Kessen Bowl has literally thousands of items in stock and you need an hour or so to take it all in, stocktaking must be a nightmare!

Plate 171

The porch on the immediate right of 'Kessen Bowl', is the entrance to the former 'St Martins Lodge', where Marie Marguerite Lowden lived. Marie stands in the doorway to her house, with matching bonnet and house coat, awaiting customers to purchase her crackly homemade toffee, on sale at 5d per bag.

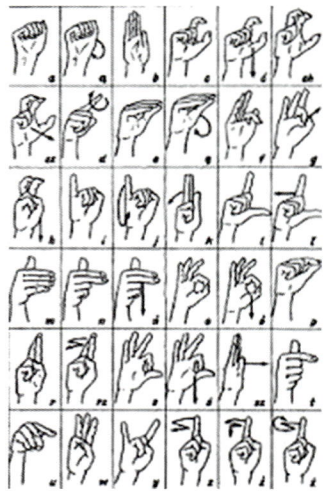

Marie was totally deaf and half blind from her teens, her husband was totally deaf and dumb. Sadly when her husband died of Leukemia, she was left with a hefty mortgage and several large bills for house renovations. To make ends meet it was suggested that she sell toffee apples and she regularly advertised 'Lovely Crackly Home Made Toffee' for 5d per bag. She worked into her 70's and paid all debt off within 9 years. She was widely known as 'The Toffee Lady of Staithes' and at a suggestion from James Herriot, who stayed there, the house name was changed to 'Toffee Crackle House' and remains so today. Local entrepreneur Maurice Selby, resides here today.

Marie was also an author, writing three small books during the late 1980's, one of which was titled 'Behind the Scenes in Yorkshire'.

Plate 172

The open wire waste basket to the left, was part of the 'Keep Britain Tidy' campaign.

The advertising enamel sign, 'Senior Service Satisfy' adorns the 'Gift Shop', where toys and fancy goods could be purchased. W. Cundy ran this place in the 1950's and a lending library was within. 'The Gift Shop' shown here is of course run today by the talented local photographer & entrepreneur Terry Lawson, his wife Anne (bonnets fame) and daughter Jane. Terry's trade mark of 'if I have'nt got it, I will by Friday!' is a tribute to his desire to please and offer true service.

Locals and all visitors to Staithes utilise this shop for anything from firelighters to flying kites. 'Kippers Corner', cottage (one time Willy Gargett's barber shop/Tommy Ward's fish & chip shop) lies on the corner of the High Street and Hugill's Road, which is sharp right here and out of view. Indiana Truefitt had the Victoria Family Hotel built in 1868/69 and this is the site, now housing The Gift Shop, but not the same building. During the early 1890's Joseph Brown Newton JP had his grocery, butchers and drapery business here and John Peirson his former apprentice was recorded here as a grocer/draper in 1901. It would appear that Joseph had new business premises built on this site around 1901 and carried on with his butcher's business until at least 1911. His old butcher's hooks are still in the ceiling of Terry Lawson's Gift Shop today. Newton was known to hang his bacons and store other items for his business in 'Meal House'(now demolished), close to the slipway adjacent to the Cod & Lobster.

Pierson was running the grocer/drapery side of the business in his own right by 1905 and carried on in business here at least until the mid 1940's, almost until his death in 1948, aged 83.

Plate 173. Francis Frith c1955

Many years later this mid 1950's view, shows the lower village post office, when Mark Somers' was the incumbent, as indicated by the sign above the Telegraph Office plaque over the doorway. Model boats, picture postcards, ices, sweets, Lyons cakes and Kodak developing and printing were available here, including a lending library at one time. He advertised that he stocked 'Everything definitely Holidaymaker'.

During the 1920's, this was not a Post office and Matthew Trattles ran his Drug Stores here, selling Toilet Articles, Soaps, View Cards and crested china. This view shows how the old Co-Op shop has extended to the corner of the opening to Chapel Yard with its Butchery Dept. to become double fronted.

Plate 174

The unknown artist of this original watercolour of Staithes Post Office on the High Street, has signed his work in the bottom right hand corner. The steps on the right lead to 'Middlesbrough House' where at one time Abraham Manship lived, who allegedly gave his name to Abrahams Lane, which runs at the side, to the bridge over the Beck. Abraham Manship died in 1914, aged 73.

'Lyn House' stands to the left of the post office and was formerly called 'Custom House' and this was home to coastguard Henry Quick in 1911. Jean and William Peter Eccleston took over the reigns from Eric Preston in 1982, until their retirement in 2010, it was they, that produced the book 'A History & Geneology of Staithes', published in 1998.

Plate 175

Situated away from the busy High Street a large enamel sign advertising 'Wills Capstan' cigarettes, adorns the lower front of the newsagents & tobacconists shop (George & Hannah Daniel's old general dealers shop, in 1911) on Church Street.

Mary Ann Cole was an earlier occupant, being recorded as a grocer & general dealer in 1881.

Mary lived with her two sons William Cole and John Trattles Cole, both became joiners and this eventually led to their fame as Staithes boatbuilders.

The former premises of the White Horse Inn (now The White House!) are just above and the narrow opening to Dog Loup is just below, with Kirkhill House and café opposite. This relatively modern view was taken in the mid 1960's, when the shop housed a former Doctors Surgery (Doctor Brash 1912-1969, sadly killed in a road crash on Boulby Bank in January 1969) and now forms the private residence of 'Hazeldene'.

Other shops on or near the High Street, existing during the 1920-1930's are as follows:

Proprietor	Business	Proprietor	Business
L. Armstrong	Butcher	EE Hodgson	Butcher
Tom Bennison	Joiner/Cartwright/Undertaker	Jas W Legg	Newsagent, tobacconist etc
John Bennison	Carrier	John Peirson	Grocer & Draper
Arthur Boyes	Butcher	Seymour's	General Dealer
J.T. Cole	Builder & Contractor 'Springfield'	S.H. Thompson	Grocer & General Dealer
Daniel Cole	Baker	W Thompson	Draper/Boot & Shoe Dealer
M. Cole	Fruiterer & Confectioner	Matthew Trattles	Drug Store
W. Cole	Joiner/Undertaker/Builder	A.S. Umpleby (station depot)	Coal/Coke/Gas/ Lime dealer
Emily Hanson	Fruiterer & Confectioner	Joseph Verrill	Grocer/general dealer

During the Edwardian period, ex deputy miner Richard Dix opened his general store on the land adjacent to Staithes telephone kiosk on the corner of Hugill's Road (long since demolished and land used as a private car park now)

Plate 176

William Francis Verrill Longster' shop on the High Street is easily recognised by the fancy brickwork above the shop lintel, this brickwork is found also on the adjacent house 'Sandringham' and both formed a single dwelling in earlier times.

This shop is now the house named, 'The Coppins', a former home to the infamous fish seller Vera Marsay, situated next to the former Golden Lion (now Greystones).

William Francis Verrill Longster, was the son of Fish Merchant, James Longster and born in 1905. He married nurse Elsie Ward of Belmont House, Staithes, the daughter of Staithes joiner Matthew Trattles Ward in 1941.

At this time William was living in Chapel Yard and working as a Burner in the Steel Works.

'Will' became a Fruiterer and Grocer and he has fresh rhubarb and plums for sale in the boxes at the front of the shop and two dispensing machines, close to the doorway, behind his two female assistants.

SECTION 16.0 – THE 'BROTHERS' CLUB WALK

Plate 177. H.C.Morley

Morley did not have far to travel from his nearby photographic studio, to capture the 'Club Walk' at Staithes in c1906. The Staithes women wear their pristine whites from top to toe.

The High Street is overrun with locals who are in every doorway, to witness this important day, to watch the 'Brothers'; who all wear their green woven silk sashes, bearing the emblem of the Good Shepherd. This is the Ancient Order of Shepherds Lodge No.245 who arranged the Club Walk to coincide with the Staithes Fair.

As Staithes men began to earn a regular wage, through fishing, farming or iron-stone mining, a small deduction was made to contribute to a Benevolent Fund, to cover hard times, such as illness or deaths in the family. John Trattles Cole was the first secretary and the Club Walk commenced around 1892. 'The Brothers' were summoned to attend and a fine was levied if you did not attend. The Friendly Society was widely supported and with tragedies not far round the corner, Staithes families were able to bury their loved one's without resorting to pauper's graves.

Other societies such as the Loyal Order of Druids, Staithes Fishermen & Miner's Benevolent Provident Society and the Loyal Brotherly Love Lodge No 3781 of Oddfellows (Manchester Unity) had existed earlier in the area.

Plate 178a
Matthew Verrill (left) & Willie Verrill proudly wear their 'Brothers' sashes for the much later Club Walk during the 1940's

Plate 178b
The women dressed up too for the Club Walk and Sarah Hannah Cole(nee Verrill) and Margaret 'Margit'Ward are on the lane above the Station Hotel.

Plate 178c/d
A Staithes 'Brother' wearing the full sash, possibly taken in H.C Morley's studio.

Plate 178e/f
Such Ancient Order Societies always favoured woven silk and they are highly collectable today

Now known as the Shepherds Friendly Society, (The Loyal Order of Ancient Shepherds) was a UK Friendly Society and one of the oldest mutual insurers in the world. Shepherds Friendly Society started as a sickness and benefits society called Ashton Unity in Ashton-under-Lyne, Lancashire. It was later renamed as the Loyal Order of Ancient Shepherds.

SECTION 17.0 – THE BUTCHERS OF STAITHES:

The title conjures up all sorts of images!

For a fishing town, Staithes has had more than its fair share of butchers shops, spanning a period approaching 200 years. The following butchers were recorded, the years shown are only a 'snapshot' of the time they were in business, but the time is indicative and at its height Staithes would have had 4 or 5 butcher shops for several years.

Butcher	Year Recorded (not complete)
Thomas Parkes	1823 - 1871
William Gibson	1834
Christopher Mann	1834
Thomas Walker	1834
Samuel Dougherty	1851
Robert Parkes (1833 - 1907)	1861 - 1872
Thomas Henry	1890 - 1897
Robet Dunn (also a carter)	1890
James Andrews	1891
John Wilson	1891 - 1893
Joseph Newton Brown	1890 - 1911
Thomas Hodgson (1852 - 1926)	1891 - 1925
George Gibbon	1897 - 1909
John William Stainthorpe	1909 - 1911
Ernest Edgar Hodgson (1881-1952)	1920's - 1930's
Arthur Boyes	c1890 - 1920's,
Leslie Armstrong	1925
George Race Hodgson (xx - 1993)	1950's
J. Parkinson (The Pork Shop)	1950's
Richard Lyth junior & Marianne Lyth (nee Hodgson) - Richard Lyth senior was at the Hinderwell shop only	1970/80's - present day (Hinderwell & Staithes shops),
James David Lyth (1996 –present)	Hinderwell shop only

The Parks family are interesting and the following provide links as to how the Parks managed to be involved in butchering, for nigh on 90 years.

Thomas Parks, Staithes early butcher (born c1793), was a well known Wesleyan in Staithes and he was instrumental in the first Wesleyan chapel building, on the Beckside in 1824. Thomas and his wife Ann had two sons; Thomas & Robert and they lived with their house servant Elizabeth Readman in Staithes.

Robert Parks became a staunch Wesleyan and he was one of the original trustees of the new Wesleyan Chapel of 1866 and he was recorded as a butcher and local preacher in 1871. Robert's sermons were always well received here in Staithes and surrounding districts. He preached the whole of the Guisborough Wesleyan Circuit by travelling on his infamous, sturdy white horse. He married Sarah Ann and they had a son Ralph Thomas Parks (born c1857) along with daughters; Hannah and Ann.

Robert also lived and farmed in Dalehouse, but infirmity forced him to move and he had his new house 'Westgate', built on the corner of Bob Bell's Bank, Staithes, close to his beloved Wesleyan Chapel.

Ralph Thomas Parks carried on the the family tradition and he was recorded in Borrowby/Dalehouse as a butcher in 1890.

Joseph Brown Newton J.P. who was also a Staithes butcher and draper, with his business premises on the High Street, on the site of the former Indiana Truefit's Victoria Hotel. Joseph married butcher/preacher Robert Parks eldest daughter Hannah and they had seven children. In 1891 it is recorded that John Peirson and Jane Hugill were living in the same household as Joseph Brown Newton and his wife Hannah. John Peirson was Joseph's apprentice and they are both recorded as working up to at least 1911 (Joseph as butcher only and John as grocer & draper). Peirson went on to take over Joseph's business when he eventually retired, maintaining a High Street business well into the 1940's.

Plate 179. c1923

Staithes folk stroll on the cobble stones in the vicinity of the Cod & Lobster. This view was taken in the early 1920's, where a 'giant' of a man is strolling past Slip Top on his way to the High Street.

The small butchers shop belonging to Thomas Hodgson, who was also a flour dealer, can be seen behind the lady in her mourning dress and bonnet, this building has been utilised as an electricity board/company housing for some time now.

Both black and white bonnets are evident with peg rugs and fishermans socks hung out to dry on the railings.

The 'Ices' sign on the right hand wall, possibly belonged to the nearby Marine Café, formerly Seymours General store, just around the corner.

STAITHES 'BETWEEN TWO NABS'

Thomas Hodgson was born in 1852 and he ran a very successful butchery business in Staithes for well over 40 years. In 1882 he and his wife Ann had a son called Ernest and shortly before Thomas died in 1926, Ernest took over the butchers shop, shown above and carried on the family business.

Plate 180. c1940's
The former Thomas Hodgson original shop, close to the opening for Gun Gutter, is shown here during WW1 time, where Ernest Edgar Hodgson had been in charge since the 1920's.

Ernest is second from the left, with large cap and equally large smile. The man on the extreme right is believed to be Arthur Boyes and he assisted Ernest Hodgson for a while, but eventually opened his own butcher's shop in the village. Arthur was the son of tailor & draper, John H Boyes of Cowbar Bank and he was recorded as an assistant butcher in 1891.

The two dark haired men either side of Ernest were Italian prisoners of war, who were seeing their time out, by working at the well stocked butcher's premises at the end of the High Street.

Plate 181. Sue Young
This picture was originally a fine pastel painting, of Richard & Marianne Lyth's butcher's shop at No.12 the High Street, produced in 2007 by the talented Sue Young of Beckside, Staithes. This painting, titled 'Quiet Moment', was entered in the pastel Society Exhibition during February 2007 at the Mall Gallery, London and was sold for just under £2,000 and now adorns the wall of a country manor house. Richard in his trademark striped butchers 'uniform' takes time out to read the news of the day, before the morning rush!

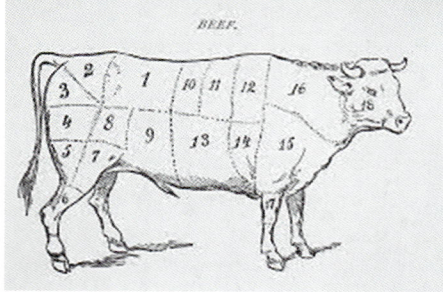

One of the novelty features associated with Marianne and Richard's shop is the use of pre-decimal pricing tickets, where many items are priced in 'old money', providing much amusement for locals and visitors alike.

Richard's wife Marianne (nee Hodgson) is the granddaughter of early Staithes butcher Ernest Edgar Hodgson and she married butcher Richard Lyth (junior) and so the tradition carries on. The Hodgson-Lyth partnership now outstrips the Parks family as they have been butchering for 120 years or so and still going strong, especially with the young James David Lyth further extending the tradition.

SECTION 18.0 – 'STAITHES CO-OPERATORS'

Lofthouse in Cleveland Industrial Co-operative Society, held their opening meetings for the proposed formation of new Co-operative Stores during the period 1874-76.

Loftus Co-operative Society had their Offices & Central Stores in Loftus, with branches on the High Street in Brotton and Staithes. They published a society magazine called the Wheatsheaf, which tells us that by January 1907 they had 2,050 members, with sales of £73,000 and profits of £11,000 for the year; which would be divided quarterly amongst its members. They supplied all manner of domestic items, 'all genuine, unadulterated and without sweated labour'.

The first Staithes Co-op opened on 14th September 1889, within a former convenient, well positioned, High Street shop, that had become vacant and the society duely rented this property. John Buchanan was the first manager of the Staithes store and Skelton Fenby, shortly replaced him, before leaving in 1892 to take up a General Manager position. Thomas Fawbert took over the reigns for a shortwhile, until he transferred to Brotton in 1894 and handing over to James Turnbull. It took nearly seven years for the membership to reach 125 and by the end of 1905, the members had increased to 333. The turnover/profits from trading in groceries, butchers meats, coals, tailoring, bootmaking orders and furniture were such that the new premises, which had been talked about for years, were becoming justifiable. On 31st August 1896 an oil lamp that had been suspended in the front window, became detached and created a fire within the window. A crowd soon gathered, buckets were requisitioned and all was soon put right.

Enid Lucy Pease Robinson (obviously a local girl!) states in her diary on Monday 26th August 1901 that she wanted to go to the art exhibition in the Fisherman's Institute and that a furious storm was brewing, she left The Bank House where she was lodging with Mrs Mary Brown, wife of a Master Mariner.

Enid was nearly blown over, she looked up the street to see Staithes Group artist, Ernest Rigg walking down with a friend, as she went to greet them, Rigg was blown across the street nearly into the Loftus Co-op stores and she was hurled against Mrs Browns Bank House window. We can assume Rigg was blown roughly in the same direction, hence the old first store must have been in a previous vacant shop close to the former Matthew Trattles drug store (later the post office) and is thought to be the old shop, where 'Newholme' is situated (has lintel of former shop).

Plate 182. Co-op Delivery Cart c1910

The Society then purchased by public auction, some old property fronting onto Staithes High Street and their architect Mr Kitching, drew up the plans for a new store and arranged for the two old cottages and rookeries behind; to be demolished (Thomas Rodham's old boatyard). The build contract was awarded in May 1906, to Mr J.T.Cole (established 1878) and his chief builder Mr John Henry Roe ('Barber Jack') and they worked most expediously, using mainly Staithes labour (nearly all members!) such that the new premises were ready for the opening ceremony on 12th December 1906. The weather was poor on this day and the opening ceremony at 3pm,, was mainly held in the Primitive Methodist School Room. Staithes representative on the Society's Committee, was George Bowman and it was he, that was given the pleasant task of opening the store for business. In his opening speech George declared, the building as being the most commodious, well built and well arranged business in the whole of the Urban Councils District.

At 4pm tea was taken in the Wesleyan school room and the two rooms of New Hall up Webster's Steps, substantial spreads were laid and presided over by several Staithes ladies and over 400 people enjoyed the rich spread.

At 5pm a Cinematograph entertainment was given, in the PM schoolroom, where the children had a half hour of enjoyment. More speeches took place at 6.30pm, as this was a grand and special day in Staithes. There was an excess of food and over 500 children enjoyed the left overs, with a film show the following day.

An attempt to purchase the small adjoining cottage to the new store initially failed, as did the attempt to provide a cartway to the rear of the premises. Messrs Kitching and Lee the architects, had great difficulty with shaping the crooked, unsightly site, with its old bricked buildings behind, but all were agreed that they had made the best use of the position, providing a roomy and lightsome shop. It had a butchers shop, fronting the street, although a bit backward. In the main building, a convenient Drapery and Boot Making Department was provided upstairs and the Grocery Dept had ample cellarage, a warehouse, flour stores and a packing room were also provided. Stabling for three horses was provided behind the main building, with hay loft, harness room, manure pit and large yard with open shed; underneath which was placed the Gas Generating House. The whole of the premises were lit by the Thornton Steel Empire Patent Gas Generator and Automatic Producer. There were 17 burners attached to it and it was stated to take less attention/time than to trim one paraffin lamp.

The Society were shareholders in the North Wales Quaries Ltd and the roofs of the new Co-op were of course covered with their slates.

Plate 183. JT Ross 1906

J.T. Ross of Whitby took this important view, sometime around August 1906 from a lofty perch at Aukness (Hawkness) looking towards the new metal girder bridge, over the beck, constructed in mid 1905. He has recorded the construction of the new Co-operative store buildings, in the immediate right of picture, which were built on the former Thomas Rodham's boat building yard. It is noted that new bricks have been placed onto older bricks alongside the old pathway, formerly known as Simpson's Road (the older bricks were much later faced with rendering and several coble and fish icons added).

In the distance lies Penny Steel and Slate Heap Steel the well known surfing reef, known today as 'The Cove'.

This photograph provides a good view of the rear of Matthew Trattles Drug Store (later the P.O.), Lyn House and Ravenscraig House. It is an extremely important photograph as it positively dates the replacement of the old wooden trestle bridge, before the new Co-op opened in December 1906.

Plate 184. HC Morley c1906

James Turnbull, manager of the old store went on to become the manager of the new 1906 store. James held the reigns until the early 1920's, when Will Main took charge until the late 1930's.

Local delivery man, believed to be John Bennison, with his large horse and the new Co-op manager James Turnbull and staff are all 'frozen' by the photographer. All manner of products are offered for sale, from starch (Irl-Am & Robin) jams, packet teas, rice, candles and of course the Co-op dividend. The store in the picture right, is yet to extend into the adjacent property on the corner of the opening, leading to Chapel Yard.

Thomas Verrill was an assistant grocer here in 1911 and Valentine Hugill was a cobbler for the Co-op store.

By the 1920's this became the East Cleveland Co-operative Society and visitors were told 'that they would find the pleasure of their holiday enhanced by making their purchases at this branch!'.

The Loftus Co-Operative Society became part of the East Cleveland Co-Operative Society in 1911 and by 1974 it was part of the North East CS. Up to 1951 the only store in Staithes was the High St store near the Chapel Yard opening.

The Co-op directories for both 1966 and 1972 show that the High St store had a butchery, drapery & grocery, whilst on Jubilee Terrace the small store (former Grace Shippey premises) had a grocery only. Many stores were closed during the various mergers and it may well be that Staithes High St Co-op closed in the late 1970's. The Jubilee Terrace store is now the Excelsior Fisheries Fish & Chip Shop and has been replaced by the Co-op super store on the A174 on the former site occupied by the Cleveland Garage (Tawn & Crooks) who were Motor & General Engineers.

SECTION 19.0 – CAFÉ CULTURE' IN STAITHES

Refreshment Rooms were in existence in the fishing village of Staithes over one hundred years ago and that tradition continues today.

The early café's and refreshment rooms, date from the late 1890's and they all served amongst other dishes, a popular hearty plate of Ham and Eggs, no doubt a product of locally kept hens and of course several houses also had their own 'p-g housings'. Local superstition does not allow the use of the word p-g and alternatives have to be found, when used in conversations (years ago it was grecians but curly tails, grunters etc are often used even now!).The influx of artists, walkers and as Staithes developed as a tourist attraction with many well off visitor's, this brought demands for refreshments, dinners and of course cakes.

Following research it would appear that the earliest recorded café was that of Margaret Winspear, who ran both a grocer's shop and café in 1893.

Plate 185

It was a gated road that led to Staithes station and in this photograph a team of eight horses, are hauling a large tree trunk up the rough track towards the station.

The Cabin Café can be seen sandwiched between the large dormer bungalow of 'Cosy Cottage' and the fishermans store house (garage like structure).

Plate 186

This busy photograph has captured a British Rail Standard Class 4-2-6-4T locomotive, with several additional coaches, on the viaduct, travelling towards Saltburn. A motorbike LVN 495 is parked up alongside another motorbike with wind screen and a vintage motor car close to the dormer bungalow of 'Cosy Cottage', now extended to the rear. The Cabin as advertised lies to the right of the bungalow, where snacks, jugs of tea, bed & breakfast and Car Park were advertised at the time of this mid1950's photograph.

Plate 187

The Cabin Café advertising sign is just visible to the right of 'Cosy Cottage'.

It was later renamed as the Tea Shop and this is still a flourishing café today where kipper breakfasts and snacks are served by owner Angela Cox. Angela has run The Tea Shop Café since 2006 and prides herself on her friendly service. It was previously known as 'The Cabin Tea Shop' which in the 1960's/70's was a sort of Coffee Bar, where a juke box was regularly played and somewhat unusually a Mr & Mrs Downey held their wedding reception there!

SECTION 20.0 – BECKSIDE

John Walker Ord (1811-1853) had but a short life, but in this time he wrote some important books and his Prospectus of his projected 'History and Antiquities of Cleveland' first appeared in 1843, in 12 monthly parts, costing 2/6d each. He wrote about Staithes as follows: "The roads are three – Old Church, Dale House and Coburn Road, the last of which terminates in the rough, rocky, shingly channel of Coburn Beck, over which carriages of every description entering Staithes here are forced to pass".

Plate 199
This exceptionally rare 1890's photograph, was titled 'A snapshot of Staithes, showing Old Bridge'. This snapshot' is very important, as it confirms the use of a ford across the beck from Coulthirst Slip, towards the slipway, at Granary Yard; close to the boat building yard, of John Trattles Cole. With whip in hand, the carter drives his faithful horse and seemingly empty cart, diagonally across the beck, eagerly watched by three small boys in the beck, with their trousers rolled up. A cottage opposite here on the Beckside is named 'Fordside', (see photograph below), giving further credence to the existence of the old ford.

Plate 200. c1900
The left hand of the central, three story houses, close to Rodham's Boatyard, is 'Fordside' and a low stone shed lies between it and the beckside.

The wide area in the front of 'Fordside' was drastically reduced in width, once the old buildings lining the beckside were demolished. Hence the beck width increased here, leaving just a narrow road from Back Road to the bridge at Abraham's Lane, this narrow road was formerly known as Simpson's Road. The wall and bank in front of 'Fordside' collapsed in May 2013, taking a small brick shed into the beck, probably due to the actions of a digger, removing a large boulder from the bankside, during Council improvements to the beckside bank.

Plate 201. c1904
The washing hung from a makeshift line, the tumble down buildings in the Beck and the rickety reinforcements, present a true picture of life by the Beckside in 1904. The young woman with bonnet, is carrying a pale, no doubt in order to draw water from the Beck. The low lying building in front of 'Fordside' and what is now 'The Cottage Beckside' has smoke emanating from the rear chimney, where fish will be curing. The tiny building to the left of 'Fordside' was a fisherman's store and still exists today.

Plate 202. c1923

Fish have been hung out to dry, on the fence opposite 'Cowbar View Cottage', lining the narrow beckside path, formerly known as Simpson Road. In 1911 this was the home of postal clerk, William C. Featherstone. The small glass panel above the door of this fine cottage carries the date 1732. To the right lies the narrow nick, leading to Ruby House Yard/Simpson's Yard. The adjacent right buildings belong to the Loftus No.2 Branch of the Co-op Society.

The crude Beckside bank has yet to be strengthened, in this early 1920's photograph, taken from a glass negative. Coble 'Polly' (WY83), can be seen moored just below the old baiting and salting sheds, built low in the Beckside.

Badger Castle stands proudly to the top right, on prominent ground, this being the first building erected at the top of Staithes Bank. It was erected by William Thompson a former fish curer and jet merchant, who built it illegally, in defiance of the Marquis of Normanby.

Plate 203. Rod Jewell c 2007

This young seal, caused quite a stir in 2007, when it became stranded on the Beckside, after swimming from the sea and up the beck; before becoming exhausted. The baby seal took rest, on the rocks opposite 'The Granary' and 'Pilot Me ' cottages, on Granary Yard, before members of the RSPCA managed to coax it back into the water and out to sea.

Plate 204. 1920's

Neat allotments existed on the left hand side of the beck and coble boats were stored to the right, in an area known as Low Coble Gardens, in this view of the upper reaches of the Roxby Beck, taken from the railway viaduct. The old bridge in the vicinity of today's stepping stones (The Battlestones), is still in place and the Staithes first Board School is just in the picture, top right. Opening in 1878 and closing seven years after its centenary. The large house to the left of the school, close to the edge of the cliff, is Badger Castle. The message penned to the reverse side reads, "Having a lovely time especially with our 10/- ticket, obviously a reference to their 'rover railway ticket'. We have been to all the places up the coast as far as Staithes. This is quite a nice little place for an afternoon, but not for much longer"

SECTION 21.0 – THE YARDS & NICKS OF STAITHES

Plate 205. A private yard off Chapel Yard

Staithes contains several Yards, accessed through narrow Nicks or passageways and most exist off the High Street, hidden from view down narrow alleyways. During the mid19th Century and at the turn of the 20th Century, these yards were very busy and industrious places, being in constant use; associated with the fishing industry and other trades. The women folk would sit in the sheltered yards, knitting and of course chatting continuously!

The Yard names being associated with former Staithes vessels, or former eminent people; mariners, tradesmen, chapel ministers or preachers or as in several cases the yards take their name simply from the ordinary local people who lived in the immediate vicinity of the yards for many years.

Plate 206. JT Ross c1909

Ross titled this photographic viewcard, as 'A Bit of Old Staithes.' A narrow yard in Staithes, has been recorded, with lady seated, wearing the traditional Staithes bonnet, whilst knitting (their hands were never idle). The fisherman behind, is in the doorway of a very small one up, one down cottage. It was originally thought, that this very small yard was sandwiched between, the rear of the houses fronting Broomhill and the rear of the houses fronting Darlington Terrace, as an identical building to the one on the immediate right exists here. However following a thorough search, this yard is thought to have been situated off the Barris, but now demolished.

BACK YARD

Housed a single dwelling, situated off the North side of the main street.

John Seymour the shoemaker was recorded as living in Back Yard, Staithes in 1851 with his wife Lydia, grand daughter Lydia, servant Mary Harker and his two shoemaker apprentices: Thomas Moor & Stephen Nicholson. John employed five men in total, so it must have been an extensive business. In the 1851 census, John Seymour is listed immediately after fishermen John Robinson & Burton Verrill, who were in Boathouse Yard. Hence as there was only a single dwelling in Back Yard, which was off the North side of the main street, it is assumed that this yard was a small yard off Boathouse Yard, probably the narrow portion to the right.

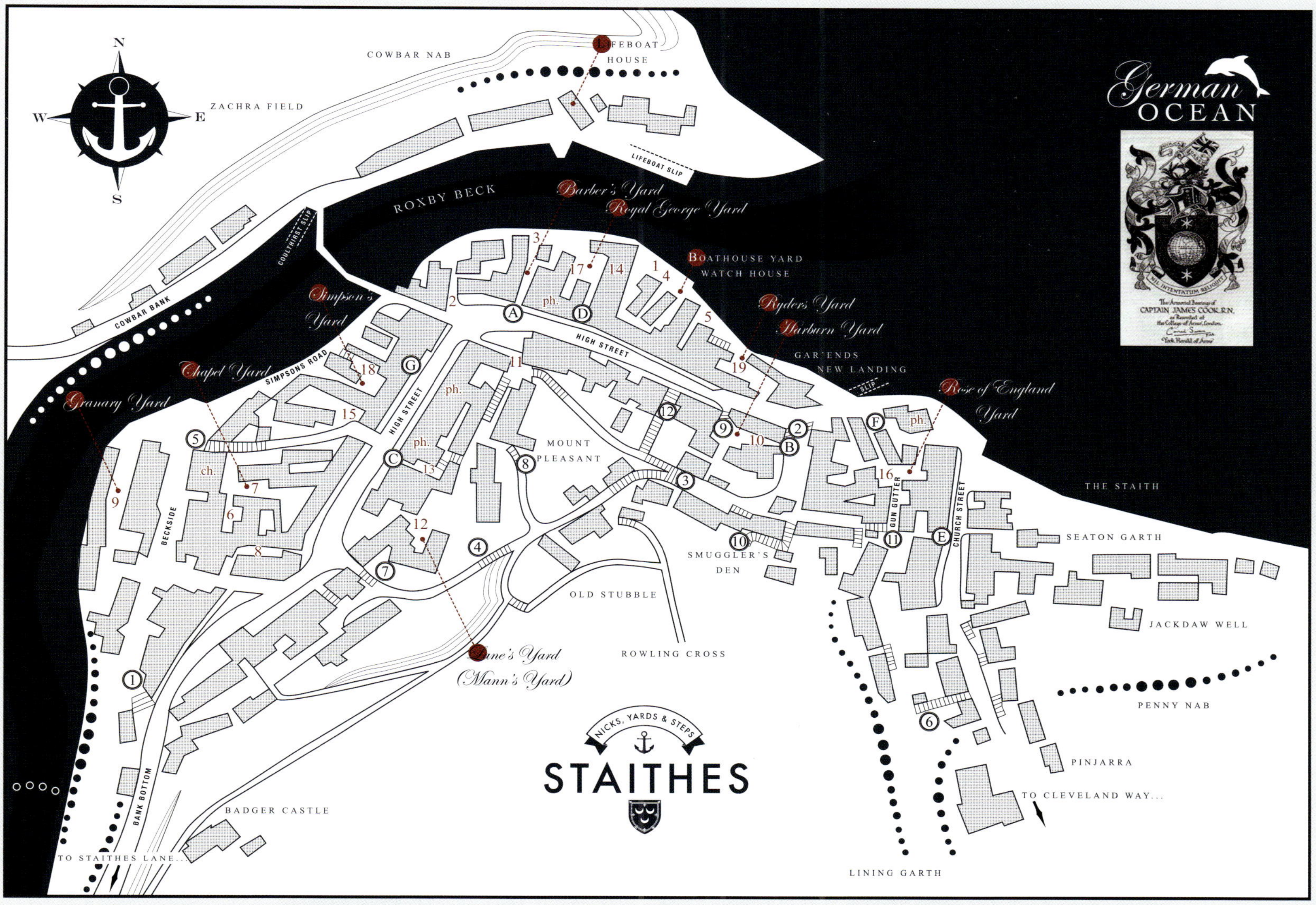

THE YARDS & NICKS OF STAITHES

STAITHES
NICKS, YARDS & STEPS

1. Back Yard
2. Bank Yard
3. Barber's Yard (P.O. Yard)
4. Boat House Yard
5. Browns Yard
6. Bulman Yard
7. Chapel Yard
8. Elliot's Yard (Ward's Yard)
9. Granary Yard
10. Harburn Yard
11. Hugil's Yard
12. Lane's Yard (Mann's Yard)
13. Lion Yard
14. Narrow Yard
15. Rodham's Boatyard
16. Rose of England Yard
17. Royal George Yard
18. Simpson's Yard (Ruby Yard)
19. Ryder's Yard

The Nicks

- Ⓐ Alley Toner Nick
- Ⓑ Barris Nick
- Ⓒ Lion's Passage
- Ⓓ Mary Crispin Nick
- Ⓔ Nanny Nick (Dog Loup)
- Ⓕ Slip Top
- Ⓖ Sotherby's Passage

The Steps

1. Back Road Steps
2. Barris Steps
3. High Barris Steps
4. Bennison Steps
5. Chapel Steps
6. Lining Garth Steps
7. Morley's Steps
8. Sarah Cole Steps
9. Slippery Hill Steps
10. Smuggler's Den Steps
11. Waller's Steps
12. Webster's Steps

SIMPSON'S YARD (RUBY HOUSE YARD) & SIMPSON'S ROAD

Access to this small old Yard is off the former Simpson's Road running parallel with the beck on Beckside, from the opening, situated to the right of Cowbar View house. Alternatively access is off the High Street, via a small alley between Ruby House and Newholme house and the yard area lies behind 'Newholme' and to the side of 'Ruby House'.

Ruby house was named after the yawl belonging to Richard Verrill.

This small yard contained just two dwellings in 1871, one occupied by James Jefferson, his children & housekeeper, the other by Elizabeth Simpson and her tinsmith son Christopher. Simpsons Road is recorded as running from the Chapel Steps area along the beckside towards the nick and steps leading to Ruby House Yard or Simpson's Yard, as it was known in 1871. The yard name is derived from the Simpson family where Elizabeth Simpson, 84 years old in 1871, lived with her two daughters, Mary and Sarah, together with grand daughter Mary Ann Cummings.

Simpsons Road contained seven dwellings, including homes to fishermen Joseph Crispin, Isaac Crooks, Francis Harrison and coastguard David Grant.

RYDER'S YARD
(See also BROWN'S YARD)

This large yard is situated to the rear of the former Fisherman's Institute (now Beckfoot Cottage). Seaton Garth has its northern limit at the opening to Ryder's Yard near Garth Ends (Gar'Ends). Access to this wonderful yard is off the High Street, via a narrow passage between the 'Mariner's' the former Shoulder of Mutton PH and the former Mason's fruit shop (now empty but being refurbished) or alternatively between the wide access between 'Singing Waters' and 'Beckfoot Cottage'.

Daniel Cole had his bakery in this yard for many years.

William Ryder was not born in Staithes, he entered the village as a draper and lodged with retired farmer John Crossley in 1851. By 1861 William Ryder was listed as a shipowner at the age of 33 and living in Browns Yard, this being one of the only two dwellings at that address and believed to be part of Ryder's Yard.

By 1881 he was farming 18 acres down in Dale House and Ryder's Yard is believed to take it's name from this man.

It is worth a look in Ryder's Yard to see the tall 'Tudor Rose', home & studio to the 'Fabulous Czainski's, artists extraordinaire and to see the life like seagull painting above the doorway and the coble wall painting too.

THE NICK WITH NO NAME!

If you turn immediately right after the cottage named 'Sea Crest' with the large protective bulwarks, before you reach the Cod & Lobster, you enter a very narrow nick. This leads to a small hidden yard where the houses on the Barrass back onto this yard, as do the houses at Slip Top.

Plate 220a

WARD'S YARD

See Elliot's Yard for details.

SECTION 22.0 – THE STEPS OF STAITHES

Plate 221
Stone Steps are abundant throughout the lower village of Staithes and are a necessity for gaining access to the yards and properties that have been built in precarious places on the higher ground, in all areas of the village. Most of these steps have existed for close on 200 years and several take their name from local yards, people and places. Large groups of properties exist on the higher ground of Broom Hill, Darlington Terrace and Mount Pleasant, where many steps can be found. This area was dominated by iron-stone miners from the Grinkle Mines during the period 1861-1911.

BARRIS STEPS

The Barris Steps are 8 in number, situated at the end of the High Street, and lead to one of the largest openings within Staithes, the Barrass Square (a corruption of Barris).

Please refer to Section 23.0 for more details.

Plate 223
The eight relatively new steps leading to Barrass Square are clear to see in this post 2nd World War 2 publication, where the title was given as Barris Steps. Tom England's Cottage lies on the left hand corner, adjacent to Seymour's old shop and eventual Marine View Café.

BACK ROAD STEPS

Plate 222
Although this may not be it's official title, a series of 8 steps lead off the lower portion of Bank Bottom into the former Back Road where Back Buildings were situated to the rear of the Congregational Chapel (Bethel), as listed in the 1861 census. These steps exist between Valley View and New York House and lead to 'Bob Bell's Bank' and Beckside.

HIGH BARRIS STEPS

Plate 224a/b
Walking up to the top right hand corner of Barrass Square there are 21 steps leading to High Barrass (Top Barris) and a further 28 steps to Mount Pleasant.
The High Barrass Steps can be seen above, close to York House and leading to Burton's Cottage on high, hence the name.

BENNISON STEPS

Plate 225
These steps 23 in number, exist above Morley's Steps and take you from Browns Terrace towards Mount Pleasant. John Bennison was the one time Staithes Carrier and the Bennisons, resided at the nearby Popular House, which was the first house on the south side of the Main Street after passing the Ropery (Browns Terrace). Popular House became a Guest house in the 1930's.

John Bennison was a well known Wesleyan and his preaching was warm and well received within Staithes and both he and his father Henry Bennison were local Carriers and in 1881, they lived and worked together, until Henry moved to Scarborough.

The steps take their name from The Bennison family.

CHAPEL STEPS

Plate 226

The Chapel Steps number 19 and can be accessed via the opening between the former Co-Op (now Coble Cottage) and 'Rock Lea' house, off the High Street or from the Beckside (start of former Simpson's Road, between Potter's Cottage and the Chapel building itself). These steps lead to the Wesleyan Chapel built in 1866 and to Wesley Square, Chapel Yard and Bulman Yard.

SLIPPERY HILL STEPS

Plate 230a/b

In 1911 local fishermen, Edward and William Verrill, Matthew and John Thompson lived in four out of the six dwellings here. Slippery Hill is accessed off the High Street between 'Salmon Cottage' (former Maggie Cole's Bakery) and 'Kirstie's Cottage', this area is more of a hill than steps (as the name suggests!), however there are just 5 steps from the High Street leading to Slippery Hill.

LINING GARTH STEPS

Plate 227

These steps total 20 in number and take you from the upper reaches of Gun Gutter (Lining Garth) to Church Street. The top of the steps emerge between 'St Helier' cottage (right) and 'Holme Crest' (left) on Church Street.

WALLER STEPS (GUN GUTTER STEPS)

Plate 231a/b

Wallers Steps run from Gun Gutter towards the Barris and are 21 in number.

Fisherman Francis Verrill and his wife Margaret Ann lived close to these steps at 'Green Hill View' (now 'Gamvik', a four roomed' house, with their four daughters; Sarah Jane, Esther, Margaret Ann & Lillie' and two sons Francis and William (Willie). Typical of many Staithes families and in particular the Verrill's, the siblings bore the same names as their parents. Francis junior was an iron-stone miner and also assisted his father with fishing.

These steps were named as Waller Steps from c1903-1912, and take their name from the Waller family who were both sailors, master mariner and iron-stone miners. The address Gun Gutter Steps (or Gutterstairs) commenced around 1912 and by 1927 the address for Frank Verrill had changed to 'Green Hill View', Barras Top. The steps are adjacent to the large 'Friendship' house Frank Verrill had his 80th Birthday in 'Green Hill View' in 1936

MORLEY'S STEPS

Plate 228

These steps, 23 in number, can be found off the High Street, with access between the former first Primitive Methodist Chapel (opened in 1838) and 'Popular House'. These steps lead to Bennison's Steps and Mount Pleasant.

Henry Charles Morley, photographer and artist had his photographic studio close to here at the end of Browns Terrace, opening in 1903 and closing towards the end of WW1 in 1919 and the steps here are named after this artistic man.

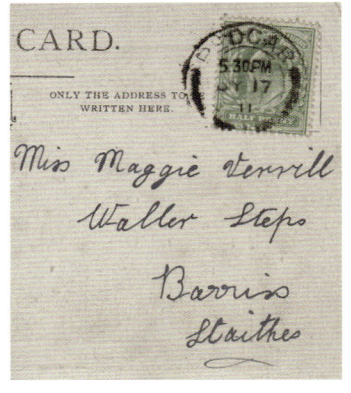

SARAH COLE STEPS

Plate 229

These steps, 31 in total take you from the Mount Pleasant area, along Darlington Terrace, towards Broomhill, where it is possible to follow the path and re-join the High Street.

Sarah Cole was born in 1852 and she was married to JB Cole and they had a son also named JB Cole and daughter Elizabeth.

Sarah Cole was shown as the head of the household as JB was always away at sea. Sarah was a strong lady and this enabled her to cope without her seafaring husband for lengthy spells and to bring up her family almost single handed. Their address in 1891 was recorded as High Barris and the steps were named after this Sarah Cole (there were six other Sarah Coles in Staithes at this time, but none resided close to these particular steps)

SMUGGLER'S DEN STEPS

These steps are situated to the side of Barris View House on the Barris and lead directly to Smuggler's Den'.

WEBSTER STEPS

Several other local names existed at various times, for these important steps e.g. New Hall Steps, Drill Hall Steps or Johnny Do'son steps – Rachel & John Dawson were recorded as living on Front Street in 1861, with daughter Hannah and son John Dawson (junior). John (senior) was drowned at sea in the tragedy of 21st September 1870, but John Dawson (junior) was saved (read John Howard's 'Triumph and Tragedy book for the full story). By 1871 Rachel was recorded as living off Webster's Steps with daughter Ann and son John. However the correct name is Webster Steps, consisting of a total of 48 steps. They are located off the High Street between Blue Jacket House (former shop of John Richard Verrill) and the present butchers shop of Richard Lyth and they are the largest run of steps in Staithes. These steps led to 'New Hall' one of Staithes early 'entertainment centres' and led to an area once known as Halfpenny Hill, where a couple of small houses existed here, for newly weds to start life together. A lion head, cast iron, fresh water tap once existed here.

New Hall was created from a dilapidated property situated towards the top of Webster Steps (often referred to as New Hall Steps) and opened in 1904, thanks to the vision of the Reverend H. Weale of the Congregational Chapel. He was supported by Captain James Pinder of Prospect House, Deacon of the Congregational Church, prominent Conservative and Crimean War hero. New Hall was a popular venue for the Liberal Association and Juvenile. Temple Independent Order of Templars – the Hope of Staithes. New Hall was often referred to as the Drill Hall and Webster's Steps were nick-named the Drill Hall Steps as the Territorial Army became one of the main users.

Plate 232a/b
They were first known as Webster Steps in c 1850, simply because the Webster family had two dwellings here. John ('Jack') Webster was a mariner in 1841 and recorded as a fisherman in 1871 and he lived in the first house with his wife Alice. Thomas Webster lived next door to John and he also was a fisherman. Thomas Webster's father also a Thomas Webster is thought to have lived in this vicinity too.

SECTION 23.0 - 'BARE FOOT ON THE BARASS'

Barrass' is Scandanvian for Square and Barrass Square is just one of the few open spaces that exist in Staithes village. Various spellings, from Barris to Barras have existed over the years. The 1841 census refers to Barras, 1871 to Barass, but Barris was commonly used throughout the period 1891-1930.

Between 1871 and 1901 there were thirty dwellings here, including High Barris and Slip Top.

The Barris Square was 90% inhabited by Staithes fishermen (Coles, Verrills, Shippy's and Harrison's), with nearby Slip Top, containing 22 Theaker family members in 1901. Two shoemakers and the odd dressmaker were here too.

On Monday October 9th 1775, James Rice (alias Michael Rijks), murdered local Staithes man, Thomas Wastell, at the foot of the Barris Steps, in a smuggling related affair. He was executed at the Old Gallows in York on 19th December 1779.

Plate 233. Lilywhite Ltd c1924

The black bonneted lady, in her mourning dress & bonnet, draws water from the communal water tap, into her galvanised pale. Whilst the youngster just a few yards away in the centre, goes 'bare-foot on the Barrass'. The house on the corner of the High Street end is 'Tom Englands Slip Top Cottage', currently being renovated by owners Diana and Peter Sharples. Tom England acquired the cottage in 1944 at auction. William Francis (Billy 'Fanny') Verrill was born here when it was known as 'Cock Hat House', due to the slant of the roof.

A message penned to the reverse side reads, "I could'nt go to church today as there was'nt one here, nearest was a mile away'.

'Kildale' cottage lies to the right of the Square.

The steps to houses on the Barrass and elsewhere in Staithes were often cleaned using 'Donkey Stone' or painted white as can be seen to the left.

Plate 234. 1953

A fine array of bonnets as worn by left to right: Mrs R. Theaker, Mrs Florence Verrill & Mrs Mary Verrill.

All three are at one of the village water taps, situated on the Barris, the former cast iron, lion head pump, has been replaced with a modern 'push' down tap at this time.

Barris, Staithes.

Plate 235

Titled 'Barris' rather than 'Barrass', this early view shows what a rough open yard the Barrass Square was at this time in c 1903, with the steps broken in places and the Barrass Square very uneven. The Barris steps at this time were in two different sections, with narrow steps to the left and wide steps to the right. All were renewed by the 1930's into the uniform format that exists today. The house at the top behind the water tap, used to house a small shop and another shop existed to the bottom left of this view.

Plate 236. c1904

Possibly the best animated social history view taken in Staithes, with 14 inhabitants of Barrass Square in view. The women knit, outside the small shop, today's 'Sea Haven' cottage.

Whilst Tom Francis Harrison standing right plus other men carry out essential repairs to their corked nets. The women appear to be using a variety of 2, 3 and 4 needles, no doubt for differing garments and the lady sitting nearest the doorway is Tom's wife, Mary Ann Verrill (Polly Spink). At least three generations of the same family are outside the old shop, with its ornate lintel, on the Barris, on this fine day in c1904. The Barris was a stronghold for the Theaker families for several generations, where they had up to 7 dwellings here. The white bricks of the centre left house 'Sea Crest' were possibly brought back, prior to 1883, as ballast from Aberdeen, by Yawls returning from the Scottish fishing grounds.

Plate 237

This is a good place to be when the sun is out on the Barris. Tom Francis Harrison, 'Polly Spink', pet spaniel and several other family members and friends, take time out to pose for the photographer on this sunny day.

Plate 238. c1932

Jas. W. Legg sold this postcard view of the area known as Slip Top from his Confectionary and newsagent business on the upper part of the High Street (now the 'Emporium').

The lady in the dark bonnet appears to be crossing the cobbled street in order to visit the old Seymour's shop, whilst the other aproned lady, Ruth Cook is about to ascend the wide flight of eight stone steps leading to Barrass Square.

'BARE FOOT ON THE BARASS'

Plate 239. c1933

Joseph Verrill, published this postcard view of the Barrass steps, from his High Street shop. A small gathering of seven young local ladies are posing for the photographer, on the edge of the Barrass Square, outside 'Sea Haven' cottage. As expected at least four of the ladies are wearing their Staithes traditional bonnets, but all are smiling and appear very happy on this sunny day. The house behind the group was restored to a high standard during 2012 and the large stone bulwark, to the left of the steps, is there to protect 'Sea Crest' cottage from the ravages of the North Sea.

HIGH BARRIS

Plate 240. FMS C1903

All are aware of the photographer, apart from the lone hen in this photograph of High Barrass, situated off the top right of Barrass Square. Burtons Cottage stands high above the far steps on Mount Pleasant and the carpets are out above the well worn steps, left, leading to 'Ocean View'. A similar wooden staircase exists today as does the doorway underneath leading to the lower part of the house, where the young fisher lad is standing. 'Hillside', 'Malmo' (Dog Fighting Plaque here) and 'Grimes Nook' cottages all lead up to the tall 'York House', former home of Master Mariner George Delavel Laverick, on the top LH corner.

Plate 242. HC Morley c1906

A scarce view of High Barrass, taken from outside York House, looking towards the top of Barrass Square. Grimes Cottage/Grimes Nook lies to the right and Hill Cottage to the left of the steps. James Grimes and family lived on the Barrass for many years. The beautiful ornate iron gates on the immediate left have either been relocated to the front entrance of York House or an identical set of gates exists here. The two small outhouses opposite the washing line still exist today.

Plate 241

Steps with a wooden canopy at the top, are rare and it has been very difficult to identify this location. The photographer titled this view 'Friendly Gossip at Starthes!'(spelling error). It is believed that this may be a much earlier view of the steps to Ocean View on High Barrass, as shown in the previous photograph.

SECTION 24.0 - 'COFFIN LANE – THE ROAD TO SEATON'

   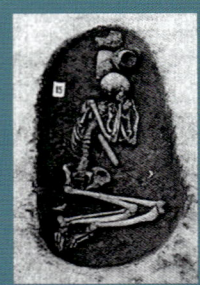

Church Street was formerly named Weatherill Street, after the Staithes Master Mariner, ship owner and merchant Edward Weatherill who had his house built here. His house became the National School and eventually St Peter The Fisherman Mission Church. In its upper reaches Weatherill Street, consisted of Kirkhill Bank which leads onto the Cleveland way today. The ancient parish church of Seaton is said to have existed between the top of Kirk Hill Bank and Hinderwell – (the road to the Kirk). It was named/recorded as Church Street prior to the formation of St Peters Mission Church in c1878 from the old National School on this site and the census from 1841-1871 proves this point. Thus giving further credence to the existence of the old church of Seaton, where it is alleged that funeral processions used to follow the route up Kirk Hill Bank to the old church. Sometime between 1871-1891 the name changed to Weatherill Street.

Coffins were also transported to Hinderwell Church via this steep route, hence the reference to 'Coffin Lane'. There were two cast iron water taps situated on Church Street to serve the villagers at this end of the village for many years.

Plate 243

Hands on hips was the usual stance for these two young Staithes women, as they chat and pose for the photographer on a sunny day in Church Street during the late 1890's.

The woman in the street carries a large basket, probably containing lines for baiting or for 'tanning' or simply for drying on the grass at the top of Kirkhill Bank. The woman on the steps leading to Kirk Cottage (hidden from view to the right), is stood outside Unity House, where various fisherman's paraphernalia such as boots, oilskins, hats and socks line the fence.

Plate 244. Francis Frith c1920's

Francis Frith & Co of Reigate visited Staithes during the early 1920's and this is one of their original proof photographs. These two fine characters were photographed (No. 85271 in their series) in the upper reaches of Church Street, close to Felicity House. This house was built in the early 1800's by local ship owner James Theaker (1849-1931), who owned 'The Felicity', one of the fastest yawls on this coast.

Both carry receptacles in readiness for drawing water from the nearby water tap.

Plate 245

The bonneted ladies baskets appear to be full of blackberries, no doubt picked from the hedgerows along the upper reaches of Kirk Hill Bank above Church Street. Although this view card was late posted in 1954, the card itself dates back to c1907. Hens run freely on Church St at this time, outside St. Helier, Holme Crest and Windsor House where the terrain to the right, below 'Hilary Cottage' and 'Hillsover' appears extremely fragile and ready to be washed away. All is much safer today as a retaining wall exists here now and the builder, E.Hansell (Eric), 1984 inscribed his name on one of the lower left stones.

Plate 246. Lilywhite Ltd c1909

Church Street's upper reaches look barely made up in this view, where the bonneted lady plays with her young child close to 'Pinjarra' cottage above the slope to the right. The building on the left contains Felicity House and the attached 'Felicity Cottage.'

Plate 248

Taken approximately 50 years later, when Church Street was completely empty, there are several archictectural changes if you look closely.

This photographic postcard, bore the title 'Sleights' and even the people who wrote the card, penned a message to say that they had enjoyed a good time here in Sleights, before moving onto Whitby!.

Plate 247. H.C. Morley c 1909

Photographer Morley, has captured a very atmospheric morning in Church St, where several young girls in their smock dresses make their way towards the Church Mission Room of St Peter's The Fisherman. The house on the right with the steps does not yet have the 'Captain Cook's Cottage' sign inscribed above the door lintel. The house on the immediate left was drastically reduced in size following the dreadful storm damage in 1905, when the end of the house was ripped away, this house was the former Tom Verrill's abode. The adjacent house with top window open is 'Brown Haven', home to Robert Brown (1865-1942), who had his memories of Staithes made into a 'paper' called 'Staithes in Olden Times'and it was published in the Whitby Gazette in three parts in 1924.

Plate 249. Friths 1930's

John William Metcalf, supplies a broad grin for the photographer. He is balancing two large galvanised milk churns on an old fashioned wooden yolk across his shoulders, probably for delivery to 'Pinjarra'.

Mr Metcalf was a local farmer and the horse pictured below outside St Peters, may belong to him.

The far steps lead to 'Hillsover' cottage, with its neat porchway.

Plate 250

This coloured photograph, clearly records the position of the 'Barking Copper' at the top of Church Street, in front of 'Felicity House' and 'Cliff Cottage' to the left. This was where the lines and nets were treated to afford some protection from the North Sea. This process was referred to as tanning or 'barking' by the local fishermen.

The actual message pencilled on the reverse side reads, 'the object in the bottom left hand corner is a furnace for heating pitch for painting the boats'.

The top of Church Street leads to an area known as 'The Bogs'.

Plate 251. Pictorial Stationary Co c 1907

A Staithes couple are pictured outside their house 'Unity House'' talking to a young fisher lad on Church Street. The steps on the right lead to Kirk Cottage and the small pent roofed shed (now a garage) was once Ernie Gibbons Cobblers shed, who was also a former ironstone miner.

Plate 252. R.Johnston & Sons, Monarch Series C1940's

The old sign has been removed from the White Horse Inn, leaving the bare metal stay. The iron railings and steps left, belong to the old Master Mariner's house of John Joseph Robinson, which is now the grand 'Balmoral House', where well known actor 'Ace' Bhatti once resided. The two young girls enjoy their lollipops, as they follow behind a bonneted Annie Metcalf past Kirk Hill House, having passed Captain Cooks café with its enamel sign above the steps. Most of the houses from the lower Captain Cooks Cottage through to Balmoral House are Grade 11 listed buildings of architectural or historical interest, as is Kirk Hill house and 'Seaholme'.

Plate 253

William Metcalf turns the handle on the old mangle for Annie Metcalfe, outside their home 'Kirk Cottage' next to the tall 'Aunt Pat's Cottage', opposite St Peter's on Church Street.

SECTION 25.0 – 'LIFE IN THE GUTTER'

Gun Gutter is mentioned in the Bye Laws of the Manor of Seaton in 1704. This peculiar name was thought by famous Staithes artist Laura Knight (nee Johnson), to be because it was just wide enough to shoot a gun down!, whilst there are other tall stories regarding the site of a large gun during the Napoleonic Wars 1803-1815! It was near here, where Laura Johnson would listen to tales from Isaac Verrill (the younger) when they gathered round his kitchen fire, in his cottage in Gun Gutter. The local butcher had his slaughterhouse towards the end of Gun Gutter, which also had a brief life as an amusement arcade (penny slot machines). The smallest house in Staithes can be found in Gun Gutter, often referred to as 'The Doll's House' or 'Noah's Ark'.

In the 1901 census, Laura's friend and fellow Staithes Art Group member, Arthur Friedenson was recorded as lodging at George Porritt's house in Gun Gutter and he was listed as an artist/sculptor.

In 1871 the only Porritt living in the Gutter was Patience Porritt, but later, The 'Gutter' became a stronghold for the Porritt families and six dwellings out of a total of ten were taken up here in 1901 by George Porritt, Isaac Porritt(1), Richard Porritt(1), Richard Porritt (2), William Porritt and Isaac Porritt (2)

A small stream runs down Lining Garth into Gun Gutter where this is eventually culverted.

Plate 254. Walter Scott, Bradford c1920's

Scott, published this scarce image of the upper section of Gun Gutter, leading to Lining Garth taken from the elevated pathway off 'Rolling Cross' and shows the rear of the houses on Church Street that back onto Gun Gutter.

The pantiled lean-to on Windsor House has long been demolished and a pull in for motor cars now exists here. Also backing onto the Gutter are Everest, Lyne's Garth, Felicity House & Felicity Cottage, with some noteable changes to the rear of these properties, where the old pig sties and wash sheds have long since been demolished.

St Helier cottage has always had a useful sitting out area with garden as shown here.

Plate 255

Mrs Verrill has just washed a variety of fishermans clothing, including smock and gansey and an amateur photographer has captured this everyday occurrence in c 1917, where she can be seen hanging them out to dry at the side of her house in Gun Gutter. The steps (Lining Garth steps), going right, lead up to Church Street in the vicinity of St.Helier's cottage, just above the Mission Church of St Peter The Fisherman.

Plate 256. HC Morley c 1907

This is a rare social history photograph, of the lower end of Gun Gutter and Morley titled it 'Sorting Crabs, Staithes'. It depicts a large crab table in the narrow yard, to the rear of Captain Cooks Cottage, which fronts onto Church Street. The curved stone wall is still there today close to 'Bramla Cottage'. The fisher couple, believed to belong to the Porritt family, have assembled the crabs by their size, with some very large crabs indeed.

Plate 257. c1930's

Sarah Hannah Cole (nee Verrill), complete with fur lined slippers, is sitting on a small bink, in the sun outside 'Friendship' cottage, off Gun Gutter, with her bonneted friend and husband George Cole (1889-1973) observing from the doorway.

Friendship cottage was once the home of William Henry 'Enny' Verrill (1867-1937) and his wife Patience 'Paashy' Ward Verrill (1869-1921)). They had two daughters, Sarah Hannah Verrill (1898-1976) and Margaret Ward 'Margit' Verrill (1907-2001).

This was the Verrill family home for 'Margit', from 1907-1927, until she moved to 'Seacot' on the High Street and she became Margaret Ward Suckling.

Plate 258. c1937

Willie Verrill sitting on a bink, in front of Friendship Cottage, carries out essential repairs to one of his pots, just below the stone steps from Gun Gutter leading up towards the Barrass Square and High Barrass. The former Green Hill View cottage, where Mrs Frank Verrill used to rent out 3 bedrooms, with sitting room and organ, lies top right and is now called 'Gamvik'.

Crab pots consisted of the following: 4 bows, 4 side sticks, 1 top stick, 2 end sticks, 2 deear sticks, 2 bait bands, 1 slip band, 2 deear bands & 2 spoots.

SECTION 26.0 – 'SEATON GARTH' – FORESHORE & THE STAITH

Seaton Garth was the name given to the sea front area running from Penny Nab to Garth End.

The word Staith has several meanings from a sea wall for protection, hole in the wall, a quay by the waterside for shipping or landing goods or as exists here in Staithes a landing place for vessels.

The Staith comes from 'staeth' the Old English version of the Old Norse word 'stoth', meaning landing stage.

Plate 259. Nelly Erichsen
A c1886 engraving by Nelly Erichsen, depicts the basic structure of Seaton Garth, Staithes. A skeel of fish can be seen on the ground just before the wooden staith commences. The cottages on the staith have changed dramatically since this view, with several being much taller today.

Nelly Erichsen (9 December 1862 – 15 November 1918) was an English illustrator and painter. Born in Newcastle upon Tyne, she was the daughter of a wealthy professional Danish family and first came sketching in Staithes around 1894.

Plate 260. c1896
The landing stage (Staith) was very restricted as can be seen in this early photograph, where vast portions of Seaton Garth, are without support to its quayside. Only the portion nearest to the Cod & Lobster has the wooden supports and planking. The smoking chimneys have created quite a haze over most part of the village and the shutters are closed on the Cod & Lobster, which is about four years from being ripped apart from a great storm to come in 1900.

Plate 261. c1898
Ten small children are gathered around coble 549 WY during the early 1890's, one of the far cobles is thought to be 'William' (138 WY).

The old Jackdaw Well is hidden from view to the rear of the Staith end cottage, 'Mizpah', however the old 'barking' copper can be clearly seen. The small two story house (known as 'Hard Struggle') third from the left, with upper wooden doorway openings, is to undergo several structural and cosmetic changes over the next decade or so, as can be seen in the following two images. This old dilapidated building will eventually be demolished and rebuilt to form today's large house,'Ocean View'.

Plate 262. c1895

The beach and the Staith are very much alive, in this important early photograph, found in an old Victorian photograph album. There are no railings and no seats around the old Cod & Lobster, where the pent roof is clearly visible to the right of the picture. However there does appear to be a small gathering of people and two fishermen are sitting on a large barrel, outside the pub. Several large herring fishing cobles are within the beach area, with their masts erected. In this c1895 photograph, the third house from the left on the Staith front, eventually belonging to the James family who were fish sellers; is being re-constructed from its original two story cottage into a three story house. This house became known locally as 'Hard Struggle' as the materials were hard to come by. Two houses appear to be thatched, 'Mizpah' on the far left and the small whitewashed cottage now the 'excellent Sea Drift café, half hidden from view.

Plate 265. Francis Frith c 1920's

The Staith is relatively bare, except for a lone black cat and two ladies close to fish salesman James Clemance James house with the staircase, which looks as if it has just had a re-paint. The height of the Staith surface seems unusually high in the vicinity of the small low lying 'Harbour View' cottage, this was a crude defence from the sea, known locally as 'Golden Hill'. The old cast iron water tap was behind the 'wall' here.

The large house with ten windows facing the sea, with the huge wooden lintel, at one time belonged to fisherman, Robert Longster who married Sarah Crossley. Their son fisherman, John Francis Longster and family lived here for several years. Many years ago it housed sail lofts and in modern times it housed two flats upstairs. In more recent times it housed a small fish & chip/restaurant, whilst today 'Harbourside' is the largest holiday let in the village, being very well appointed and sleeping up to 10 people.

Plate 279. c1903

This old bridge over Roxby Beck, leading to Cowbar and Aukness was much higher up the Beck than the bridge from Abrahams Lane. The early wooden structure had three support pillars firmly fixed into the Beck with open wooden rails above. This early coloured picture postcard, positions the bridge in the vicinity of where the Battlestones (stepping stones) over the beck exist today.

At the right hand end of the bridge the various buildings in and around Granary Yard are visible, the first house on the right of Granary Yard has long been demolished and now forms the private garage close to 'Longhouse', a former Dames School.

Plate 280. Judges Ltd c 1908

Two bridges for the price of one in this view of the old bridge over Roxby Beck near the stepping stones of today, with the railway viaduct dominating the background. This early wooden bridge had three central support columns and is believed to have been constructed in the last quarter of the 18th Century.

Fishing nets are hung out to dry on the old bridge, in the afternoon sun, whilst a few chickens are just visible in the beck close to the left hand support. The site of an old early Lime Kiln, was close to the Aukness side of the bridge. The interesting message penned on the reverse side reads "Captain Cook lived here, but the house has been washed away, the only house in the row remaining is 'The Cod & Lobster Inn'. Used to be a great Smuggling place, now particularly honest hardworking population. Many Merchant Captains come from here".

THE LOWER TRESTLE BRIDGE – (ABRAHAMS LANE TO COWBAR)

Plate 281 Similarly in this view nets were also draped over Staithes second bridge further down the beck leading to Abraham Lane. This trestle bridge had just the one central support column. This practice came to a halt when notices were posted, mandating fines for anyone placing their nets on the bridge.

Plate 282
A 'one-off' photograph taken from a glass lantern slide in c1900, depicting a tranquil scene, looking up the beck through the old trestle bridge, towards the iron railway viaduct, with Jane Ward's Kipper House to the right. Everybody seems to be aware of the photographers prescence, with their overly posed stance.

Plate 283. Brittain & Wright c1905

At one time horses were quite common place in Staithes, playing their part in the huge fishing industry that flourished here and stables existed on Beckside.

The two children walking in the Beck, don't even look up as the lone unsaddled horse, is led over the narrow primitive wooden bridge, possibly to stables in Granary Yard. This postcard was posted from Whitby without stamp and incurred a postage due penalty. A pencilled message on the reverse reads, 'found on West Cliff Platform'.

Plate 284. Valentine c1900

The house to the right hand side of the bridge with the lean-to building, we know belonged to Robert Featherstone the shopkeeper and postmaster on the High Street; as his name is painted in white letters on a board above the stable doorway. This place was 'The Bridge House' and Mr Featherstone had a small Café here for several years. Note the buildings within the beck, with the rudimentary barrier to keep the beck at bay.

Fourteen cobles, take up most of the room on the quayside, near the lifeboat station along with five handcarts, lobster pots and seven large fish barrels.

Plate 285

A magic lantern slide of Staithes in c1901, where a bonneted lady peers towards the Lifeboat House and Beckmouth, with locally caught fish drying on the fence close to Abrahams Lane. The ladders near the bridge were also used for drying the split fish on. Laura Knight described this bridge as being 'a graceful structure, slender and strong, its trestle supports formed a pedestal to the stretch of footway and rail'.

Plate 286. c1908

One of the many artists to visit Staithes is dressed in his 'uniform' of tweed jacket, plus fours and floppy hat. He sets up his easel just behind the old smoke house in readiness of 'capturing' the view looking towards the Beck Mouth.

People are gathered at either end of the new replacement single span bridge.

Boats over many years had been tied to the old wooden bridge and the friction of the rope wore the oak in waists, due to the boats pulling and slackening with the water movements. The old bridge was an inspiration to the many painters and they were saddened when it had to be replaced by a hideous iron girder bridge as described by Laura Knight; who complained it cost as much in fresh red paint, than the old one had with replacement wood.

A postcard of Staithes posted in August 1905 shows the new bridge to be in situ, hence the construction is likely to have been completed by mid 1905.

Plate 288

This c1930's view, taken from the high ground off Cowbar looking towards Abrahams Lane, where nappies' are hung outside 'Beck View' cottage to the right of Abrahams Lane. Telegraph wires now stretch across from the village side across to Cowbar. Coble WY254 'Mizpah' appears to be being tethered to one of the mooring posts, this boat was the first motor powered coble in Staithes.'

A clear view is given all the way across to the farm buildings of J.W. Metcalf, on the cliff top.

Plate 289. c1960

The fencing to the right looks as if it has been renewed and painted white, replacing the former drab brown fencing. The former Robert Featherstone's small outbuilding has now become a modern extension with railings to the flat roof and a glazed doorway from the main house installed. This will have paved the way for the future extension into the popular North Lea holiday cottage of today.

SECTION 28.0 – 'O'WER THE BECK' – COWBAR

The Cowbar side of Staithes was in the parish of Easington and at the beginning of the 18th Century there were two main roads into Staithes – the one from the north skirting the cliff tops from Red House Farm to Cowbar, where it descended down Cowbar Bank to the beckside. The other route into the village, was from the old village of Seaton, across the fields and down Kirkhill Bank and Church Street onto Seaton Garth; which of course was in Hinderwell parish.

Plate 290. T.Butterworth 1890
Cowbar Bank rises steeply past the sash windowed cottages, lining the right hand side of the steep roadway, leading to Cowbar Cottages and Boulby. At the end of the old tressle bridge on the side of Cowbar Bank stands the old smoke house, where local herrings were treated. The heavy coated fisherman, takes time out to gather his thoughts, alongside coble 229 WY and he is believed to be Francis Unthank, who lived in the right side of the old iron stone cottage behind him, close to the upturned coble WY 1. This photograph was taken in 1890, just nine years before he was to lose his life along with his two sons, when their coble, WY99 'Knight Commander', was hit by fierce storms on 30th September 1899.

'GATEWAY TO THE GERMAN OCEAN'

Plate 321
This view was taken from a glass stereo plate and shows how rudimentary the ground was, close to the old lifeboat slipway

Plate 322. c1907
Looking towards the Lifeboat House and slipway, it is noticeable just how narrow the pathway leading to the Beckmouth was, when this photograph was taken. The old wooden cart contains several skeels and baskets used in the fish trade. The fencing leading to the old bridge, certainly had some character with its random shaped posts and hap-hazard wooden rails. Coble 'Perseverance' (250WY) is moored in the Beck alongside other cobles.

Plate 322a
The far cottages, beyond the lifeboat house, belonged to 'Joe Ben' Verrill and John Coulthirst.

Plate 323. 1897
The area around the old lifeboat house is strewn with cobles, in this view taken from a magic lantern slide, showing the two levels alongside the Beck and the rough stone sides, without any form of handrails, along the way to the lifeboat slipway and Beckmouth.

Plate 324. c1897
What a delightful scene and not a ripple in sight, this well composed photograph, has captured three Staithes children posing on the rocks at the Beckmouth, with coble 71WY in the background. The boys both wear thick full length, knitted heavy leggings with breeches on top. Taken from a late Victorian, magic lantern slide, two of the above children can be seen in an earlier photograph at 'Jackdaw Well'

'GATEWAY TO THE GERMAN OCEAN'

Plate 325. c1924

Developed from an early 1920's glass negative by unknown photographer, this view has captured cobles 'Rebecca' (WY147), 'Ellen' (WY22), and 'Guide Me' (WY72).

At high tide, landing was easier in the Beckmouth, when cobles would be moored up to two wooden posts set for the purpose.

Plate 326. Judges Ltd.

Crab & lobster pots adorn the Lifeboat slipway where four small children have been photographed on the slipway walling at the Beckmouth.

A shed like structure has appeared on the cliff top.

Plate 327

The cobles are no longer grounded, in this lower area of the Beck close to the Beckmouth, due to tidal changes, brought about by the introduction of various sea defence alterations.

Washing is laid out on the bushes of Cowbar in the distant background.

Plate 329
An unusual photograph of the old fisher folk dwellings facing the Beckmouth.

Plate 328. Valentine's c1968
R. Porritt's boat lies in calm water at Beckmouth in this late 1960's photograph.

Plate 331
This 'one-off' photograph was taken by an unknown photographer, in the immediate post 1st World War period and has captured five young Staithes lads with their model sailing boats at Beckmouth.
Large coble WY185, 'Margarets' lies on the beck bottom, this coble was registered c1890. A large gathering is evident on the slipway down from 'Meal House' and the Cod & Lobster PH.

SECTION 32.0 – 'ROUGH SEAS' AND FEWLES O' MUCK

John Walker Ord historian, wrote in 1843, 'The trade of Staithes might be considerably improved by the establishment of a breakwater, or harbour of refuge and proposals to that effect have been published in the local papers, but without adequate encouragement'. The cottages on Seaton Garth have been ravaged by severe storms and high tides for well over 300 years. The fierce storm of 1767 washed away 13 houses, including Sandersons grocers shop where the young Cook, Captain to be, worked as an apprentice. Some of the highest tides ever, were recorded in 1771 and there were many severe storms, on average every seven years or so, throughout the 18th Century, with the loss of many lives. The 1890's and early 1900's witnessed some of the heaviest storms for years and some of the fiercest were in the September to December of 1899, forcing the eventual rebuild of the wrecked Cod & Lobster in 1900. The damage continued through the 1st World War, culminating in two great storms in 1924 and 1925 when the Fish Quay (Staith) was nearly destroyed.

Plate 335. A.C.Bruce 1905

During the early months of 1905, severe storms wreaked havoc in Staithes and photographer A.C.Bruce entitled his photograph, 'Sea Wrecked House, Staithes'. The wrecked house is the 'Homestead', former home of Tom Verril who was away working on the 'screws' (screw propeller ships) in Antwerp. It was here where he received a copy of this very same postcard, recording the damage to his cottage (what a shock he must have had!).

This real photographic postcard was part of the Weatherill family correspondence and was posted by Annie in February 1905 to Miss Weatherill, Chubb Hill, Whitby and provides evidence that the small cottage to the left was thatched at this time. This is now the Sea Drift Café on the sea front at Staithes.

Plate 334. Butterworth c1903

The Staithes fishermen erected some crude sea defences, by driving piles of timber into the ground as far out to sea as possible, in order to make a groyne and to break the force of the waves.

The rudimentary sea defences consisted of an assortment of crude wooden posts, which became well worn by the ravages of the sea and their effectiveness was questionable. Proposed new Breakwaters were being spoken of in January 1883 and on January 4th 1884, Charles Mark Palmer offered free materials to build the Breakwater.

Plate 335. H.C.Morley 1905
Further 1905 devestation, where a large section of the Staith itself near the Cod & Lobster, has been destroyed . Cobles 'Margaret & Rose' (WY36) and 'Edward Campbell' (WY181) have been lifted onto the Staith for safety, along with what appears to be coble WY 218 and unknown coble. A dozen or so children are captured within the Staith wreckage, where they have formed a 'gang-plank' for their amusement.

Plate 336. C1908
Titled 'Rough Sea at Staithes,' this view shows just how high the water could reach during stormy weather, before the new piers were completed in 1924. The message penned on the back reads; 'It is so funny all the houses look as if they are one up on the other, it is a funny place'

Plate 337
This photograph, titled 'Rough Sea High Street Staithes, clearly illustrates the power of the sea, as it reaches towards the steps of The Barrass Square.The large stone re-inforcements (bulwarks) outside 'Sea Crest' cottage act as a barricade to defend the houses from the high water. Various properties in this vicinity had additional 'door shutters' to protect from the ingress of the sea water. This was partly one of the reasons why the new sea defence piers were built in 1924 to combat the risk of flooding and damage to properties.

Plate 338. 1924

The crude sea defence with its random stone and mud filling, stands left, and was an attempt to protect the properties lining the back of Seaton Garth, from stormy seas.

Mains water was not laid on in Staithes until the late 1930's and only fully completed in 1950. As you can see in this 1920's scarce photograph, the bonneted Staithes lady has just filled her pale from one of fifteen water taps strategically placed around the village. This daily chore was always carried out by the women or girls of the village. This particular 'lion-face' pump was situated right outside 'Harbourside' house on the seafront and you can just make out the shaped beams carrying the wooden lintel above the windows.

The water was piped from Ellerby Resevoir and installed in c1892. The houses on the High Street were the first to receive mains water and in August 1933, Whitby Rural District Council were charging Mr Hansell 13s 5d per year for the privilege. The payment being collected in cash by the Water Rent Collector.

Plate 339. c1926

In this late view the water is calm within the confines of the early rudimentary sea defences, where coble 'Hannah Dawson' (WY 261) lies in the centre. This photograph was titled 'The Piers and Harbour, 'Staithes-by-the-Sea'. These piers were completed in 1924, using steam driven cranes and local Staithes labour; which included Edward Verrill, amongst many others.

The rail structure mounted on blocks to the right of the cobles was latterly used for tethering the boats and along with the post mounted sign inscribed 'No Road This Way', are believed to be remnants from the rail track laid during the construction of the new piers. This postcard view was posted on 22nd of December 1925, hence proof that all pier works were complete and did not go on into 1928 as once wrongly recorded.

STAITHES 'BETWEEN TWO NABS'

The RNLI produced a black & white 35mm 'Silent Movie' in 1924, in order to celebrate their centenary and to raise monies for new Motorised Lifeboats. It was called 'Saved by a Motor Lifeboat' and was one of the earliest examples of a promotional film for any charity and featured the Whitby and Staithes Lifeboats. During an improvised 'shout', the local workmen building the new piers, abandon their tasks to man the lifeboat, hence futher proof of the work on the piers being completed around 1924.

Plate 340
The three piers were known as Big Pier (North), South (Stean or Stone Garth) and Little Pier.
The new harbour was badly needed and as good as it was, it should have been bigger to attract larger vessels and this led several fishing families to leave the area, for work elsewhere in Whitby and further afield.

Plate 341. 1924
The great storms over the years, have created huge devastation to the village of Staithes and in particular to the Staith itself and the cottages behind it. The huge gaping hole in the Staith opposite 'Harbour View' cottage, in this 1920's scarce photograph was probably caused by the great storm in late 1924. The bonneted lady carries a wooden skeel on her head as she walks across Seaton Garth perilously close to the edge. Note the large hut like structure that has now been constructed at the end of the Staith abutting Penny Nab, possibly for cleaning fish/storing fishing related items at this time.

Plate 342. AE Graham, 1925
Despite the new piers being in situ, Staithes again received a battering, when just one year later, severe storms wrecked the wooden sections of the Staith. A huge hole has opened up in front of Harbour Side, Harbour View and Spray Cottages. We know the precise date of this disaster as A E Graham of Redcar, recorded the 5th September 1925 on the front of their photographic publication. Extreme high tides were experienced both in 1924 and 1925. A similar breach in the Fish Quay during January 1899, brought some condemnation from the local council regarding repairs, who stated, "the lack of public spirit among householders and fishermen was much deplored".

Plate 345a. Eglan Shaw of Whitby 1953
The new piers completed in 1924, were not sufficient to stop this storm ravaging the side of Staithes sea front public house. Eglon Shaw published this and other photographs of the Cod and Lobster during the great Storm of January 1953. This photographic card was actually posted in August 1955 from Mrs Iris Kirton to her daughter Ann Elizabeth Kirton who became Ann Lawson, wife of local photographer & entrepaneur Terry Lawson, who runs the successful 'Gift Shop', on Staithes High Street.

Plate 345b. 1953

This is the third Inn on this site and the previous two were both severely damaged by storms or washed away, requiring re-builds. This pub has suffered much damage for over 150 years and it was severely damaged due to extreme storms during January of 1767, when thirteen houses near the Staith were washed away. A large portion of land in the vicinity of 'The Cod' run by Matthew Trattles at the time, was broken and swallowed by the sea in February 1844, exposing several retreats (Smugglers Gin Holes). The fiercest storm for generations on November 27th 1862 forced it to be re-built in similar style. Another storm in November 1875 flooded the Inn. During 1890 a Lavinia Lane was recorded as the licensed victualler and Thomas Lane by 1897, the year of Laura Johnson and Harold Knight's first visit to Staithes. They witnessed a part of the Cod & Lobster being washed away during their early years here, before the large bulwarks were built to give added protection (1900/1901).

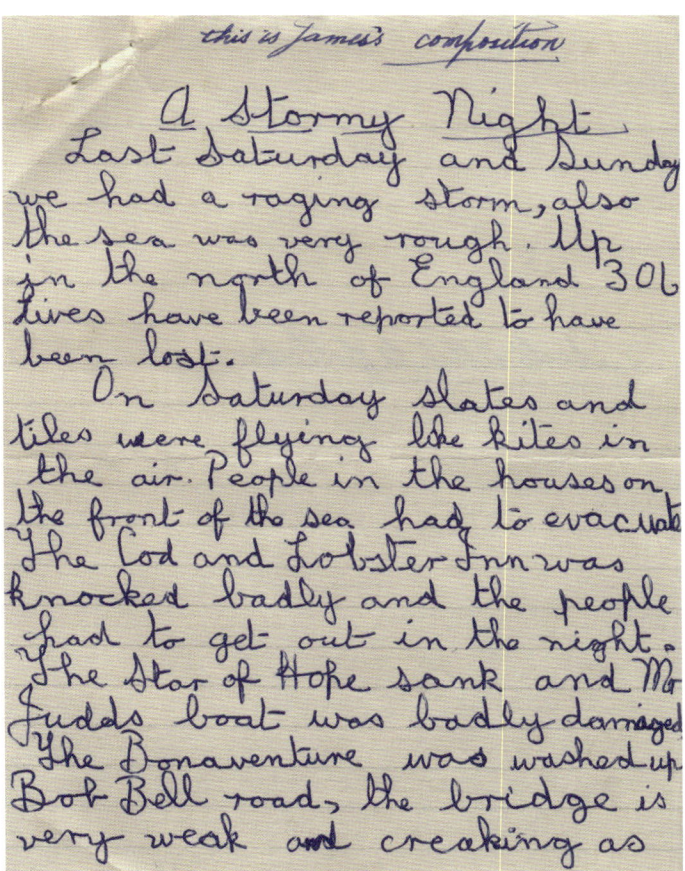
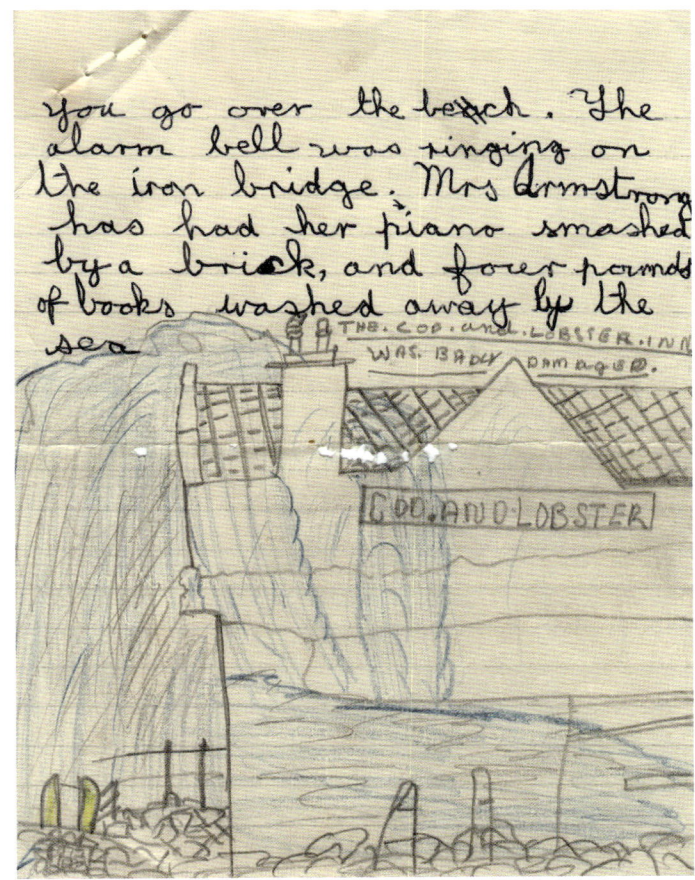

Plate 345c/d. "A Stormy Night" by James Rodham Longster
Young schoolboy, James Rodham Longster (Jim), who now lives at the restored Smokehouse on Granary Yard, produced a very pertinent and informative, school composition on the Great Storm of 1953, entitled 'A Stormy Night', reproduced above, complete with sketch.

Plate 346. c1903

Plate 347

For well over a Century, this well weathered rock, shaped by the movement of the sea, was likened to a ship's capstan or mushroom and some locals referred to it as 'Table Top'.

Two mules are anchored (brought up) in the Wyke, this being as close as they could get.

The small inset picture right is the SS Aberdonian, which became grounded on Cowbar on 18th June 1930 in the vicinity of this landmark rock.

During the modern installation of new sea defences during 2001-2002, involving the ferrying of huge Norwegian boulders, the above well known landmark, was destroyed when a ship collided with it.

Plate 348. FMS 1901

Who else would pay boys 1d each to take off their clothes! Yes this is an animated photograph from 'The Master' allegedly taken at low tide in Staithes, according to the label on the photograph sent to the author from Australia! This classic Sutcliffe image, reminiscent of his famous medal winning photograph titled the 'Water Rats' has six naked local lads showing their skinny rib cages for all to see. This photograph was titled by Sutcliffe as 'Sea Urchins' and was exhibited by him at the Royal photographic Society on 2nd January 1901. However the dates of this and the previous view together with the amount of tidal wear on the rock do not tie up, so maybe there were two such rocks or the Sutcliffe view was taken on home territory in Whitby.

Plate 349. c2003

Staithes most recent sea defence & slope stabalisation work was completed in 2002, at a cost of £3.5 million and a plaque was unveiled in April 2002 by Sarah Neson, Head of Flood & Consolidation Division of the Dept. of Environment, this can be found on Seaton Garth, opposite the Sea Drift Café.

SECTION 33.0 – BETWEEN TWO NABS

Staithes is sheltered by two prominent Nabs, in the west by Colburn Nab, now called Cowbar Nab and in the east by Old Nab, now called Penny Nab (Piercy Nab).

Colburn Nab has been stated as the second highest point on the English Coast at 666 feet, with Old Nab at 400feet. This Yorkshire coast section exposes the Cleveland Ironstone of the Middle Lias (Lower Jurassic). A stretch of coast of only about one kilometre in length from the old fishing village of Staithes to the small headland of Old Nab, provides a fine section through a sedimentologically unusual and quite fossiliferous, Lower Jurassic marine succession. The Cleveland Ironstone Formation of Middle Liassic age is very well-exposed. It consists of shales with prominent ironstone beds, where Siderite nodules are abundant in the shales. The trace-fossils at Old Nab are quite remarkable in their excellent preservation.

Smuggling was rife in Staithes during the early days (1700-1840's) and smugglers operating in Staithes beck, would place a lookout on the cliff top, so that they could be warned of any visits by the Preventative Officer/Coastguard.

The lookout allegedly lit a fire on the cliff top, using coal to warn the smugglers, hence why it was called Coalburn, corrupted to Colburn Nab and now Cowbar Nab.

Plate 350 H.C.Morley 1910

In their 1890 directory, Bulmer's wrote 'The village of Staithes is situated in a narrow creek, between Colburn Nab, now known as Cowbar Nab and Penny Nab (Piercy Nab) which completely seal it from the view of the approaching traveller until he reaches the summit of the cliff above'.

This photograph clearly illustrates how the bay and the village of Staithes are encapsulated between the two Nabs.

Four cobles, one in sail, have just left the confines of Staithes, hoping to be lucky out in the German Ocean.

Plate 351

Sandstone is present at the village of Staithes, particularly at Cowbar Nab (on the east side), it disappears under the beach at Penny Nab, the headland on the west of the harbour, shown left. From here onwards the shales and ironstone are well-seen when the tide is out. The Cleveland Ironstone Formation is well-exposed in the intertidal ledges and in the vertical cliff.

Plate 352

Staithes was just a bay when this Victorian photograph was taken, with very rudimentary sea defences. A bonneted woman stands along with two dogs on the slipway and a very busy scene exists on the Lifeboat quayside, where the lifeboat house doors are open.

Large, but yet narrow, herring cobles 459 WY and 548 WY, lie at the waters edge and the 'Watch house' flag pole in Boathouse Yard is evident. The end shape of Cowbar Nab has changed considerably in the 100 or so years since C.N & Co produced this photograph, No.2573 in their series.

Plate 353

Taken from an unusual angle in c1912 this unknown photographer has captured the pantiled 'Burtons Cottage' in the foreground on Mount Pleasant, with Penny Nab dominating the background. A gap exists today, where the small cottage is pictured, immediately below Burtons Cottage. The Brown family were well established fishermen and sailors within Staithes. The double dormer windows of Seymour's old General Store('Singing Waters') are at the bottom of the High Street, on the extreme left together with Tom Englands Cottage ('Cocked Hat house') and the Cod Lobster Inn also in view. Penny Nab was also referred to as Piercy Nab in the 1890's.

Plate 354

Cowbar Nab dominates the background in this 1939 view where the the pub has a new sign, 'Cod and Lobster Refreshments' and as usual attracts a small gathering of locals. This view was published by 'The Holiday Fellowship' and was available from the Trig Point Holiday Camp, Staithes.

Plate 355
Taken shortly before Queen Elizabeth's coronation this c1952 view shows how the fishing village is situated between Cowbar Nab and Penny Nab with the new harbour/sea defences erected in 1924, in place.

Plate 356
Three local Staithes lads pose sitting and paddling for the photographer. This 1897 magic lantern slide shows the lads in their gansey's and caps, in the vicinity of the old anchor and chain that lay on Staithe's beach for many a year. Penny Nab has changed shape over the years and the small outcrop seen here is no more.

SECTION 34.0 – THE HOLIDAY RESORT - UNSPOILT BY MODERNITY

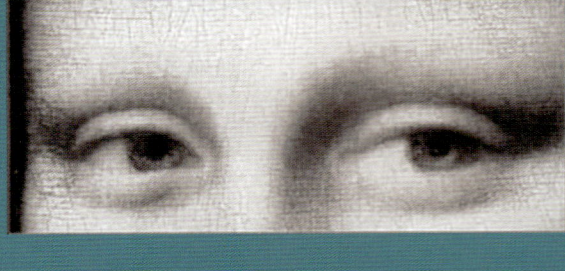

The picture postcards sent by the Edwardians, all record Staithes quaintness and picturesqueness and what a jolly good time they had here.

A Staithes, Yorkshire Coast brochure, published by Staithes Advertising Association, issued in 1924, carried the title: 'Unspoilt by Modernity'. This being a quote from author and poet J.S. Fletcher, who wrote three volumes on the History of Yorkshire, from his journey through the three Ridings.

More and more tourists visited Staithes after the 1st World War finished and it is often stated that more visitors came in the period 1930 to late 1950's than today. Thankfully Staithes has never succumbed to amusement arcades, fish & Chips, Candy Floss and Kiss Me Quick Hats, it has always been tasteful and understated and remains so today. The nearest Staithes came to having an amusement arcade was when penny slot machines existed in the former slaughter house in Gun Gutter and next to the lifeboat house, for a brief while shortly after the 2nd World War.

HOLIDAY RESORTS IN THE NORTH.
STAITHES.
(From a Photo by Payne Jennings, Ashstead.)

Plate 357 1896
Laura Knight once described Staithes beach in c1903, as a 'Sordid stoney beach that was a dump for the refuse of the town and fish guts'. However the Northern Weekly Gazette issued seven years prior on July 18th 1896, advertised Staithes as a Holiday Resort in the North and certainly tourists have steadily visited Staithes since the Railway was completed in 1883.

Plate 358
A typical Raphael Tuck Oilette postcard of the day, with a cryptic message;'Would you rather be here or on an aeroplane'. The heading title of Staithes would be added later and equally this card could have been used for any resort.

'NORTHERN HAUNTS OF ARTISTS AND LITTERATEURS'

From the 1920's through to the 1970's, Staithes was advertised as having boating, bathing, tennis and fishing along with village cricket. With a Carnival Committee providing various Summer Entertainments such as: aquatic sports, fancy dress, band music and open air dancing on the sea front. The United Automobile Services Ltd, ran a regular service with a quarter hourly service in the peak holiday season, with direct buses to Whitby, Scarborough, Redcar & Middlesborough & Summer excursions. The adverts stated that the district around Staithes offers in epitome, an ideal background for a seaside and country holiday with unrivalled sea views, majestic cliff scenery, moorland and pastoral beauties all become part of the same exciting panorama!

There is no doubt that Staithes attracts certain types of clientel, generally quite fit people who are prepared to do some walking and who do not want a funfair front!

Artists have come here for around 150 years and possibly there are more artists operating on this part of the East Coast than ever before. The area has inspired artists and bookwriers alike and it is quite difficult to find the words to describe, just what a special place Staithes really is.

Plate 359
What a delightful scene where the four sailed model boat, is launched into the warm water of the large 'Skate Hole', rock pool on Staithes scaurs. All but one boy and the girl are without head cover. This model boat would have been a prized possession at this time and nearly every boy in the village would have a model boat, but not necessarily with four sails. If this had not been taken in 1908, you would have thought the girl was operating the boat by remote control!

Plate 360 c1897
At least twelve Victorian local children are captured paddling and playing on Staithes beach, during the early evening. The beach at the time of this photograph in 1897, contained very little sand.
On the horizon a sailing ship and a steam trawler are just visible, with Penny Nab outlined right, against the bright sky.

Plate 361

All appear to be overdressed in this early evening Victorian magic lantern slide of 1897, where a trio of well heeled, pretty young women sit on the beach with their daughters.

Plate 362 J Valentine & Sons 1958

This photograph was titled 'The Quay and Nab, Staithes.'

Most of the nets and all of the crab/lobster pots that used to line the quayside, have disappeared in this c 1958 view where 'DPT 516' takes up a prominent position on the Staith. Holiday makers bask in the sun, lounging in their deck chairs which could be hired from the end of the Staith. A Mr and Mrs Unthank from 'Harbour View' rented out chairs as did George and Ann Cole from 'Friendship' Cottage. The message sent in August 1958, on the reverse reads," Having a grand holiday, never known so many seagulls as at Staithes, make life rather hazardous at times! The beggars scream all day & all night long!"(they still do today!)

Plate 363 FMS c1939

Taken from a very lofty perch off Penny Nab we can see that the Staith has 22 cars parked on the sea front as tourism greets this part of the North Yorkshire coast. The Lifeboat house is out of commission and the large doors have been replaced by windows, as it has become a private residence.

THE HOLIDAY RESORT

Plate 364   **Francis Frith**

Plate 365   **Francis Frith**

The above Frith photographs were taken in the late 1950's and capture a time when tourists could take Sea Trips around Staithes harbour and on a good day they would venture beyond the harbour and out to sea. Boats Frank & Elizabeth (WY170) and Sunbeam (WY14) would take up to a dozen or so day trippers. The local fishermen would refer to the visitors boarding their boats for trips, as 'running spors' and was a useful source of income to the fishermen.

Plate 366

There were 4 or so Staithes cobles operating as 'pleasure boats' from the beach front and T.C. Theaker's boat WY127 is being launched with a dozen or so day trippers aboard. Other boats in view are Sunbeam (WY14) and the empty Frank & Elizabeth (WY170).

SECTION 35.0 – DIGS IN STAITHES

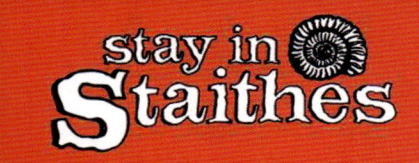   

Prior to the Whitby, Redcar & Middlesborough Union Railway, opening in 1883, there was little or no official accommodation in Staithes for visitors. The North Yorkshire Directory of 1890 has no record of accommodation other than the Station Hotel, run at that time by Edward Henry Hutty and none recorded in Hinderwell. However we know that a certain Indiana Truefitt, started her business career in 1864, with a Milliner/Dressmaking business, eventually opening the Victoria Family Hotel (allegedly a Temperance Hotel) on the High Street in 1868/9. By1872 she was recorded as a Beer Retailer (so much for temperance!). Hence this would probably have been one of Staithes very first places of proper accommodation for visitors, outside of the public houses and it was probably nothing grand, more of a basic lodging house (however her terms were not cheap at 4/6d per day). Indiana was born about 1812 and her death was registered in Whitby in April 1877, aged 65.

Basic accommodation for local and itinerant workers however, was provided in abundance in the form of Lodging Houses and both Rachael Cook and Ann Bake in 1841, ran their Lodging Houses on Back Lane, Staithes, mainly catering for labourers. It was common practice for certain tradesmen to lodge in Staithes, so the practice of 'putting people up' was not unusual. James Harburn the Staithes chemist to be, stayed with Mary Sanderson on Front Street, when he was just a medical student and alum worker Samuel Smith stayed with grocer Hannah Simpson, again on Front St, both recorded in 1851. Many people took in lodgers such as apprentices, iron-stone miners, labourers from Ireland and some of course put up servants. Anthony Thompson at No. 92 Back Street, was in 1851 'putting up' a chimney sweep (figuratively speaking), three hawkers, a miller and two travellers. John Busfield at No.108 Main St. was also 'putting up' a chimney sweep/wife together with a seamstresss, a miner and a hawker, plus a servant and three young family members. Six lodgers are recorded staying with Robert Garnett at No. 37 Back Road, namely; a 70 year old optician from Malton, Irish labourer, an 84 year old smelter from Ireland, a 74 year old sailor, a dressmaker and young 20 year old sailor. During the period 1851-1861 there was a very large influx of iron-stone miners, into the district and Staithes was nearly at breaking point in accommodating this demand. Boarding houses started to spring up, including those of Mary Crooks and Hannah Atkinson on Church Street. However many of the miners were boarded into local families, where they remained for several years. There are examples of small 3 & 4 roomed houses boarding miners, with up to 11 people in total recorded in John Metcalfe's five roomed house in Mann's Yard (top/tail!). Miners were accommodated at the larger roomed Royal George (x10 rooms), Golden Lion (7rooms), Free Masons Arms (8rooms) and the larger 12 roomed Black Lion.

Many of the miners were forced into the areas off the High Street such as Gar' Ends, Boathouse Yard, Mann's Yard, Lion Yard, Hugill's Yard, Slippery Hill, Webster's Steps, Chapel Yard, Seaton Garth and Church Street and Old Stubble (The Hill), often creating small mining communes.

Most houses in Staithes had 3/4/5 rooms, there were a few with 2 rooms only, so it was the larger houses that were able to assist with the need to board the influx of miners, labourers e.g. Felicity House (10 rooms), Ravenscraig (8 rooms), Ruby House (8 rooms), Bank House (8 rooms), etc

Plate 367 GWW c1900

This photographic 'positive' poses a problem, in so much as the two properties towards the centre right on the High Street are 'Sandringham' with the fancy brickwork and the adjacent Black Lion PH, but no sign of the building housing today's Gift Shop or the earlier Indiana Truefitt's Victoria Hotel or Joseph Brown Newton's former butchers/drapers shop, as the gap must mean the building is low lying or has been demolished awaiting a re-build. It is believed that the former Victoria Hotel was demolished around the turn of the 20th Century, to eventually make way for the new 8 roomed Victoria House, built for Joseph Newton Brown (the Gift Shop building that exists today).

By 1897 the Commercial Hotel had opened its doors in Hinderwell with proprietor Robert Taylor, but no further official accommodation shown within Staithes until 1904 where a Mrs Ann Porritt was renting out apartments within Captain Cooks Cottage at the bottom of Church Street.

It is likely that visitors may have rented a room at one or two of the public houses, outlying farms as did Laura Johnson & Harold Knight or stayed with locals who were prepared to let them lodge within their own homes in order to earn some extra income.

It was a mixture of the advent of the Railway and the influx of artists during the period from 1883-1910 that changed the situation in Staithes, with a whole stream of visitors and artists arriving in Staithes. A lot of visitors only came for the day from nearby towns such as Middlesborough, Whitby & Redcar but the artists stayed as long as their money would last and as a result of this new demand, several locals started to rent out apartments or provide board residence.

The advent of the motor car, brought several more visitors to Staithes, but invariably, most came here by train or bus. The period from 1903-1914 was the 'golden age' for picture postcards and several messages are pertinent as follows:

- A message from 1907 reads as follows; "Ask Lizzie are you coming by the M.R. or G.C.R. we came by M.R. will she drop me a postcard what train. I will meet you at Whitby if by the M.R. come by the one leaving Sheffield 12.45, the one we came by, love Mother"

- A message from Frank, staying at the Cod & Lobster in 1963 read, 'stayed the night here, The English here is queer'.

Post WW1, Staithes started to open up to the visitors and several apartments, rooms and cottages became available.

Several early recorded places to stay in Staithes were as follows:

ACCOMMODATION	OWNER	NOTES
Victoria Family Hotel, High Street	Indiana Truefitt	1868/69, Hotel was built adjacent to a low lying thatched house attached to the Black Lion PH
Bank House(former Midland Bank), High St.	Mrs Brown	1901 as recorded in Enid Lucy Pease diary (socialite & 'artist')
Blue Jacket House, High Street	J.R. Verrill	1910 – Furnished Apartments
Bridge House, Abrahams Lane	Mrs J.W.Crooks	1920's onwards
Captain Cooks Cottage, Church Street	Mrs A Porritt	1897-1938, where artist Harold Knight lodged for 12s/week, all in
'A low cottage,' probably 'Mizpah'	Mrs Thompson	1901-1909, near the Staith on Seaton Garth.
'The Cliffs'	-	1903, Cliff Road.
House on Church Street	Mrs Crooks (widow)	1897 where artist Laura Johnson stayed, 10s/week all in, Mrs Crooks lost her husband John Crooks in the lifeboat tragedy of 27th November 1888
9. Grinkle Terrace	-	1928 Lodgings
House on Church Street, probably Balmoral House	Mrs Robinson	1897 – the English artist Romilly Fedden (1875-1939) was a watercolourist & came to Staithes to paint, lodging with Mrs Robinson
House next to Captain Cooks Cottage, Church Street	Margaret Ann Verrill	1898, where artist Harrington Mann and Mrs Mann lodged
House on Church Street	Mrs Harrison	1949
Popular House	Mrs Bennison	1930's Guest House

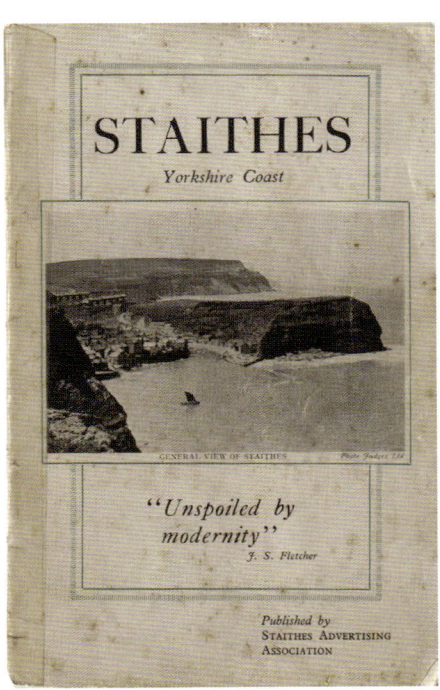

Plate 368 1924

A brochure issued by the Staithes Advertising association in 1924, with the very pertinent title 'Unspoilt by Modernity,' listed the following accommodation in Staithes:

ACCOMMODATION	OWNER	DETAILS
Bridge House	Mrs Crooks	Sitting room+3BR, WC
Boulbly Cottage	Mrs Bennison	SR, 1BR, attendance & central
5. Broom Hill	Mrs R Hick	SR, 2BR with attendance
Church Street	Mrs Dohring	SR, 2BR, attic, furnished cottage
Cliff Grove	Mrs Duell	2SR, 1BR with or without board, bath h&c & wc inside
Darlington Terrace	Miss Cole	SR, 2BR comfortable apartments
Glen Dene	Mrs Stonehouse	SR, 3BR no board, attendance, ½ hour sea, ½ hour moor
Green Hill View	Mrs F Verrill	SR, 3BR, organ, board if required
Granary Yard	Mrs Legg	SR, 3BR, near sea, wc
High Street	Mrs A Boyes	SR, 2BR, near sea
High Street	Mrs B Shippey	SR, 2BR, near sea & station
Hill View	Mrs Adamson	2SR, 3BR, attendance, piano, wc
Popular House	Mrs Seymour	SR, 3BR, organ, attendance, wc, pleasant situation near sea
Sea front	Mrs Worthy	SR, 2BR, organ, sea view
Sunnylea	Mrs Shippey	SR, 3BR, attendance, bath h&c, wc
Westfield	Mrs Theaker	2SR, 4BR, attendance, sea view
Westgate House	Mrs J Hugill	SR, 3BR, piano, pleasant situation

The added attractions of organ or piano would be the equivalent of today's Wi-Fi or coloured flat screen TV and of course the WC inside was always a bonus!

Plate 369
The replacement chapel of 1880, stands proudly to the top left of this photograph, which shows a busy High Street. The horse and cart is making a delivery to J.W. Legg's shop, whilst another horse and cart are stationary outside of 'Beaumont', with it's nick/alley leading to Elliots Yard. This house adjoins 'Westgate' the former home of well known preacher Robert Parks. The house to the right is 'Sunny Lea,' which was a boarding house in the 1920-1950's period when Mrs G. Shippey was in situ. Today this is home to local character Willie Wright and 'Sunny Lea' looks different at this time, with the exposed stonework, without the rendering, as does the adjacent house, 'The Nook' with it's large bay window. The Nook was later the premises of Sarah Hannah Thompson, who ran a small confectionary, grocery and general dealers shop here, where she was known as 'Sarah Hannah Cream Buns' for obvious reasons.

The stone steps to the right, lead to 'Coastguard House' and 'Coastguard Cottage.'

The boy in the centre walks barefoot along the cobble stones and hens wander free on the High Street.

CLEVELAND GEMS

STAITHES, HINDERWELL & RUNSWICK BAY

It is clear that all 35 or so establishments for accommodation were run by women (you can't beat a woman's touch!)

A very useful brochure entitled Cleveland Gems, issued in the 1950's advertised accommodation in Staithes, along with The Official Guide to Staithes, Hinderwell & Runswick Bay and both give an insight into accommodation facilities within Staithes, as follows:

ACCOMMODATION	OWNER	DETAILS
Akenside, off the Barrass Square	Mrs F.M. Verrill	Furnished Cottage to let
Asbury House	Mrs Cole	Apartments only (2BR)
Black Lion Hotel	R.Lewis	B&B, Russell's Ales
Bulman Cottage	Mrs R. Longster	Board with H&C Bath (3BR)
Captain Cooks Cottage	Mrs Ann Porritt	Apartments
Cliff Road	Mrs Bell	Board Residence (2BR)
Glen View	Mrs R. Davis	Private Hotel (near beach, overlooking sea)
Kirkhill Café & Private Hotel, Church Street	Apply to Proprietess & later A.Rudduck	Board Residence, comfortable with reasonable terms
Marine View, High Street	Misses Kitching	Board Residence for eleven, with two private balconies, plus holiday cottage with balcony
Merlewood, Jubilee Terrace	Mrs Dunn	1st Class Board&Lodgings 15/-, B&B 10/-, modern conveniences
Newlyn	Mrs M.Theaker	B&B and Board (4BR)
Ravenscraig, High St.	Mrs Verrill	Apartments (4BR)
Ridgemount, Lane End	Mrs Dickens	H&C, Homely & Comfortable
Royal George Inn	H.Pearson	B&B, Scarboro' Ales
Sea View Cottage	Mrs Crispin	Furnished Cottage with sea view
Seymour's Café & Boarding House	-	Board residence, B&B, Liberal tables, 2 minutes from sea front
St Annsville, Cliff Road	Mrs Duell	Board Residence (3BR)
Staithes High Street	Mrs Boyes	Board only
Sunnylea, High St, next to Elliots Yard	Mrs G. Shippey	Indoor Sanitation (2BR)

DIGS IN STAITHES

Plate 370 'Ravenscraig'

Ravenscraig was home to fishmerchant, Dinah Alice Hick, in 1911 and is situated between Lyn House and Ruby House.

By the 1950's, Mrs Verrill had apartments to let, including two sitting rooms and four bedrooms at the three story 'Ravenscraig' on the High Street, next to Ruby House with the upper bay window; pictured on the right of picture above.

In 1911. Ruby House was the home of grocer's assistant, Mary Ellen Laverick. She was a friend of the artist Laura Knight and it is alleged that the now famous Laura Knight had stayed at Ruby House on more than one occasion, in the early years that she visited Staithes.

Plate 371

Wilf Mannion (1918 – 2000) the famous Middlesbrough & England inside forward used to stay at Ravenscraig from time to time. The current owner often jokes that Wilf has visited her bedroom!

SECTION 36.0 – 'THE BANKS OF STAITHES'

Plate 372
Staithes Bank, with the 'Battlestones' below
by Terry Lawson.

Staithes Bank was not in situ during the early part of the 18th Century, when only two roads existed into Staithes:

1) – the road from the old village of Seaton down Weatherill Street (Church Street), onto Seaton Garth/The Staith and

2) – the road from the North/Cliff tops & Red House Farm to Cowbar, down Cowbar Bank to the side of the beck and access to the village was via fords across the beck.

As the fishing trade grew, this demanded a more convenient access for the horse & carts and Staithes Bank was created by blasting away the cliff side to create a rough and ready access road down Staithes Lane, Byron Bank & Staithes Bank onto today's High Street.

Staithes Bank runs from the 'First & Last' house as you leave Staithes up to the site of the former Board School area where new houses now exist (c1996).

Byron Bank is the portion roughly from the top of the bank where the stone steps to the car park exist, up to the Captain Cook Inn.

Plate 373
This sepia viewcard was on sale in M. Cole's shop on the High Street. The Staithes Board School built in 1878 stands to the centre of this view.

The former National School on Church Street was replaced by the new Board School at the top of Staithes Bank which opened on 30th December 1878 & closed 107 years later in 1985. (now demolished and 8 new houses built on the site in 1996).

To the left of the school stands 'Badger Castle/Seacliffe'.

To the right of the school, two new residences have been built; 'The Haven' & 'Roselands', with the third, 'Northern View' under construction. The wooden huts of the old army camp/former Staithes Holiday Fellowship Camp can be seen in the background. The land in the foreground appears to be well cultivated at this time.

Painter and author Gordon Home wrote in his book 'Yorkshire Coast & Moorland Scenes' in 1904: "The steep road leading past the station drops down into the village, giving a glimpse of the beck crossed by its ramshackle wooden footbridge, the view one has been prepared for by guide books and picture postcards. Lower down you enter the village street, here the smell of fish comes out to greet you and one would forgive the place this overflowing welcome if one were not so shocked at the dismal aspect of the houses on either side of the way".

One hundred and nine years later, Staithes village and houses are in a much better state of repair today, than they were at the time of Gordon Home's visit and the fishy smell has gone too!.

'THE BANKS OF STAITHES'

Plate 374 1920's
This previous reference above by Gordon Home, to the old bridge would be the 'upper' trestle bridge as seen in the photograph here, looking down Staithes Bank towards 'Valley View' cottage and the old Smoke House close to the trestle bridge.

Plate 375
It is difficult to date this photograph titled 'Staithes from Bank Top' but it is probably late 1930's. The High Street is in the centre of this view with the old Midland Bank at the bottom corner. The area to the upper right hand is where you would find the houses at Broom Hill & Darlington Terrace, whilst the prominence to the extreme right is an area above Mount Pleasant affording superb views over Staithes village and harbour.

Plate 376 JT Ross c1909
Matthew Trattles sold this post-card from his High Street Drug Store, taken from a photograph by Whitby photographer Ross. The house on the right is both the First and the Last house as you enter/leave the village of Staithes and was once a little known public house during the early part of the 19th century. 'Caves' exist to the rear of this house. The house on the left is 'Valley View' and following heavy storms in 1924 this house partially slipped towards the ravine containing Roxby Beck and required shoring up. Close by was the site of a former Blacksmith. The arched windows of the Bethel Chapel (Independent) are just in view.

Plate 377
A horse and cart has just reached the top of the Bank and several children are playing just below 'Valley View' cottage. Tom Bennison, cartwright & joiner, is believed to have had his shed near to 'Valley View'. The two women wearing their Staithes bonnets coming down the bank, are just about level with the former public house the 'First and Last.' The un-metaled road looks to be no more than a rough track in this c 1917 photograph.

BELL's BANK (BOB BELL's BANK)

Robert Bell was a well known early blacksmith in Staithes as was his father, also a Robert Bell. Robert Bell junior lived on Back Road and was married to Ann Bell (nee Calvert, from Runswick) and initial thoughts were that this was how the name was derived.

However after extensive research there is a link to the Rodham family. Thomas Rodham the boat builder, married Ann Elizabeth Robinson in 1878 and they lived at 'Belmont' on Bell's Bank, between the High Street and Beckside. Ann Elizabeth gained the distinction of reaching 100 years of age on 13th September 1945 and a suitable celebration tea was held in the Wesleyan Chapel, to which she had been a life long member. Their daughter Sibbel Smales Rodham married, miller Albert Bell (1884-1918), who was the son of John Thomas Bell the flour miller at Dalehouse. They also lived at 'Belmont' for sometime(there were houses No.1 and No.2 here, built as houses for the coastguards) and the steep lane in front of 'Belmont' was initially known as 'Bell's Bank' and has since been corrupted into 'Bob Bell's Bank'.

Robert Parks (1833-1907) the Wesleyan preacher and farmer had his residence 'Westgate' built on the top left hand corner of Bob Bell's Bank.

Plate 378 T. Lawson 2006
This photograph, clearly shows the link from Beckside to the High Street, opposite the former 1880 Methodist Chapel via 'Bells Bank'. The lower bank to Granary Yard was known as 'Silver Street'. 'Belmont' houses No1 & No 2 have the white bay windows and stone steps to the top left of the steep bank.

The house on the left, with small garden, almost out of view is 'Long House', a former Dames School. The former sail lofts and stables on Granary Yard, lie to the right. Behind the dilapidated part tiled shed right, lies the narrow lane formerly known as 'Back Road', this winds a corner to Back Road steps and joins Staithes Bank. According to the 1861 census 'Back Buildings was the name listed for properties that existed here.

COWBAR BANK

Plate 379 c1905

A classic photograph of Cowbar Bank, from just past the old Alum House up to the top of Cowbar Bank and Dawnas Row (hidden from view). This of course is in the parish of Easington and is one of the two roads into Staithes.

The former Ward's Kipper House to the right of the bridge was eventually demolished and the stone was largely re-used to strengthen the side of Cowbar Bank in 1947.

During a severe cold spell in 2012 a huge rock fall occurred, weakening the upper side of Cowbar Bank, this unfortunately has led to some unsightly strengthening and provision of uniform stone cladding.

SECTION 37.0 – 'UP TOP' - STAITHES LANE END

Although it is spoken of in a very friendly way, locals refer to the 'Uppers' and the 'Downers'; a reference to whether you live up-top or down in the village itself. Up Top is considered to be from the top of Staithes Bank to the A171 main Whitby – Saltburn road.

Plate 380 Frith Ltd c1958
The main A171 road from Hinderwell sweeps left as it enters the old Staithes boundary. This photograph is taken from opposite Seaton Crescent where the new Co-Op store exists. The former council houses eventually reach Lane End as shown in the view to the left. Eleven new bungalows now exist on the left and finish at Captains Cook Close. The Boulby Cliff can be seen in the distance.

Plate 381 c1915
The Staithes lady, dressed in black walking past the Catholic Church, is carrying a basket of washing on her head, possibly for drying on the hedgerows on Staithes Bank.

The catholic church of 'Our Lady, Star of the Sea' stands to the left and where Staithes Lane meets the A171 main road from Whitby to Loftus we can see the former Grinkle Miners Hospital which opened midway through the 1st World War in 1915.

The iron-stone miners within the Lane End cottages and the more recent Geenbank Terrace cottages, were from Staithes and Hinderwell and several from further afield such as Durham, Scotland etc. The Dunn's, Simpson's, Bennison's, Adamson's, Welford's and Dix's were here when the mines were going strong and generally father and sons lived & worked together.

Plate 382
The precise date for the opening of the Miners Hospital was 20th March 1915 and a large crowd have gathered for the opening ceremony. Mrs Jane L Tyreman was recorded as the matron, working at this hospital during the 1930's.

R.W. Longster's pay slip for March 1915, shows that he worked 12 days, and after deductions he received £4-16-10d, where a deduction of 4pence was made for the above miners hospital (nothing is free!). This closed to become a private house, sometime towards the end of the 1930's. Its glazed turret gives this house a unique feature.

Plate 383 Frith Ltd c1958
Taken from the corner of Seaton Close, this photograph shows the gentle rise in the roadway past the neat row of terraced houses towards Bank Top. The 26 former iron-stone miner's cottages, formed Grinkle Terrace, finishing at Palmers Close and include the former Willie Verrill's Fish & Chip shop now a Pizza shop. The Greenbank Stores and Post Office (former Heseltine's shop) stands opposite Palmers Close. These cottages contained machine workers, ratchet men, plate-layers, chargers, putters, trappers, drill changers, wood sawyers, banksmen/bank riders, horse drivers, blacksmiths, engine fitters, powder magazine keepers and deputy underground managers. A Mr King who was blind lived in one of the Grinkle Miners cottages and he was the former Bellman for Staithes. Ivor Ridley ran his Plumbing & Electrical Business from No.24 Grinkle Terrace. The cottages above Palmer's Close originally formed Greenbank Terrace.

SECTION 38.0 – THE SUPREME SACRIFICE – WAR TIME IN STAITHES

   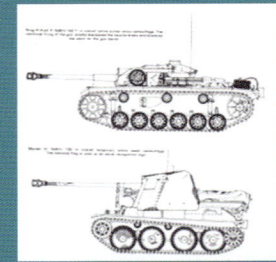

Plate 388a

Thomas Verrill (1895-1942)

There are still those who remember World War 2 in Staithes when barbed wire was strung along sea walls and slipways, concrete boxes and tank traps were built.

The Local Defence Volunteers (LDV)/Home Guard was formed.

There were few wartime casualties within Staithes itself, and little or no direct attacks on the village/harbour, however on 23rd January 1941, two small local boys found an unexploded bomb and despite warnings, they were unfortunately both killed when the bomb exploded.

William Henry 'Enny' Verrill of Gun Gutter Stairs, took out Aircraft and Bombardment Insurance to the sum of £200. His dwelling was insured for damage by shells, shots, bombs and missiles or bombardment by hostile guns, so long as they had not landed on British Territory at any time before 4pm on 8th May 1917. If these conditions were met the Government promised to make good all losses within 30 days!

Plate 388b

Three alleged Staithes men in full uniform each wearing black arm-bands, hats fastened up on the left hand side and carrying short rifles.

Little if nothing is known about this photograph from a Staithes family album.

Plate 389

This close up photograph from the early 1920's, records the Staithes men who made the supreme sacrifice for King & Country during the Great War 1914-1918. They were all part of the Yorks Regiment and the higher ranking Sergeant William Green and Corporal Thomas Rigg are inscribed first, followed by 24 of the Privates.

It is difficult to mention all, but the local names of Harrison, Porritt, Laverick, Theaker, Shippey, Verrill, Cole, Thompson, Hick and Trattles, are all celebrated on this elevation of the Memorial.

A further memorial to the fallen residents of Cowbar and Boulby exists at All Saints, Easington.

Plate 390 FMS c1930's

Frank Meadow Sutcliffe captured 'The Cod' and Slip Top, in this photograph which bears an FMS number, but will have been sold by Thomas Waterfall Gillatt, who bought the business, including all his negatives and photographs from Frank in 1922. Note the two remaining old tank traps, huge concrete blocks placed on the slipway next to the Cod & Lobster during World War 2.

JUNKERS JU88 M2+EK NEAR STAITHES.

On the night of 9th/10th July 1941, three Junkers Ju88's set out from Schipol in Holland to carry out anti-shipping patrols over the North Sea, they had possibly set out at different times.

All three aircraft flew into mist as they neared the English coastline and were separated. This Bernberg manufactured aircraft headed north and hit the cliff top at Brackenbury Wyke, Staithes at 00.06hrs. The tail of the aircraft fell back down the cliff and the rest of it broke up and was spread over the fields, at the top of the cliff on land near Cliff Farm. The incident is well known of locally.

Plate 391

Plate 392

Plate 393

Plate 394
All four German airmen died and Observer Rudolf Bellof, born 1919 was one of those killed eventually being buried at Thonaby-on Tees cemetery.

The Junkers Ju 88 was a World War II German Luftwaffe twin-engine, multi-role aircraft, designed by Hugo Junkers' company in the mid-1930s to be a so-called Schnellbomber. Which would be too fast for any of the fighters of its era to intercept. It became one of the Luftwaffe's most versatile combat aircraft of the war. Affectionately known as "The Maid of all Work" (Mädchen für Alles), it was used successfully as a bomber, dive bomber, night fighter, torpedo bomber, reconnaissance aircraft etc.

Plate 395 A general view of the area of the above crash on 10.7.1941

Plate 396
On a more sombre note, the ship, pictured below, was the SS Empire Heath, a 6,644 tons Catapult Aircraft Merchantman (CAM) ship, completed in June 1941 for the Ministry of War Transport (MoWT). On the 11th May 1944 when on route from Victoria Bay, Brazil, to Loch Ewe, Scotland for orders, via Freetown, carrying a cargo of Iron Ore, she was torpedoed by U-Boat U-129 and sunk. All but one of the complement of 58 were killed, the only survivor was taken as a POW.

This was a sad day for Staithes as the following eight crew members, all from Staithes, were lost:

Name	Title	Age
William Thompson Brown O.B.E.	Master	45
Joseph Gargett	Able Seaman	24
Richard Harrison	Boatswain (Bosun)	43
Tom Porritt Harrison	Able Seaman	23
James Thomas Laverick	Senior Ordinary Seaman	20
Leslie Longster	Able Seaman	30
Burton Verrill	Able Seaman	25
William Ward	Able Seaman	32

The War memorial close to the Captain Cook PH at the top of the bank, recognises the sacrifices by the above Staithes men. They are all listed on the stone cenotaph under the heading of 1939-1945 Merchant Navy Captains

SECTION 39.0 – STAITHES HOLIDAY FELLOWSHIP CAMP (TRIG POINT)

The Holiday Fellowship was founded in 1913 and its objective was to provide for the healthy enjoyment of leisure, to encourage the love of the open air, to promote social and international friendship and to organise holiday making and other activities with these objectives.

In 1924 the charges to stay at Staithes Holiday Camp varied according to age from 20/- to 27/6 inclusive. The facilities were aimed at Schools, Welfare Clubs, Scout troops, Girl Guides and Lad's Brigades.

By 1935 The Fellowship Camps in Wales, Suffolk and Staithes had provided holidays for over 45,000 boys and girls. Each Camp was composed of large well built wooden buildings, which gave ample and well ventilated accommodation for sleeping, dining and recreation. The sleeping huts at Staithes in 1935 accommodated 30 children with separate adjoining cubicles or rooms for the leaders. A Common Room, with piano was available for recreation, dances, concerts etc and both this room and leaders rooms were equipped with heating stoves. A dry canteen supplying all usual requirements was established within the camp. The Staithes Camp was advertised as standing on high ground immediately above the quaint fishing village of Staithes, close to the sea and Staithes Station (L and NE Railway). The district abounds in delightful cliffs, rocky pools and wooded glens. The moors are within easy walking distance and there is good bathing in the vicinity.

Plate 397
Obviously berets and 'flannels' were in, at the time of this photograph of the Main Avenue through the Camp.

The former WW1 Army Barracks have provided accommodation for schools, colleges and uniformed associations for many years.

The message on the reverse side of this postcard read as follows; 'Holiday Fellowship, Senior Camp, "Dear Louie, This is a great life, I cannot describe it very well, but will tell you all about it when I see you, Love Madge"

Plate 398
The wooden buildings of the Holiday Camp were quite extensive, as can be seen in this view taken in c1936 when open fields existed and neat allotments were in situ off Cliff Lane. The poor grammar of the message from a child at the camp in 1935 was addressed to a Mrs Riddel, 17 Peacy Rd, Sheperds Bush, London W12 and reads: 'Dear Mum, this is our camp. I have a letter from Miss Main. Will you right to me if you can send me a 2/- post a loda. The Master will chang it, thake 2/- out of my box'. In 1935 the accommodation was available from Easter to the end of September and could accommodate 180 per week.

In 2000 the owner Geoffrey Walker restored several of the wooden buildings to provide 4 Self Catering Lodges and 5 luxury en-suite Letting Rooms and retained 3 of the barracks as 'bunkhouse' accommodation for large groups.

The new facilities are now advertised as Trig Point 49 Campsite and Keel Cottages.

STAITHES HOLIDAY FELLOWSHIP CAMP

Plate 399
This was the Holiday Fellowship brochure for the season of 1935, for organised parties of boys and girls.

Plate 400   Raphael Tuck & Sons c1936
This sepia view card of the Camp shows that the males outnumber the females, as the youngsters pose for their photograph in the Main Avenue of the Fellowship Camp. The message on the reverse side reads; "Dear Kathleen, We are having a good time at GLB Camp, this morning we are going on a bus tour around the district. We went dancing in the Common Room on Saturday night and June & I met two nice boys, Love Sheila & June"

Campsite facilities are available today or letting rooms if preferred. Jazz and Real Ale festivals have also been held here for the past few years, organised by the landlord of the nearby Captain Cook Inn.

Plate 401
Lilywhite Ltd c1935
The Dining Room looks very presentable and brand new, with perfect cutlery settings for over 30 in view. The message on the reverse side of the post card reads;' Dear Mother, Very nice place up here, plenty of air, perhaps too much wind'. The Fellowship advertised that 'particular attention was paid to the dietry, quality, variety and preparation of all food, which was done by fully qualified, camp staff!'

Plate 402
1928
Arkala and Assistant and their 17 Girl Guides all smile for the photographer during their stay at Staithes Camp during 1928. This believed to be the Staithes troop, but the actual site of the Camp may not be the Holiday Fellowship camp as the simple message on the reverse side stated 'Staithes Camp 1928', although they did cater for such parties of girls.

SECTION 40.0 – THE 'HALLS OF STAITHES' – FARMING IN STAITHES

THE EARLY YEARS:

The earliest recorded farmer was John Boyes in 1523 and he was a farmer-fisherman, earning his living from the land and the sea. Francis Bigod of Seaton Hall was farming several farms by 1536 until his demise in 1537. A certain Philip Lewis was recorded as a husbandman in 1721, pasturing cattle in the Staithes Field, now Seaton Hall Farm and John Gill a yeoman was farming here too. In 1866 the following trustees of Staithes Wesleyan Chapel were recorded as farmers; Thomas Watson (Seaton Hall), Andrew Chapman and John Plews. A certain James Spink the licensed victualler of the Golden Lion, divided his time 1870-1890, between farming at Cowbar Farm and running his High Street public house, with the help of his wife.

Many of the local farmers were involved in the clearing of sites and transporting stone for Staithes new chapels in their horse & carts.

In the 1880's, Joseph Tyreman was farming on the cliffs at nearby Red House Farm, Isaac Duell in Dalehouse, Francis Newton on Home Farm in Roxby, William Judson at Twizziegill Farm(Betwixt two gills), John Willis at Boulby Grange and Matthew Codling at Cowbar Farm. The Staithes Wesleyan preacher Robert Parkes also farmed at Dalehouse as did William Ryder who farmed 18 acres here in 1861.

In 1851 George Webster, the fish merchant, farmed 8 acres above Staithes, with his son William and employed two labourers and a servant boy of 12 years, who's occupation was listed as 'Boy of all work!'

Thomas S. Cole farmed 21 acres in 1851 and employed one labourer.

In 1881, fishmerchant Johnson Ridley of Gun Gutter was recorded as farming about 6 acres and Thomas Wake who lived at the top of Church Street, was a Carrier and farmer of 3 acres.

The following farms are considered to be in or near Staithes;

SEATON HALL FARM:

Seaton Hall Farm is the oldest farm in the Staithes area and George Adamson was farming here in the 1760's. Seaton Hall the surviving Manor House was built in 1548, but evidence exists of an earlier dwelling dating back to the Norman Conquest, when it was home to de Seaton family and has alleged connections to the Knights Templar.

In Tudor times the Hall passed to the Bigod family and Sir Francis Bigod was an alleged 'spy' for Henry VIII, reporting back on any misdeeds in the Dissolution of the Monestries. Richard switched sides after the Reformation and became one of the leaders of the Catholic Uprising in the North – 'The Pilgrimage of Grace', for which he was hung, drawn and quartered at Tyburn.

The Hall & Farm later became part of the Mulgrave estate, where The Marquis of Normanby became the Lord of the Manor of Seaton.

In 1851, Paul Wilkinson was farming 166 acres here, with four farm servants/labourers and his son as help and by1861, Jane Campion was recorded as a farmer, farming 160 acres here, with her two young daughters, brother and five servants!

The acres increase! As in 1881, Joseph Wilson was farming 174 acres here.

Date	Farmer
1760-1800's	George Adamson
1851	Paul Wilkinson
1861	Jane Campion
1866-1880	Thomas Watson
1881	Joseph Wilson
1893-1909+	Will Dawson
1925-c1929's	Aeron Hart
1930	Charles Dennis

Plate 403a

Plate 403b

The Manor of Seaton (includes Staithes) passed from the Mulgrave family to Charles Mark Palmer the 'Iron-Master' in 1868.

William Kidd, conservationist, collector and engineer bought the place in 2002, when it was somewhat run down and spent around £1million in restoring it as holiday accommodation for large groups and themed breaks for garden and art appreciation. Here lies renovated barn and servants quarters now Seaton Cottage and Seaton Court and they contain among other fine features, some of the panelling from one of John Lennon's former homes at Tittinghurst Park, rescued by collector William and re-used here.

The Hall contains a 700 book library, made from Peggy Guggenheim's library in Venice and there are Staithes Group paintings too.

Plate 404
William Kidd rediscovered the original moat during extensive renovation work on the old Hall and estate.

CLIFF HALL FARM (FANCY HALL FARM)

Farmer Thomas Trattles is recorded as having a house on Abrahams Lane in 1841, next door to fishmonger John Hick, possibly associated with his fish merchant work, however there is also a note on the census form referring to Fancy Hall.

Thomas Trattles was a hard working Staithes Fish merchant who also had a great interest in agriculture and he employed several local men to assist him in his endeavour to farm successfully at Fancy Hall Farm on Cliff Road, Staithes. He continued here until his death in 1850.

In 1851 this farm was recorded in the census as Cliff Hall Farm, where Thomas Trattles widow, Frances Trattles at the age of 63 was farming 350 acres, with the help of four farm labourers and a maid.

By 1881, John Kirby was farming 110 acres here.

Date	Farm	Farmer
Early 1800's	Fancy Hall Farm	Weatherill's
1830's-1850	Fancy Hall Farm	Thomas Trattles
1850-1860's	Cliff Hall Farm	Frances Trattles
1866-c1881	Cliff House Farm	Walter Thompson
1881	Cliff House Farm	John Kirby & Robert Willis (joint occupiers)
1881-1911+	Cliff Farm	Robert Willis
1919-1930's	Ciff Farm (Fancy Hall)	Arthur Willis
1930	Ciff Farm (Fancy Hall)	George Dobson

Plate 405 1964
A clear aerial view of Cliff Hall Farm (Fancy Hall) on the cliff tops, taken in July 1964. The pile of white stones in the field are all remnants from the Staithes viaduct demolished in 1960.

This was where famous marine artist George Weatherill (1810-1890) was born ('The Turner of the North'). Fancy Hall farm was later farmed by Thomas Trattles, Staithes, fish merchant and later by Robert Willis (the Willis's were also at Cowbar and Red House Farms)

Plate 406a/b

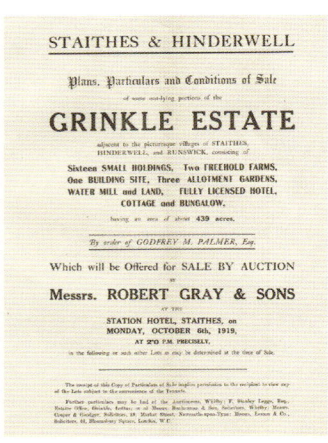
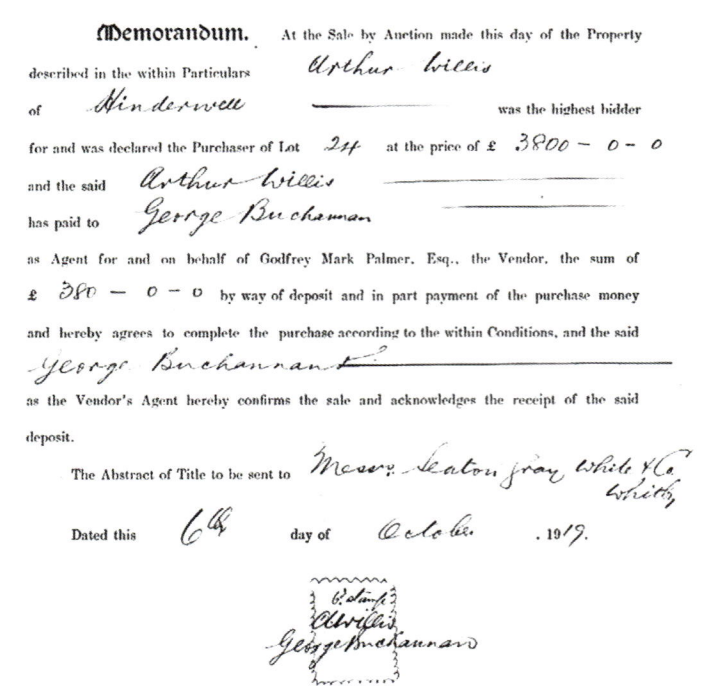

The privilege of working for jet in the cliffs was not part of the Sale as this was already allocated to Mr Thomas Trattles estate. Cliff Farm was sold inclusive of the following: The farmhouse containing, Entrance hall, 2 Sitting Rooms, Kitchen, Scullery, Dairy, 6 Bedrooms, 2 Attics & 2 Staircases.

Plus the farm buildings, including; Coach House, Cartshed, 2 Piggeries, Boil House, 2 Loose boxes, Beast House (10), Turnip House, Beast Shed (10), Horse Wheel House in working order, Barn, Implement Shed and Granary over, Cow House (10 & 6 calves), 5-stall stable and chambers over and Poultry House. A total of 143.900 acres (grass, tillage & cliffs) were included with the farm sale. In 1919 Arthur Willis who had been renting the farm from the Palmer's at £173-10s-0d, bought the farm for £3,800 from Godfrey Mark Palmer as part of Lot 24 at the Grinkle Estate Sale of 1919, held at the Station Hotel, Staithes. The present owners Sharon and Alan McMahon have been in situ since 1995 and the land is currently farmed by Mr Blackett.

RED HOUSE FARM (HIGH COWBAR)

This farm is situated in the parish of Easington.

Joseph Tyreman was farming in 1891 with his grandson John Tyreman and two farm servants.

Date	Farmer
1880 – 1890's	Joseph Tyreman
1897 -	Thomas & William Willis

COWBAR FARM (LOW COWBAR)

This farm was situated in the parish of Easington.

Date	Farmer
Pre 1800's	Weatherill's
1880's	Matthew Codling
1890	James Spink
1891	George Dove
1893-1909+	Robert Willis

CLIFF GROVE FARM (HANSELL HOUSE)

Cliff Grove Cottage was sold in October 1919 as part of the Grinkle Estate Sale as Lot No.8, complete with kitchen, scullery, 2 sitting rooms, 5 bedrooms, WC, plus additional buildings containing; wash kitchen, coal house, cow house (4), stall for horse with granary above. The Beck adjoining this lot and the right of fishing were not included. However a total of 6.143 acres including grass, scrub, cultivations and gardens were part of additional lots 52-54. The Lots were described as Two Closes of Grass Land with Dwelling House, Farm Buildings, Plantation, Orchard and Garden.

In 1911 John Richardson was the 'head' at Cliff Grove and he lived there with his wife, eight sons and two daughters (ample farm servants!)

Plate 407   HC Morley c1908

This scarce photograph was taken from the railway viaduct. We can see three ladies and two gentlemen all dressed in their summer 'whites,' outside the entrance to Cliff Grove Farm with its neat vegetable plot, haystack and greenhouse to the rear.

Up above lies Cowbar Farm (Low Cowbar) and the distant cottages of Boulby, whilst to the right the Roxby Beck flows down towards Staithes. It was here that the Hansell family ran their Fulling Mill during the 1790's, where cloth already woven would be treated, using Fullers Earth & soaked in water from the Beck, to remove grease and impurities. The cloth was then trodden on, to flatten it and hence the name 'Walk Mill,' which eventually became corrupted to 'Warp Mill'. The cloth was eventually stretched on tenter hooks in the adjoining field which became known as 'Tenter Field' as depicted on the 1856 ordnance survey map.

By 1924 a Mrs Duell was renting out her two sitting rooms and just one of the five bedrooms here, with or without board.

Date	Farm	Farmer/Owner
1841-1861	Cliff Grove	William Hansell
1881	Cliff Grove/Hansell House	Edward Stewart (deputy miner)
1891	Hansell House	Edward Stewart
1909 - 1919	Cliff Grove	John Richardson

In 1841 William Hansell and his wife Hannah Hansell ran Cliff Grove and their son, also William worked as a vetinary surgeon from here.

Not all had grand farms and a few were generally referred to as cowkeepers and often had the most rudimentary buildings for their livestock. Phillip Lewis was recorded as a Staithes husbandman in 1721 and kept cattle and oxen, other known cowkeepers were as follows:

Date	Cowkeepers
1893	John Adamson
1905	Thomas Hansell

George Ward and S. Dix were recorded as Dairymen in 1933 & 1937 respectively (dates are not precise as the directories are often released in four or more year intervals)

SECTION 41.0 – STAITHES RAILWAY & VIADUCT

The Saltburn-Whitby line of the Whitby, Redcar & Middlesborough Union Railway first opened on 3rd December 1883 and remained in use for 75 years until closure on 3rd May 1958. The first Goods train here was 26th December 1887. The Whitby to Loftus section was opened on 3.12.1883 and this joined up with the former Cleveland Railway at Loftus, allowing a through route from Whitby to Saltburn and later the NER connection from Brotton to Saltburn was used. The railway was of huge importance to the fishing industry and many tons of fish were transported away from Staithes for delivery to fish merchants far and wide. The advent of the railway opened up many new horizons for the people of Staithes, who up till 1883, either had to walk or travel by horse and cart. Many were suspicious of this mode of travel and never travelled by train, preferring to stay within the confines of Staithes village where they felt safe and self sufficient.

Alfred Worthy from Staithes Bank Top/Old Stubble was recorded as a railway platelayer in 1901, along with Robert H. Shipley.

Plate 408
The station platform and waiting rooms were situated just to the rear of the Station Hotel (now the Captain Cook Public House)). This photograph of the station with its hefty chimneys and original Victorian lamps together with its semaphore signals was taken approx. 20 years before the station closed in 1958.

Peter William Hill was the station master here throughout the 1890's and beyond. The station had two platforms serving a passing loop. The stationmaster's house was incorporated into the main building on the 'down' platform, with a wooden waiting shelter on the 'up' platform.

Arthur Stanley Umpleby started his career in Staithes as a humble railway clerk, before rising to the post of stationmaster and taking over from Mr Hill.

Stanley Umpleby produced a very important/interesting document titled; 'The Dialect of Staithes' – it was very akin to a foreign language course! – 'Wheer's thoo gannin' gauvin' aboot?

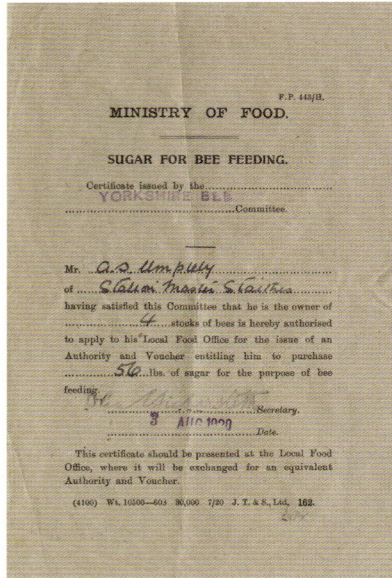

Plate 409   1920

Staithes Station Master A.S. Humpleby was a keen beekeeper and as the above certificate issued by the Yorkshire Bee Committee in August 1920 states, he was entitled to purchase 56lb of sugar during the post war period of sugar rationing. Rationing came into force during 1917/18 due to heavy losses of food ships during sustained attacks by U-Boats (230 ships sunk in February 1917). Panic buying also led to rationing and this continued until November 29th 1920.

Plate 410 1950

You could leave Whitby (West Cliff) at 7am and be at Staithes just 28 minutes later. What a tourist attraction this railway would be today!

Plate 411   **H.C. Morley c1914**

The train and five coaches look precariously perched on the high viaduct.

If you look carefully a large quantity of cobles are stored at the foot of the viaduct and the upper reaches of Roxby Beck were considered to be a safe haven by the Staithes fishermen and this area was called High Coble Gardens.

The single track viaduct at Staithes was the largest of the tubular viaducts on the route and it was built in 1875. The bracing between the pillars or piers was added in 1883 to strengthen the 790 foot long and 152 foot high viaduct following the collapse of the Tay Bridge in 1879, where the train plunged into the sea with great loss of lives. The viaduct consisted of six, 60 foot spans and eleven, 30 foot spans and was designed by John Dixon. Where the pillars stood in the Beck below was referred to by locals as Ta'' Black Watter Stream'.

The message on the reverse side is from Bella Hick of Staithes to her sister Mary Hick, saying that she is coming over to Scarborough with John and Zac. Almost certainly she would have been related to Zaccarriah Hick a local Staithes fish merchant

Plate 412 Francis Frith c1940's

Taken from the opposite side looking towards the sea, the viaduct stretches from the 'Saltburn side' towards the Station Hotel at Staithes standing right of picture.

The line consisted of a single track, but most stations had a passing loop (apart from Sandsend). Because of its height and accidents elsewhere, the high viaduct was fitted with a special device that gave an audible alarm in Staithes Signal Box, if the winds reached a certain force. The signaller would have to put the protecting signals to 'danger', on either side of the viaduct to stop trains, the viaduct would then be inspected before the train service could resume. A speed restriction of 20mph was imposed for normal windy conditions.

British Rail put up posters during 1958 to inform the public that the stations of Staithes, Hinderwell (for Runswick Bay), Kettleness and Sandsend would be closed as the line was not viable financially. The viaduct was demolished during 1960, because it would have been too expensive to maintain such a structure in order to meet strict Health & Safety criteria.

Plate 413

A two coach steam train crosses the viaduct on its journey towards Whitby in May 1958. The steam train locomotive is a British Rail Standard Class 4 2-6-4T and its number is probably No. 80116. The bracing added to provide greater strength, is much clearer in this photograph.

SECTION 42.0 – STAITHES SPORTING HERO's

With few local facilities it must have been difficult to produce a 'home-grown' team for any sport from within Staithes, however both football and cricket teams did exist within Staithes and the villagers played hockey in nearby Hinderwell. The visiting artists who congregated in Staithes and Runswick, played cricket and artist Fred Mayor's team played Charlie Lyon's team from Whitby on 23rd August 1901. The artists team included: Mayor, Friedenson, Knight, Bagshawe, Brown, Richardson, Swinstead and Jones.

Plate 414
The Staithes team at this time sported eight moustaches out of eleven players

Plate 415
Staithes Crusaders Football Club are pictured above, during their 1912-13 season and the whole team was made up from Staithes villagers only.

From left to right are: standing, Tommy Ward, Joseph Verrill (goalkeeper) & Tommy Unthank; Back row, Jack Sherwood, Tom Johnson, Middle row, George Longster, Tom Newton & George Hugill; Front row, Jack Hugill, 'Tich' Longster, William Newton, John Verrill & Joe Cole (not the Chelsea player!)

Plate 416
This was the Staithes Juniors team and they played in the Whitby & District Junior League.

Back row: Ken Gibson, Joe Garget, John Stone, R. Nicholson, Tony 'Tosh' Welford, 'Fudge' Evans, John Hicks & Jack 'Cockbod' Bowes.

Front row: Alan Crossman, Michael Hollingsworth, Don Burleaux, Dave Prothero, Richard Lyth.

John Stone later played for South Bank FC in Middlesbrough before joining 2nd Division Middlesbrough (1970-71), followed by York City (1972-75), Darlington (1976-78), Grimsby Town (1979-82) and finally for Rotherham United (1983-84) Stone was a polished right back, noted for his retention of the ball and he retired following the 1983-84 seaon with Rotherham United, having made 10 appearances and scoring one goal.

EDWARD VERRILL

Plate 417
Edward Verrill the son of Richard Verrill and Zipporah Verrill, was born in Staithes in 1885, he had three sisters and three brothers. There were at least five other Edward Verrill's living in Staithes around this time!

His father Richard, was initially a fisherman in Staithes, earning his living from the sea, however the whole family moved to 149. Victoria Road, East Middlesborough and the 1911 census records him as a Dredger Man. By now Edward ('Neddy' or 'Fishy') has become a Professional Footballer and commenced his Wing Half career with Middlesborogh FC during the 1907-08 season.

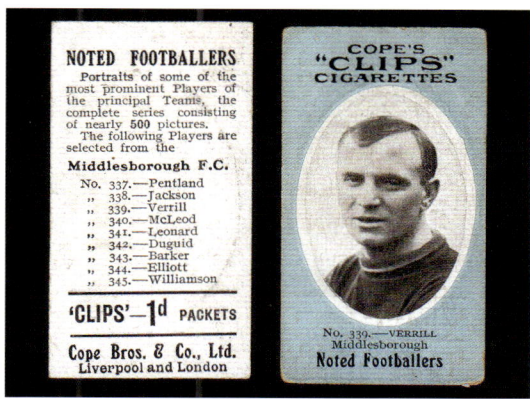

Plate 419
The 'Noted Footballers' portraits of the most prominent players of principal teams, consisting of 500 different pictures, were issued in 1910 by Cope's Bros & Co Ltd. Number 339, featured Edward Verrill a Staithes sporting hero when playing for Middlesborough F.C. and eight other Middlesborough players formed part of this large set. Edward was also featured in an earlier series produced by 'Taddy' cigarettes, issued in 1908.

His playing career with Middlesborough is listed below:

Season	No of Appearances	No of Goals Scored
1907-1908	26	0
1908-1909	27	0
1909-1910	39	3
1910-1911	36	1
1911-1912	35	0
1912-1913	21	0
1913-1914	6	0
1914-1915	2	0

He played for three seasons alongside the famous England player Steve Bloomer (1907-1910), where Steve scored 36 goals during the period. The war curtailed any further Middlesborough games until the 1919-20 season. His final game was his 192nd appearance for his only league club 'Boro'.

Plate 418
Edward Verrill (wing half) pictured here in the centre, during a training session with Middlesborough F.C.

COBLE RACING

It may be pushing the boundaries a little to call Coble Racing a recognised sport, however to the men of Staithes, there could be no doubt.

Coble racing events were organised well over 200 years ago and the following is recorded:

A notice announcing the annual fair is very interesting, the wording was as follows:

"Staithes Feast will be held on Tuesday, June 20th. 1797, when the prizes as advertised below will be offered to all those skilled in such matters, as well as divers others not herein stated, to wit: - A coble race for £1 1s., a lyke sum will be given to the best kept coble, to be equally divided; W. Hymers to adjudge.

The 1st Staithes Regatta was held on 14th June 1898, as part of the Staithes Fair. The coble race was open to cobles used for crab fishing and was an open rowing race over a four mile course. E.W.Beckett M.P. was the president of the Regatta Committee, Thomas Spink the vice president and J.V.Laverick J.P. the secretary.

Position	Cobles	Crew	Prize
1st	Martha & Elizabeth	William Francis Verrill (stroke)	£3.0s. 0d
		Isaac & Robert Longster (bow)	
2nd	Olive Branch	Matthew Verrill (stroke)	£1.10s.0d
		Edward Verrill (bow)	
		Matthew Theaker (bow)	
3rd	Ethelrada	Thomas Unthank (stroke)	10s
		Richard & Thomas Verrill (bow)	

'Billie Fanny' and the Martha & Elizabeth won the race by 60 yards

The following year the Ocean Coble Race (open to all England) was held on 6th June 1899, over a shorter two mile course and entries were invited to be sent to the following:

- T. Johnson (treasurer) of the Black Lion Hotel
- L. Hugill (secretary/starter) of the Shoulder of Mutton
- Robert Atkinson (judge) of the White Horse Inn

Coble racing and public houses, obviously went together!

There were just the three entries but only two competed, with the following result:

Position	Cobles	Crew	Prize
1st	Martha & Elizabeth	William Francis Verrill (stroke)	£4.10s. 0d
		Isaac & Robert Longster (bow)	
2nd	Two Sisters (WY222)	Matthew Theaker (stroke)	£3.0s.0d
		Matthew Verrill (bow)	
		Charles Horne (bow)	

Plate 420

The Martha & Elizabeth won by 8 lengths, maintaining a clean sweep, two years in succession for the powerful William Francis (Billie Fanny) Verrill & his tenacious Longster crew.

Billie Fanny, was never far from a friendly lady or two!

Billie lived on Seaton Garth and in 1909 he received a postcard from T. Featherstone, addressed as follows;

"Mr W. F. Verrill, (Billie Fanny), 2. Ould Cot, Seaton Garth, Staithes."

His reputation and his fame went before him.

CHAMPIONS OF THE GERMAN OCEAN 1866

Coble Racing began well before Staithes 1st Regatta of 1898. In 1866 the Great Ocean Coble Race took place, between a crew of fishermen from Staithes and a crew of miners from Blyth in Northumberland.

The event was 'brokered' by Staithes fish curer and rough jet merchant William Thompson. Thompson was a wealthy man, always extremely well dressed, but very in touch with the people of Staithes.

The race was held on September 11th 1866, over a 10 mile course from Staithes to Whitby and the crews, boats and result are listed below:

Position	Cobles	Crew	Prize
1st	The Jane	Burton Verrill	£200 and a Silver Cup worth £15
		Thomas Cole	
		Simeon Robinson	
		Thomas Crooks	
2nd	Temperance Star	Leslie Hope	Nowt!
		James Auld	
		Edward Barnes	
		Joseph Campbell	

Although a strong wind prevailed, the sea was relatively smooth and the race commanded much excitement along the coast, as people from far and wide took up vantage points, to see the race, which finished at Whitby Pier.

The Staithes fishermen kept ahead all the way, completing the course in a very fast 85 minutes.

Brass bands played and huge celebrations were to be had after Burton Verrill and crew became crowned 'Champions of the German Ocean'.

The following local report is worth reading:

Blyth boasted of their champion rowers, one of whom was said to be "as strong as Hercules, equal to any three ordinary men". The fishermen were considered underdogs in the 10-mile contest, between Staithes and Whitby bridge, for which a staggering prize was at stake – £200 (worth more than £86,000 in today's money). The Blyth men had rowed in races "and were versed in the tactics of aquatic struggles. The fishermen had never rowed a race, and had probably never dreamt of rowing a race. But they had on their side this supreme advantage: they were perfectly at home on the sea, they knew how to make the best way of wind and tide, and, in riding the billows, they were as perfectly at ease as any gull or duck".

And so it proved. When they rounded Rock Buoy, just off Whitby, the fishermen led by more than a minute, and by the time they reached harbour, they'd eased up but still finished 200 yards ahead. As the victors did a jig on the cobblestones of the quay, a lesson had been taught. "These Staithes fishermen were literally born to the sea, the coble was their cradle, and their whole life was spent in wresting a living from the sea, which oft-times in sudden storm tested their endurance to the utmost. What better training could be wished for in preparation for a long-distance race..."

In celebration of the great Staithes victory, Peter Kelly of Linskill's Yard, Church Street, Whitby, (who's son 'Gary' Kelly became coxswain of the Whitby Lifeboat), penned the following extensive poem, which gives an insight into the atmosphere prevailing at the time of this 1866 great race (akin to that of 1966!).

Subsequent to the above achievement, the Staithes crew threw out a challenge to any four fishermen on the North East Coast to a rowing match for a wager of £5 per side. Three Picknett brothers from Redcar, Richard, Thomas, Jack, and a local fisherman name of Thompson took up the challenge.

Anyone with any money, Mr. Picknett recalled with a smile, began to bet, and Staithes people were wagering domestic animals! Two tugs besides numerous small boats carried huge crowds of sightseers. At the start of the race the odds on the Picknett's were about 7 to 1.

The race started, and almost immediately the Redcar boat drew away, and in a few minutes were two hundred yards ahead.

The odds on the Picknett's shortened and soon no one could lay a bet. The sightseers followed and when the race was finished at Saltburn Pier the Redcar team was three quarters of a mile in the lead.

The Redcar fishermen had proved to be superior to the Staithes men in rowing prowess on this occasion.

There was another Great Coble Race in 1873 (opponents/result not known) and William Thompson was again the backer for this event. The team had just the one change from the the 'Champions of the German Ocean' team, of seven years earier in 1866 and this meant that Thomas Theaker replaced Thomas Crooks, who had been unfortunately drowned at sea, some little time after the big 1866 race.

Plate 421 C 1926

A huge crowd has gathered outside the Cod & Lobster PH in c1926, to watch the Staithes Great Coble Race and many have sought a vantage point on the lower rocks of Penny Nab; in order to witness this important local event. Each of the large cobles have three men to row, together with a coxswain to encourage the team. Such coble racing was always part of a regatta, during Staithes Fair Week and they were open to all comers.

This photograph conjures up a reminder of a time 60 years earlier when a Staithes crew of T. Cole, S. Robinson, Thomas Crooks (later drowned at sea) & B. Verrill took part in the Great Coble Race of 1866.

Maybe the above photograph was to celebrate the Diamond Anniversary of the Staithes famous victory?

THE POEM
by Peter Kelly of Whitby.

1.	Ye surely have heard of the great coble race
	From Staithes to Whitby, that lately took place
	Between the Blyth miners and Staithes fishermen,
	Who nobly came forward, their cause to defend.
	chorus
	Come take up your fiddle & drive care awa'
	And play us that tune called "Erin-go-Bragh"(chorus)
2.	On the 11th September, the day they did fix
	For the match to come off in the year sixty six,
	Both parties were willing, the sport to begin
	Each fully determined the laurel to win.
	chorus
3.	When arrived at the station they tarried a while,
	And, the signal once given, got off in good style.
	The miners tried hard, but 'twas labour in vain,
	For the fishermen brave, shot ahead in the 'Jane'.
	chorus
4.	For over 10 miles they contend for the prize,
	A fine silver cup and two hundred likewise.
	The fishermen rowed with free heart and goodwill
	And quickly displayed their superior skill.
	chorus
5.	They had not, like school boys, their lessons to learn,
	And the rest of the race left the miners astern.
	Afraid that these strangers might chance go astray,
	The kind-hearted fishermen showed them the way.
	chorus
6.	And when the 'Jane' reached near Whitby pier end,
	Her friends and well wishers their greetings did send.
	While Shaftoe cried 'Smash man, the race it is won.
	The miners are beat, boys, and I am undone.
	chorus
7.	And to see that grand race, people came far and near,
	Ten thousand assembled on cliff, bridge and pier.
	They seemed quite delighted, and loud 'hip-hurray'
	Saluted Staithes fishermen winning the day.
	chorus
8.	Ye North-country sportsmen, whose dress is so fine
	And all ye bold miners who live near the Tyne,
	Again, if you're willing to come to the scratch,
	In a village in Yorkshire you'll meet with your match.
	chorus
9.	For the young men of Staithes are manly and brave,
	From childhood they're taught to breast the big wave.
	In rough or smooth water, against wind and tide.
	They're ready to row for five hundred aside
	chorus
10.	So leave all your boasting, return to the pit,
	To compete with these fishermen you are unfit.
	Go ask your bold backers to find better men
	For the Staithes men will beat you again and again
	chorus
11.	Long life to brave Thompson and all the boat's crew.
	To Crooks, Cole, and Robinson praise is due,
	And brave Burton Verrill, as I have been told,
	Should have his name written in letters of gold.
	chorus
12.	Come, fill up a bumper and let it go round,
	Your praises are sounded through country and town;
	Hull, Manchester, Leeds and a great many more,
	And all the small towns on the brave Yorkshire shore.
	chorus

SECTION 43.0 – THE ARTS – Amateur Dramatics & Concerts

Staithes were well versed in holding concerts, often to raise funds for worthy causes and on 10th January 1899 they held a Benefit Concert, in the Board School to help Staithes Cricket Club.

An early North-Eastern Daily Gazette newspaper article, dated 5th April 1900, records that a very successful concert was held in Staithes Board School. The proceeds of this concert, amounting to £5-1s-0d were donated to the War Fund (Boer War).The first part of the concert consisted of Kindergarten, songs, games and recitations, given by the infants, under the supervision of Miss Eland and Miss Carter, who ably organised the whole concert. They were assisted by Misses Jefferson, Bradshaw and Brown.

The second part of the programme was a farce, entitled "Grumpy's Blunder', which was received with enthusiasm.

The following took part: Masters John, Tom and Willie James, Misses H. Verrill, M. Laverick, Polly Cole, P.A. Cole and Alice Verrill.

Miss Clark presided at the piano, with great success and rendered valuable assistance in the general management.

Mr M. Webster played a violin solo, which provoked much applause.

Celebrations and a concert were held at the Fisherman's Institute on 2nd March 1900 to celebrate the Relief of Ladysmith and flags of every description were hung from one house to another.

The Staithes visiting artists were well known for organising impromptu concerts in the Fisherman's Institute, also Captain Pinder is recorded as being involved with post Mafeking concerts.The artists also held artists dinners and smoking concerts at the Black Lion on the High Street.

Plate 422 HC Morley c1904

Charles Henry Morley, who rarely left Staithes, took this photograph, hence this young amateur drama group, initially thought to be made up from the art fraternity or school, were most likely to be performing in c1904, upstairs in the Fishermans Institute or at the Board School. Information received confirms some of the names as: Meggy Verrill, John Willy Verrill, Lizzie Unthank, unknown, unknown, Richard (Dickie) Worthy, unknown, thus confirming that the performers were in fact local to Staithes.Dickie Worthy married Frank Verrill's daughter Esther and they lived at both Lynn Cottage and 'Green Hill View', Gun Gutter Steps for a while.The Boer War was fought and won by 1902 during those early years of Laura Johnson and Harold Knights visits to Staithes and this play involving nurses and soldiers could well be a production remembering the celebrations of Mafeking and Ladysmith. It is now proven that the Staithes folk possessed talents outside of fishing, skaning, baiting and knitting and that they possessed real musical /acting talents that were utilised for War Fund Relief and post Boer War concerts.

Plate 423   c1911

Little is known about this group, where the photographer has titled it 'The Staithes Cheeroh Girls'. All of the actors have dark long hair and appear to be in their early twenties. Possibly a show put on at the Board School or possibly in New Hall up Webster's Steps, which opened in 1904. The stage shown here was very small.

Plate 424

The Cheeroh Girls were all smiles for this later concert

CHAPEL CHOIRS:

The Methodist movement started in the nineteenth century, when there were three chapels in Staithes: the Primitives, the Wesleyan and the Congregational (High Chapel) they were full to overflowing every night. The fishermen all foregathered on the staith on a Sunday evening, in front of the Cod and Lobster, and they marched up the street singing at the tops of their voices... and then as they come to the various chapels, which of course they all had their own ones, they peeled off still singing, and went into it. If you come down to Staithes on a Sunday evening you'd practically hear them lifting the roofs off.

STAITHES CHOIR

Plate 425

The Staithes choir goes back a long way and they were invited to sing at Crystal Palace in the early 1900's. A quintet led by Willie Verrill, were recorded by the BBC in the 1930's and included Ted Theaker, Jacob Unthank and Dickie Hick, with Lillie Verrill as the pianist. This quintet appears to have been the nucleus of the 'old choir', under Willie Verrill, which performed in Manchester during the 1950's and included Robert Laverick and the young James Wright.

Joe Skilbeck was a major influence, with his excellent writing and composing of such numbers as; Men of Steers, Song of the Islands, Heading for the Harbour Lights etc.

Local character Willie Wright is a stalwart of the current Staithes Choir and pictured here in the glasses.

SECTION 44.0 – THE 'KNIGHTS OF STAITHES'

THE STAITHES ART GROUP

Artists came to Staithes long before, the Staithes group were formed and Indiana Trufitt in 1868 advertised her Staithes Hotel, stating that Staithes was a favourite haunt of artists, with delightful good views.

A small scattered colony of painters, were already established in the area during the period between 1880 and the early 1890's. One such painter was William Gilbert Foster R.B.A. who is said to have pioneered painting at Staithes, working in the area and at Runswick from around 1880. Gilbert was soon joined by Frederick Jackson (1884), Mark Senior (c1885), Hannah Hoyland (1890), Fred Mayor (1892), Henry Silkstone Hopwood (1900), John Spence Ingall (c1895), Ernest Dade was established in Scarborough (1892), Harold Knight & Laura Johnson (1897). Gradually a whole stream of artists came to the Staithes & Runswick Bay area between 1890 and 1907 to paint the unspoilt landscapes and the everyday fisher folk, trying to capture their way of life and their pain and hardships.

The Staithes Art Group of painters was formed between 1894 to 1909 and lasted just 15 years. The group had a hard core of thirty artists, thirteen had studied in Paris, Bruge, Holland, Antwerp, Italy and Dusseldorf and the group as a whole eventually reached forty one in number. The actual Staithes Art Club was formed in 1901 having broken away from the Yorkshire Union of Artists and initially opened with 19 members and rising to 34 members by 1907 when it disbanded. Their first exhibition was held in the Fishermans Institute on Staithes High Street and this venue was chosen for the next two years exhibitions, before moving in 1904 to the Anderson Gallery in Well Close Square, Whitby. The membership in 1901 included 20 artists, such eminent names as: Henry Silkstone Hopwood, Joseph Bagshawe, Thomas Barrett, Arthur Friedenson, Robert Jobling, Harold Knight, Rowland Hill, John Bowman, Ernest Dade ('D'), Fredrick Jackson, John Spence Ingall, Frank Henry Mason, Ernest Higgins Rigg, Mark Senior, Albert George Stevens, Harold Edward Conway, Hannah Mayor, William Fredrick Mayor, Charles Hodge Mackie and Laura Johnson.

The membership of 34 artists was built up over a gradual period between 1901 and 1907 and each had their own identity and many influenced each other, as new styles were adapted.

'THE FOUNDING FATHER' - WILLIAM GILBERT FOSTER

William Gilbert was born in Manchester on 9th May 1855 and his father an accomplished portrait painter established a studio in Leeds, when he moved the family there. Gilbert went to Leeds Grammar School and received painting tuition from his father and went on to teach art at his old grammar school, before he was appointed Under Master

Plate 427 WG Foster c1890
This fine unpublished photograph taken from a magic lantern 'positive' of c1890 shows William Gilbert Foster producing a landscape, overlooking Runswick Bay.

at the Leeds School of Art. He eventually opened his own studio and gave private tuition to his pupils who included Owen Bowen who went on to open the Leeds School of Painting and joined the Staithes Art Club in 1904. Although Gilbert had stayed in the area many times before during the 1880's, it was in 1890 when he first purchased a cottage at Runswick Bay, where he took students from Leeds to the area for sketching and field trips during the summer. He was very supportive of the inexperienced artists giving advice and encouragement whenever he could. Both Fred Jackson and Ernest Rigg were motivated by Foster

It is my belief that not enough credit has been given to Gilbert Foster for his tireless energy in bringing both established artists and students alike to the area. It could be said that he is the real founding father of the Staithes Group of Artists.

William Gilbert Foster died on 3rd July 1906 at the young age of 51.

LAURA JOHNSON – 'EARLY DAYS IN STAITHES'

Laura was born on August 7th 1877 and received tuition and encouragement during her informative years from her mother, who was a keen artist.

It was 1897 before two students from the Nottingham School of Art, Laura Johnson and Harold Knight visited Staithes for the first time. She was 20 years of age on her first visit and Harold was 23 and they stayed in different lodgings. Laura stayed with a Mrs Mary Ann Crooks (nee-Verrill) on Church Street, who had married John Crooks in 1874, but was widowed when John lost his life in the lifeboat tragedy of 1888. She obviously must have left the ancestral home next to the Royal George to live on Church Street. Harold stayed at George Porrit's in Gun Gutter, along with Fred Mayor and Arthur Friedenson. Laura and Harold painted for a month during the summer of 1897 but returned the following year in 1898 for 6 months. It was Thomas Barrett a master at the same Nottingham School

Plate 428

Laura Johnson alongside friend and fellow artist Frederick William Jackson are photographed here painting down in the Beckmouth at Staithes, just below the old trestle bridge over Roxby Beck. Laura with parasol in left hand appears to be sketching rather than painting and during these early years in Staithes she was rarely ever photographed, this being the only known photograph in existence of Laura Johnson in Staithes. In the distant right hand side close to the old bridge another artist is painting at his easel and is thought to be Harold Knight. The unusual boat behind them with the tall mast is 'Daisy'.

of Art who recommended that they travel to Staithes, as it provided a rich source of material to paint.

Thomas had a cottage in Staithes and he became well aquainted with Gilbert Foster. By 1904 Thomas was listed in Kelly's Directory of North Yorkshire as a commercial artist resident in Staithes and it was in this year that both Laura and Harold shared a studio behind the Post Office of Robert Featherstone's. This studio was in fact a converted stable and loft and had been used earlier by Harold. They returned each year to spend as much time as they could painting their beloved Staithes, apart from the three visits they made to Holland, between 1904 and 1907, where they adored their time in Laren. They departed Staithes towards the end of 1907. During her time in Staithes she was influenced and helped by fellow artists Fred Jackson, Fred Mayor, Arthur Friedenson and in particularly Charles Hodge Mackie.

A vast collection of magic lantern slides of Staithes and Runswick Bay have recently been unearthed in a 'lock-up' close to the towns of Nottingham and Derby, not far away from where Laura Johnson was born in Long Eaton.

Two of the lantern slides showed Laura in Staithes, before she was married. Many of the lantern slides have captured the informative years from 1890 - 1910 and depict some of the artists that eventually formed the Staithes Art Group and hence they are of National and possible International importance.

Fred Jackson had been in Hinderwell from c1884 and was recorded as a resident artist in Bulmer's Directory of 1890, so it would be reasonable to say that Laura probably met Jackson at some time between say 1898 and the 1st Art Exhibition in the summer of 1901, hence this photograph is likely to have been taken during one of the summers of that period. Artists Fredrick Jackson and Harry Hopwood lived in Hinderwell and were particular friends of Harold Knight and Laura Johnson.

Her marriage to fellow artist and long time companion Harold Knight, took place on the 3rd June 1903 in West Leak Church in Nottingham and they honeymooned in London and Rye. After their honeymoon they returned to the area in the autumn and stayed on Bowman's Farm at Roxby not far from the Redman's Farm where she had stayed earlier, when she was single, but they still walked down every day to paint in Staithes. They returned again in the autumn of 1904 after one of the wettest summers. At some time prior to her marriage, Laura had stayed with a family at the top of Cowbar Hill, where she regularly painted one of the children, Elizabeth Alice, who became her chief model. Laura and Harold made frequent visits to Nottingham and London and worked in Holland for several months before returning to Staithes, where in 1907 their last year, they lodged with Robert Featherstone above the old post office on the High Street, which aptly is now the excellent Staithes Art Gallery. Within the art world there are slight doubts over whether Laura & Harold really left Staithes in 1907, or whether it was 1908 as little or no Cornish paintings dated 1908 are recorded!

THE LODGINGS AND STUDIO'S OF LAURA AND HAROLD

We know that both Harold and Laura had separate studio's for the greater part of their stay in Staithes and that they often visited/shared these studio's from time to time.

Pin pointing exactly where in Staithes Harold and Laura's various studio's were, can be very contentious, however the following appears to be true.

After Laura and sister Annie's impressive first visit to Staithes, with her aunt for one month or so in 1897, Laura used the large room above the Fishermen's Institute until it was turned into a picture exhibition. Laura returned with her well off pupil Rosie Good in 1898 and again initially lodged with Mrs Crookes on Church Street where the rent was probably paid by Rosie in return for being given art lessons. Rosie lodged at Ebor Cottage at the top of the hill, behind the village and Harold at Tom Porritt's at the bottom of Church St, next to Captain Cook's Cottage. By 1899 Laura and her Aunt Sissy were renting a red bricked, three story house, with steps, which was one of three at the top of the hill at the back of Staithes; where the coastline could be observed from the bedroom window. This house,

Plate 429

Laura's studio was in fact within the old building between the Lifeboat House and Joe Verrill's house as pictured here. The left hand of the central cottage was the home of Ann and Joseph Verrill (Joe Ben) who was Staithes first ever Coxswain.

Hence from this building she would have had good views along the quay and also across the water to the Staith as shown by this mid 1890's Victorian photograph, taken roughly from the position of the Cod & Lobster.

Harold certainly had his studio on the Staith in September 1899, which both he and Laura shared from time to time. It is recorded by Laura Knight that both she and Harold looked through the studio window to see the body of Francis Unthank being carried on a ladder, after the ill fated Knight Commander coble disaster, where he was drowned along with his two sons, Billy and Frank on 30th September 1899.

Plate 430
It is believed that Laura's studio, was in the upper story of one of the two cottages, behind the two hand carts, which would allow clear views of the foreshore and Fish Quay. Later in her autobiography Laura refers - "I had finished my day's work and was turning round the corner from my studio behind a public house in the main street, when I nearly ran into a grieving woman', this being a possible reference to walking from Seaton Garth, to the Cod & Lobster and onto the Hight St.

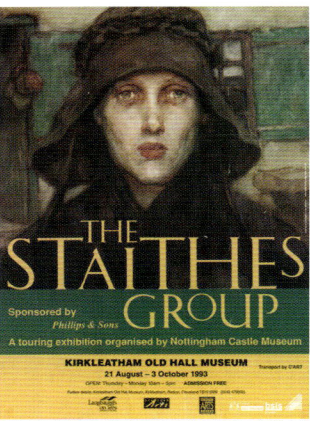

Plate 431
Laura Knight never forgot this haunting image of a Staithes woman, who's face was full of anguish and grief and one did not need to see the black mourning bonnet to know that widowhood was difficult to accept.

This subtle water colour by Laura's husband Harold Knight was a masterpiece.

Plate 432
A poster produced for the Robin Kildea Exhibitions of his watercolour paintings, which were held in the 'Little Gallery Staithes' (upstairs room of Bridge House on Abrahams Lane) in both 1990 and 1992. The first poster being a view looking at the Beckmouth and the second a view looking up the Beck towards Granary Yard.

most likely Ebor House, was near Captain James Pinder's whitewashed house, which had a 'lookout' ledge where he used his telescope. James Pinder (1840-1913) was the secretary of the Staithes Fisherman's Institute, where he was acknowledged as being "King o Steers" and was recorded as living at 'Prospect House'. Laura's first studio (1897) as described in her autobiography 'Oil Paint & Grease Paint' - "Rosie and I shared a studio on the quay, not luxurious just an empty room in a derelict house, but from the window you could see all that went on and it was easy to go out to make pencil notes when anything special happened.

Enid Lucy Pease Robinson in her 'secret diary' recorded on Friday 9th August 1901, that 'two Australians on tour had taken the old dilapidated cottage next to Joe Verrill's house, near the lifeboat house where the Johnson's studio used to be'. However this fact is somewhat contradicted by Janet Dunbar in her 1975 book titled 'Laura Knight', where she states Laura on her arrival in Staithes (1897) found a large room in a near derelict house on the staith itself, which she made into a studio: it was an ideal spot for sitting at the window and looking at the women on the quay, gutting fish or mending the dark blue nets. As Laura arrived in 1897, it is conceivable that her first studio was on the staith and that she had this for only a year or so before moving onto the lifeboat house quayside, into the building attached to Joe Verrill's house. As Janet Dunbar wrote her book 5 years after Laura's death and 39 years after Laura's 1st Autobiography in 1936, it is possible that the facts had become somewhat distant and it is unlikely that Enid's diary entry could be wrong!- Enid first visited Staithes in 1900, so it is likely that she may have seen Laura in her quayside studio during that year.

STAITHES ART EXHIBITIONS

The Staithes Group broke away from the Yorkshire Union of Artists and held their first three annual exhibitions in the Fisherman's Institute situated on the lower High Street near Gar'Ends on 26th August 1901, where it cost 2d on entry, with further exhibitions in 1902 & 1903 respectively.

By 1904 Edward Anderson joined The Group and his father had a large gallery in Well Close, Whitby, hence the 1904 exhibition was held there. There were no further exhibitions here and The Group disbanded in 1907 and most artists moved away from the area with the exception of Mark Senior who carried on at Runswick until he died in 1927, Fred Jackson at Ivy Cottage in Hinderwell with his wife Anne Hodgson, daughter of a local farmer in Hinderwell until 1918, Albert Stevens in Whitby until 1925, John Spence Ingall who owned a small terraced house at Bank Top Runswick until his death in 1936, Ernest Higgins Rigg stayed in the Runswick area until 1908 and Rowland Hill who met his wife to be in Runswick, married her and lived in Ellerby until 1952.

For a short time in the 1960's The New Staithes Art Group was formed by several professional artists living or at least working in the area and this group exhibited annually for a while. This New Group produced the well accomplished artists Lilian Colbourn, Fred Williams and Len Tabner.

A new exhibition was held in 1994 called 'Staithes Now' and was mounted in order to show the high quality works, still currently being produced from artists working the Staithes area and included some of the following artists: Heather Davies, Len Tabner, David Curtis, Fred Williams, Mark Brooke, John Carter, Eric Taylor, William Dealtry, Jill Carter & Barry Carter.

In the Easter of 2006 Allison and Dave Milnes opened their grand new venture The Staithes Gallery, in the large glass fronted building on the High Street. It had previously been used by several other businesses including the 'Central Café' run by A. Manship and from around the 1890's it was the former Post, Money Order, Telegraph Office and Savings Bank where postmaster Robert Featherstone was in charge here in 1897. It was above his premises where Harold Knight and Laura Knight slept when lodging there during 1907, their last year in Staithes, with their small studio at the rear of the premises.

The opening night of Staithes new gallery was a huge success, with the eminent artist, David Curtis, steeping high praise on this new enterprise.

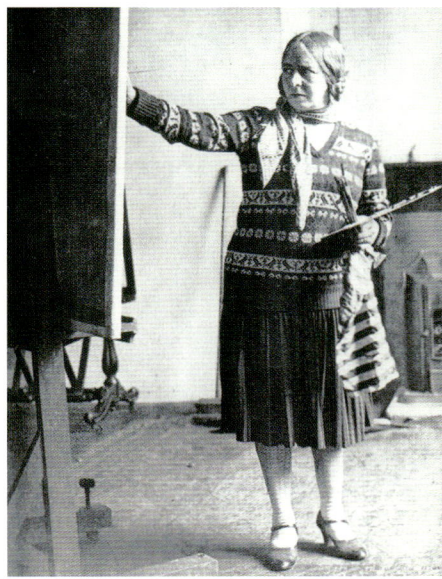

Plate 433

Laura Knight at work on one of her many compositions, where she gained a reputation as the most publicised artist of the first half of the 20th century, with high praise for ability to capture a likeness correctly.

Laura was created a Dame of the British Empire in 1929 and was one of the most successful ever female artists. She painted as an observer at the Nuremberg War Trials and has been acclaimed as the greatest female artist in Britain. She produced two auto-biographies in 1936 and 1965 titled 'Oil Paint & Grease' and 'The Magic of a Line' respectively.

Harold Knight died in 1961 and Laura in 1970 at St John's Wood.

Dear Mrs Longster,
Please forgive my delay in answering your delightful letter. To write the name Longster takes me back straight to Staithes, the memory of which is so beautiful in every way. Perhaps the happiest days of my life were spent with the dear friends I made there... great, good and wonderful people. They are all dear to my heart to-day.
I wish I could have said something about Staithes in my B.B.C. broadcast, but as your say "one cannot put a life time into a few minutes" — and you are more or less told what you must talk about.
All the same if I ever get the chance to tell of the love, help and sympathy I knew in Staithes I shall bless the opportunity.
You say you are not a good hand at writing a letter. I think yours was a beautiful letter which moved me very much. How wonderful it is that your husband remembers me. I well remember painting Sarah Jane and 'Dimples'.
With love to all my dear friends, affectionately yours
Laura Knight

Plate 435

Despite her eventual fame, Laura never forgot her time in Staithes and many years later on 26th May 1967, she wrote the following letter to Mrs Longster, praising the people of Staithes and looking back to how happy she was in that period 1897-1907.

When questioned during a TV interview, regarding what was the cheapest and most expensive painting she had ever sold, the answer came back as 2½d and a thousand guineas!

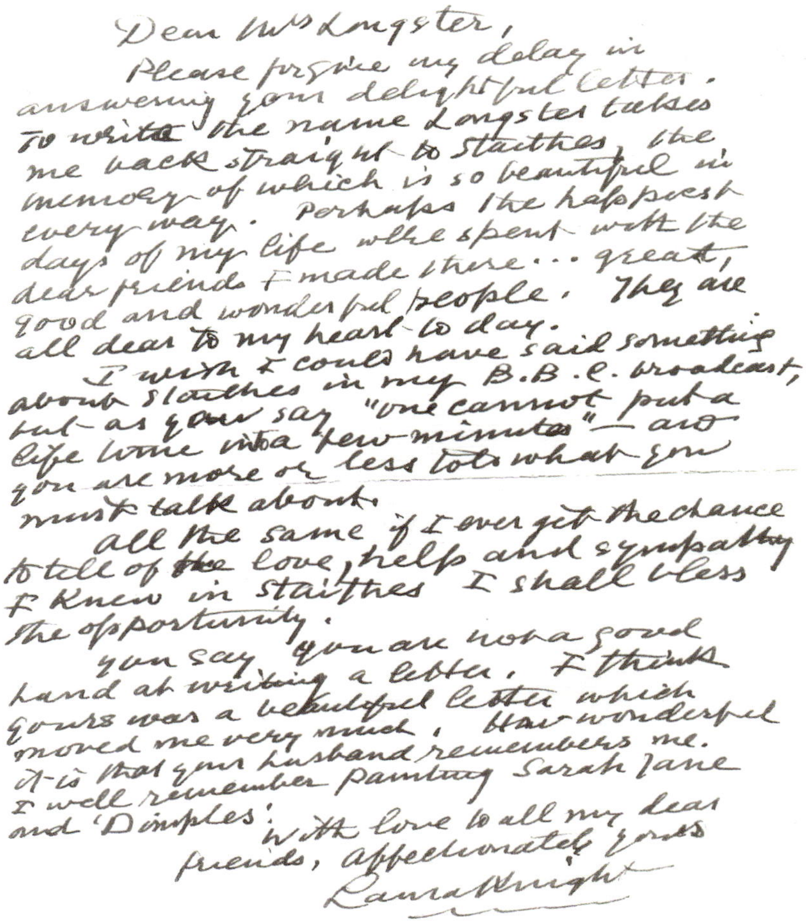

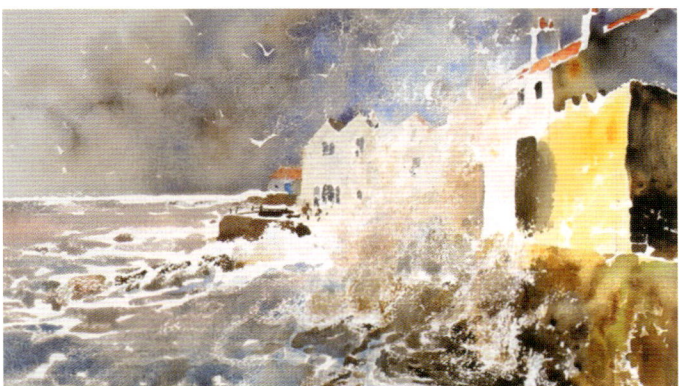

Plate 434

Frontispiece of the 'Staithes Now' exhibition catalogue of 1994 featuring a study by talented Cumbrian artist Heather Davies.

There were some stunning paintings on view and once again, proved just how much talent was still around the area. Some of the artists that have exhibited their works of art here are as follows (not exhaustive): Painters David Curtis ROI RSMA, Rob Shaw, Paul Czainski and Bruce Mulcahy; Sculptors Darren Yeadon and Michael Turner and painter & printmaker Ian Burke, to name but a few.

Al and Dave are helping to keep the tradition going, by running the Staithes Art School & Residential Painting weekends, using experienced tutors who are in turn accomplished artists. This is now their seventh year and several exhibitions have been held since the inaugural exhibition, displaying a wide range of styles and media with some spectacular fine art on display at all times, all of which has put Staithes well and truly on the map.

Derbyshire born artist Rob Shaw, with his unique impressionist style was chosen to display one of his canvases at the Royal Academy in 2012 & 2013.

David Curtis, ROI RSMA, is one of the most successful artists in the country, having won countless awards for his spectacular art and superb brushstrokes and he has been a tutor for at least three of the Gallery Art weekends. The 'Fabulous Czainski's'(Paul & Chris) continue to produce work of the highest quality with many surreal paintings receiving high acclaim from far and wide.

Ian Burke, art housemaster at Eton College is a regular exhibitor here and Rob, David, Paul and Ian's works are always on display in the Staithes Art Gallery.

Long may this gallery and the Staithes tradition of artists continue.

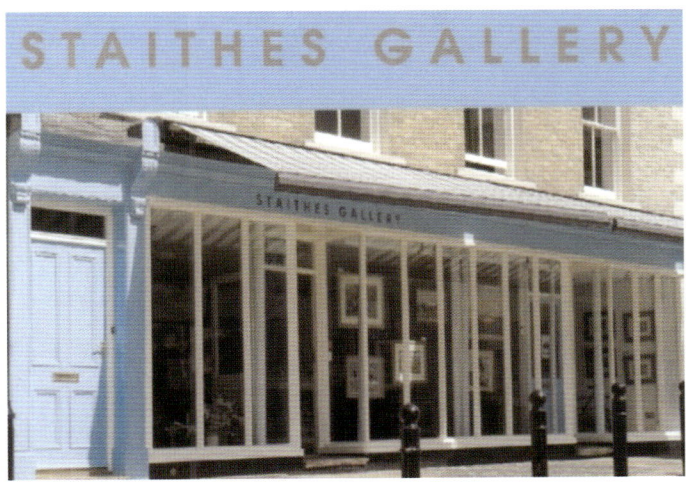

Plate 436

The newly decorated front of the Staithes Gallery on the High Street.

ARTIST DRAWN PUBLICATIONS.

Many of the famous artists of the day, produced paintings of the area and they found a way of sharing their works, without the public having to buy paintings! Many of the artists of the day, including Staithes Group artists had their work reproduced into coloured art postcards, which sold for a few pence. This had two results in that it was a way of advertising their obvious skills and afforded a small income too.

Plate 437 – JR Bagshawe
This 'Oilette' Connoisseur series was titled 'Toilers of the Sea' and was published from Bagshawe's original painting called 'In the Teeth of the Gale'. JR Bagshawe (1880-1919) had a very distinctive style and produced several postcard series often published by Raphael Tuck & Sons as part of their Oilette series. In order to study his subject he once spent a week on the yawl 'True Love' observing the fishermen's long lining techniques. His artistic cards depicted just how hard a fisherman's life really was. Joseph was the original secretary of the Staithes Group of Artists appointed so in 1901.

Plate 438 – E.T. W. Dennis & Sons
An Edwardian publication by E.T.W.Dennis, of an original painting of Staithes by W.Gibson.

E.T. W. Dennis & Sons had their publishing business in both London & Scarborough and published a number of artistic cards featuring such artists as: Hannaford, Warren Williams & W.Gibson (who's art work on Staithes and Runswick Bay were also published by J.T.Ross of Whitby).

Plate 439
J. Salmon Ltd exclusively published view cards from the original water colour paintings of A.R.Quinton. Published by Salmon in the 1920's, this view from an original water colour drawing by A.R.Quinton was titled 'The Nab'.

Plate 440 – Walter Hayward Young
Walter Hayward Young produced several artist cards of the old bridge at Staithes, the old fisher wife, Staithes etc, and his works were published by Misch & Stock Ltd, and also the 'Aquarelle' series.

This c1905 publication of Staithes old trestle bridge leading from Abrahams Lane to Cowbar, was simply signed by 'Jotter' which was Young's pseudonym used by him on most if not all of his postcard productions.

STAITHES FESTIVAL OF ARTS & HERITAGE

Another new venture for Staithes was the inaugural Arts & Heritage Festival on September 22nd/23rd 2012, where 40 plus 'pop-up art galleries' were open, for all to see the huge variety of artistic skills that existed locally and from further a field.

The vibrant event included sculpture, jewellery, salvage exhibits from shipwrecks, music, photography, live talks, food, rare film footage of the village and a display of heritage photographs and of course many styles of exciting paintings; something for everyone. It was a real festival atmosphere with great weather and the festival organisers Barbra Govan, Jill Turton and team deserve every credit for bringing in the region of 2,500 visitors to the historical fishing village of Staithes.

The author had a very successful event in the former High Street Antique Centre by displaying for the first time images of the village and its fisher folk from the 1890's. The second festival was held on the 15th/16th September 2013 with double the number of artists in their 'pop-up art galleries', alongside a 'pop-up Tea Room Trail', workshops, live music, live art and more rare heritage photography and lantern slides for those interested in the history of this magical place.

The fabulous Czainski's opened their 'Curiosity Shop' which was both weird and wonderful. The art scene was very varied and colourful, with some fabulous items on show and was again a huge success.

Plate 441
The Author's Poster for the Staithes 2013 Festival of Arts and Heritage, advertising the exhibition and sales of rare local heritage images.

SECTION 45.0 – DALE HOUSE

In T. Bulmer's directory of 1890 Dale House is described as a secluded little hamlet, situated in the parish of Lythe at a point where the townships of Borrowby, Hinderwell, Roxby and Easington meet and in each of which it is partly situated. Palmers Ship Building and Iron Company had their Coal Depot here and in 1890 William Porritt was the coal agent.

Other notable trades at that time were: farmer James Duell, miller (water) John Thomas Bell, butcher Ralph Thomas Parks, shopkeeper George Welford, joiner Joseph Welford, shopkeeper Mrs Mary Welford and licenced victualler Matthew Codling of the Fox and Hounds.

Other private residents were recorded in 1890 as Reverand David Rycroft (Wesleyan), Robert Parks, Joseph Brown and Mr William Ryder.

The population in Dale House in 1861 was 35 and it was essentially a small farming community.

Dale House was a stronghold of the Welford family who were prolific farmers and Welford's could be found in Roxby, Mickleby, Uglebarnby, Newton Mulgrave, Lythe, Liverton and Whitby, however they are not necessarily related to one another. Ralph Welford is recorded as owning Ridge Lane Farm during the 1890's, whilst at Roxby John Welford had Oak House farm, Robert Welford had Midge Hall farm and William Welford had Home and Manor House farms.

Plate 448
H.C.Morley c1910

The Staithes viaduct, miners cottages and the Station Hotel are visible on the skyline, top right, in this photograph taken from a high point to the rear of Dale House Farm. On the immediate right the small outbuilding within the garden of No.21 was the local abattoir. Amongst other things the current resident here is a professional mole catcher. The adjacent house (no 17/19) at one time used to be a small hospital for the Grinkle miners and it is alleged that Willie Gargett's leg is buried in the rear garden here!

The farm building on the left has now been converted into a separate residence, named 'Wild Thorns'.

Plate 449
H.C.Morley c1908

The horse drawn delivery cart has just passed the Fox and Hounds (voted pub of the year for 2013), where Thomas Bainbridge was the licensed victualler at this time, having succeeded Ralph Dawson and is on its way to cross the old bridge.

During 1861, Elizabeth Seymour was the Inn keeper here and a Mrs Alice Teasdale was in charge here in the late 1930's.

Today the first house past the bridge is 'Glendale' and the second next to the Fox and Hounds is 'River Cottage', which for many years was merely the old stables.

A close look on the immediate left tells us that the oak troughing, behind the fence, is full, carrying water to the Water Driven Mill, just beyond the Fox & Hounds.

John Bell was recorded as the miller here from at least 1897-1901.

Plate 450   1963

This amateur photograph was taken inside the Fox Hounds Inn at Dale House in 1963.

From left to right they are; Tom Welford, unknown, unknown, John Stanger, Herbert Wren, Arnold Dunn and Percy Tawne on the stool (Garage fame).

Plate 451   Jack Braithwaite of Leeds

An unusual aerial photograph of the Fox Hounds and the Mill House at Dalehouse in the 1940's

This picturesque hamlet was in a state of devestation in early September 2013, when flash floods caused havoc here. Several cars were swept away and many cottages were flooded.

Plate 452   H.C.Morley c1909

Behind the Wesleyan minister and his good lady, the washing is layed out to dry on the hedgerow, between the two cottages (The Cottage and Peach Cottage). Mary Welford posted this postcard in September 1909, whilst on a trip to Glasgow. Peach Cottage to the right of the washing, with plaque over the doorway, was at one time the local shop/general store and Mrs Mary Welford had been the shopkeeper here for many years. The handcart and chickens to the right belong to Dale House Farm and the road to Roxby was a gated road at this time. The other cottages after the shop are today: Rose Cottage, Holly Cottage, No 17/19 and No 21. Fern cottage stands detached on the top left.

Plate 453   H.C.Morley 1910

This excellent photographic viewcard was sent by Bessie Duell to her Aunt, a Mrs Welford in South Hampstead, London with a brief message:
"This is our house, we shall be pleased to see Uncle Joe ('Record' tools firm) when he comes".

Young John Duell complete with sturdy boots and gansey is pictured with his sister, Elizabeth Bessie Duell, posing for the photographer, outside their Dale House, farmhouse

Plate 454 The Famous 'Mulgrave Supreme'
The breed declined to such an extent that in 1962 there were only four mature Cleveland Bay stallions left in Britain. The Queen got involved and famously bought a colt named 'Mulgrave Supreme' from Dale House farm to prevent its sale to America. Mulgrave Supreme was kept busy and within 15 years the number of stallions in the UK rose to 35.

Plate 455
Long time farm worker, John Stanger holds the horse steady, whilst George Duell looks very proud of his tally of five silver cups, displayed on the table in the yard of Dalehouse Farm. George is the grandfather of current Dalehouse Farm owner owner Gerard Welford.

Plate 457 H.C. Morley 1907
A tranquil scene with lady wearing a Staithes fisher bonnet, with her three children and faithful dog, pictured by the side of the road to Roxby.

We can be very precise about the date of this photographic card by Morley, due to the pertinent message written on the reverse side, "My Dear Violet, the Mission finished on Friday night, we had a very poor time of it. But lets hope the seed 'as been sown on good ground, if did not see 'rysable' results. You will be sorry to hear of the death of dear old Mr Parks. I am sure we shall all miss him very much at Chapel, with love from your dearest friend, Lillie.

This is reference to Robert Parks(1833-1907), Dalehouse farmer and well respected Wesleyan preacher. Latterly he moved from Dalehouse to 'Westgate' house in Staithes, which he had built on Bob Bells Bank, close to the Chapel there. The card was sent by devout Wesleyan, Lillie Thompson from 'Mizpah' cottage at the far end of Seaton Garth, close to Penny Nab.

Dale House Farm pictured above was run by the Duell family during the end of the 19th Century and James Duell was recorded as farming 50 acres here in 1881 and still recorded here in 1908. James married Ann Elizabeth Welford in 1883 and they had sons George Welford Duell, James Duell, John Duell and daughters Elizabeth Bessie Duell and Annie Duell.

George Welford Duell married Ann Elizabeth Smith and they had Dorothy Mary Duell who married butcher (journeyman)Thomas William Welford in 1947.

This farm was once named Mulgrave Farm House, which later became renamed as Dale House Farm.

The current owners are Elaine and Gerard Welford, with Gerard concentrating on the beef and sheep and Elaine on their two fine holiday cottages (Mulgrave Cottage and Post Box cottage).

This has been farmed by four generations of Welford's and latterly the Welford's became famous for breeding and showing Cleveland Bays and they have Royal connections!

Plate 458
This is picturesque Dale House on a quiet afternoon in the 1930's, as captured by the Valentine's photographer stood on the Staithes side of the bridge over the Beck looking towards Dale House Farm. The main farmhouse today carries a painted wooden plaque, 'TW & DM Welford, Dale House Farm', this being a reference to Thomas William Welford and Dorothy Mary Welford (nee Duell). Ridge Lane is to the right of the old milking parlour and climbs out of Dale House eventually reaching Scaling. The wooden troughing on the right hand side was an ingenious method of supplying Dale House Mill with sufficient water, and several sections of the abandoned oak troughing can be seen today, now overgrown with ivy.

Plate 459 J.T.Ross c1915

The Whitby based photographer took this photograph (No. 48582) from the walled lane running at the back of the Fox & Hounds public house which stands to the right of picture. The Old Mill stands to the left and has now been demolished, however the imposing stone Mill House in the centre of this view still stands and is in very good order with an interesting garden rolling down to the Beck. The lane unlike now was in perfect order for cycling and also for farm/motor vehicles at this time.

The miners cottages on Staithes Lane End are just in view on the top left.

In 1841 Joseph Wood was recorded as the Innkeeper/farmer, with George Moon as the miller(water)here.

The servants at Dale house Mill were Richard Smales, John Wilson, Hannah Stoneyman and Elizabeth Jobling; with the servants for the Mill House being; Robert Wilson, John Lynass and George Burnett.

In later times c 1851 a William Heslop was both Inn keeper and farmer here and by c 1861, Ann Moon was the farmer/miller and she was assisted by dairy maid Margaret Mead, ploughman Thomas Ward and milk boy John Shaw.

By 1937 Albert Edward Evans was residing at the Mill House and Mrs Alice Teasdale was running the Fox & Hounds here.

Plate 460 H.C.Morley c1911

The cart tracks on the right indicate the presence of a ford here across the beck. This ford still exists today and can be found up Ridge Lane, which commences to the right of Dale House farm. This is Becks meeting.

Two smartly dressed young boys pose for the photographer on the old wooden bridge. The character wooden bridge was eventually replaced with a metal structure and the road/track profile changed. However the replacement bridge was itself swept away during the flash floods of September 2013.

Plate 461 Gibson c1920's

Little known photographer Gibson, titled this view, 'DaleHouse from Bridge' and a sixth of the population of this hamlet are included!

The post box for Dale House was situated in the wall of Welford's farm building on the corner of Ridge Lane and is still there today. The farm building with the skylights was the milking parlour at this time and today it is a delightful four star holiday cottage, aptly named 'Post Box Cottage,' being part of the 'Farm Stay UK' Group.

The large three story stone built house on the left was for many years the home of farmer/preacher Robert Parks. Robert was well liked and his sermons were well received. He travelled around his 'circuit' on his infamous white horse in order to reach many outlying villages. The house latterly belonged to a Mrs Stonehouse, followed by Mrs Ida Armsby and they both offered Bed & Breakfast here.

This beautiful house is now owned by Alan Morrison and Sallie Hernandez and the glazed panel over the door bears the name 'Glen Dale', this being the former name of the house when Margaret Parks, widow of Robert, lived here.

Plate 462

Over 20 miners sit in the cess of the old narrow gauge Railway purposely provided for the nearby Grinkle Mines.

Several of the miners are carrying their rudimentary lamps/lanterns, whilst three Wesleyan Ministers provide them with an 'at-work' Service.

The Grinkle Ironstone Mine, was operational between 1875 and 1930 and produced thousands of tons of ironstone, most of which was transported along the railway seen here. On reaching Port Mulgrave the stone was tipped into waiting ships, for transport to Jarrow for processing.

During the later years of the mine's operation, ore was moved underground to the adjacent Loftus Mine and then, after the construction of the Whitby - Loftus railway, ore was hoisted up an aerial runway to be loaded at a siding, close to the site of the present potash mine.

SECTION 46.0 – BOULBY

Boulby Cliff lies at a height of 690 ft above mean sea level and is the highest point on the East Coast of England.

The name may have been derived from Boll's Farm, but there is also a legend that the burial mound of Beowulf was on the cliff top here, as he had wished to be buried at the highest point.

Minerals have been extracted from the cliffs in this area for over 200years and it was this activity that led to the creation of the hamlet of Boulby in the township of Easington.

In T. Bulmer & Co's 1890 directory, Boulby was described as: "a struggling and ruinous village standing about a mile east of Easington with a bold and precipitous coastline"

The mining of aluminous shale deposits (alum) commenced as early as 1615 and works were erected for the extraction of this mineral and mining continued into the eighteenth and nineteenth centuries before finally closing in 1871.

However Boulby's cliffs had some other 'hidden treasure' in the form of thick seams of ironstone and preparatory workings and sampling commenced in the mid 1850's. The new Boulby Mine was created between 1903 and 1905 and proprietors, the Skinningrove Iron Company extracted their first train load of ironstone from the newly formed Boulby ironstone mine in September 1905. The mine closed in 1921, re-opened two years later in 1923, closed again in 1925, re-opened in early1927 but finally closed later the same year.

At its peak Boulby mine employed 238 people during 1920 and Messrs Pease and Partners took over the lease during 1922.

A different form of mining goes on today at the new Cleveland Potash Mine, opened in 1974. The mines run deep underground and under the sea in order to extract the potash deposits.

Plate 463

This photograph of the cliff top village of Boulby was wrongly titled by publisher A.E. Graham of Redcar as 'Bouldy'.

Boulby Grange can be seen to the right of the picture where the mining manager once resided. The Willis family farmed here in the 1890's and also at Red House Farm.

The proprietors of the Boulby ironstone mine, the Skinningrove Iron Company, erected 40 new cottages, between July and December 1906; to house some of their workforce at a cost of approximately £100 each. These cottages were built of corrugated iron sheeting, laid over a timber frame and set on concrete foundations and generated the local nickname of 'Tin City'. There were 32 semi-detached cottages in a row on the north side of Boulby towards Cowbar at Staithes. With a further 8 near the old alum quarries, as can be seen in this c1920's view; each had gardens front and back, together with a wash house and were initially without water & electricity.

Boulby mine was officially abandoned in 1934 seven years after its closure and the 'Tin City' cottages were demolished soon after and it is believed that some of the timber and corrugated sheeting was used to build a large shed on Ward's farm at Roxby.

In1897 a Miss Emma Souter was recorded as a shopkeeper at Boulby.

Plate 464

The single story cottages had wash houses to the rear and these housed large coppers for heating the water, as shown to the right of Mr Newton in the above photograph.

Plate 465

The unknown amateur photographer 'RWH' has penned the title to his photograph as 'Boulby Wesleyan Chapel near Staithes'.

In 1997 author Simon Chapman wrote in his booklet, Boulby Ironstone Mine, 'Window of the Earth' that one of the new Boulby miners cottages was a small general shop and two houses were knocked into one to make a Wesleyan Chapel. However this photographic post card was posted from Stokesley to Redcar on 3rd January 1905 over a year before the erection of the new miners cottages had commenced. This chapel building is in an obvious state of disrepair, indicating that this must have been an earlier chapel building to that created by 'Tin City'.

The amusing message on the reverse side reads,"I thought as you are a very religious sort of a person something like this might suit you. I am sorry to hear of your toothache, you need to take a full half pint of whiskey, hot, to bed with you and drink after you have got into bed (not before)", so wrote Dick to his friend in Redcar.

It's use as an early chapel are supported by the 1891 census which declares on the same page as Boulby Barns that an old barn associated with the dwelling of John Severs, was used as a Wesleyan Chapel. This building has been tastefully restored today.

STAITHES AND DISTRICTS ANNALS

YEAR	EVENT
1086	The settlement of Seton or Seaton mentioned in the Doomsday Book
1415	First recorded as the Staith or landing place for the early settlement of Seaton approx. 1 mile from the present village
04-Oct.1507	Francis Bigod born at Seaton Hall
12-Jul.1523	Staithes existence mentioned in the Will of John Boyes a Staithes fisherman & farmer
02-Jun. 1537	Francis Bigod Lord of the Manor of Seaton Hall executed and was succeeded by his brother Ralph.
1538	There were approx 38 cottages in Staithes
1601	Hinderwell registers began in this year
01-Sep. 1603	There was an outbreak of plague in Hinderwell from September 1st to November 10th where 49 people died
1651	Anna Verrill was the first member of the famous Verrill family to be recorded in early baptism register
1651	Quaker George Fox visited Staithes
1704	Gun Gutter mentioned in Bye laws for the Manor of Seaton
1720	From 1720 through to approx 1820 smuggling was rife on the Staithes coast, reaching its height in the 1780's
04-Jun.1722	Customs Officers discovered smugglers contraband including brandy in William Bridekirk's house on Cowbar
1745	James Cook the famous mariner commenced his apprenticeship to grocer/draper William Sanderson on Church Street
04-Jan.1767	Extreme high tides washed away William Sanderson's shop where James Cook was apprenticed
1768	Captain Cook set off on his epic voyage to Australia and New Zealand
1770	Michael Rodham, Staithes 1st Boat Builder was born
04-Jan.1771	Highest recorded Tides
14-Feb.1771	Captain Cook killed by Natives
1774	Severe storms wrecked two Staithes cobles with crew of 6 lost and houses were lost and land swallowed up.
1775	Broom Hill mentioned for the first time in this year
06-Jan.1779	High Seas and severe storm devastated much of Staithes with the old Kelp House on lifeboat site destroyed.
1779	Pirate Paul Jones attempted to plunder the NE Coast
13-May1780	A writ was issued for the arrest of Thomas Crispin & John Wastell as both were known Staithes based smugglers
1787	Thomas Rodham(1st) the Staithes boatbuilder was born
1783	First Staithes Fair held
03-Nov.1790	Francis Newton influenced by John Wesley registered a licence on Cowbar side for Wesleyan style prayer meetings
1790's	Fulling Mill (Warp Mill) operated by the Hansell family
20-Jun.1797	Staithes Festival & Sports Day held with a fish skin purse prize to the winner of the sack race, a coble race was held also.
1802	Shipowner William Weatherill built his large house on Weatherill Street (now Church St), which later became the National School & eventually St Peters Mission
10-Sep.1810	George Weatherill artist of Cliff Farm (Fancy Hall), Staithes was born
14.-Apr.1815	Yawl the 'Richard & Sarah' lost with all hands
1815	Thomas Rodham(2nd) the Staithes boatbuilder was born
1817	There were 14 five man boats and 70 three man cobles operating out of Staithes was the largest fishing port on the Yorkshire coast
1821	George Pyman JP was born and started his famous career as a simple Staithes fisherman
1822	Congregational Bethel Chapel opened (High Chapel), constructed as Independant chapel
1822	Charles Mark Palmer was born
1824	Staithes first Wesleyan chapel opened by the Beckside in Staithes
1835	Resolution drawn up preventing Staithes fishermen from fishing on Sundays
1838	Staithes first Primitive Chapel erected
1840	A bridge over Colburn Beck allegedly did not exist, hence had to use the ford to cross the beck ('Fordside' house on Beckside)
1840	Jet Mining commenced in Staithes
Feb.1844	A quantity of land near the Cod & Lobster was broken & swallowed by the sea during extreme storms, exposing several retreats (Smugglers Gin Holes)
19-Apr.1844	Charles Dickens visited Staithes
1846	John Ord visited and wrote about Staithes in his book Antiquities of Cleveland, the entire population of 383 were fisherfolk
1847	Thomas Rodham(3rd) the Staithes boatbuilder was born
1849	Staithes National School on Church St. became licensed for Anglican worship, dedicated to St. Peter the fisherman
23-Oct.1849	James Theaker founder trustee of the Primitive Methodist Chapel and survivor of the 1888 lifeboat disaster was born
Nov.1849	Several houses including that of James Theaker were all swept away during severe storms and high seas
1850	Thomas Trattles the 'King O' Steers' died farming at Cliff Farm (Fancy Hall)
1851	Mary Sanderson (83 years old) was the Staithes Bellwoman employed to announce events and news
1851	Staithes population was 1192 (688 females and 504 males)
15-Jun.1856	William Cole's 30 ton yawl 'The Thomas & Margaret, built in Whitby was launched
16-Jan.1857	Isaac Verrill, Ralph Sanderson & Francis Theaker lost to heavy storms in Sanderson's coble.
25-Sep.1858	The Most Noble Constantines Henry, Marquis of Normanby sold valuable Staithes property at the Black Lion
Mch. 1860	William Sage a 10 year old boy was killed whilst working in the Main Seam mine above Staithes promenade
08-Oct.1860	Severe storms hit Staithes causing damage
1861	Formation of the Loftus, Staithes & Hinderwell Building Society
1861	Staithes inhabitants 1330 with 305 inhabited houses
1861	Dalehouse population was 35
31-Oct.1861	Severe storms wrecked portions of Staithes, 100's of ships lost throughout the country
01-Nov.1861	Severe storms hit Staithes again
1861	97 people were listed as working in Staithes shops & businesses
27-Nov.1862	The original Cod and Lobster was demolished by one of the fiercest storms ever recorded
1864	53 businesses were listed as existing in Staithes
1864	There were 16 ship owners listed in Staithes
18-Nov.1864	Coach and Four Horse Omnibus 'Eclipse' service from the Angel Inn at Whitby to Saltburn commenced, calling at Staithes.
16-Feb.1865	Replacement Wesleyan chapel foundation stone laid by Marquis of Normanby
20-Feb.1865	Severe storm where the vessel 'Thomas & Margaret' sunk with the loss of William Cole & rest of the crew
05-Apr.1865	Charles Mark Palmer bought the Grinkle Estate for £72,500
1866	New Wesleyan Chapel completed
1866	Staithes Fishermen and Miners Benevolent Provident Society formed
11-Sep.1866	Great Coble Race, 10miles in 85minutes won by Staithes men who became Champions of the German Ocean
27-Mar.1868	James and William Harrison lost their lives along with the crew of the Ship Racehorse
1868	Charles Mark Palmer purchased the Manor of Seaton from the Marquis of Normanby which included Staithes
1868	Victoria Family Hotel (Temperance) opened by Indiana Truefit next door to the Black Lion.
14-Apr.1869	Charles Mark Palmer's first visit to Staithes as Lord of the Manor
1869	Sixteen Yawls operating out of Staithes
06-May1870	Hinderwell Board stipulated that all dung, ashes, rubbish etc must not be dumped and that the Scavenger would collect, each morning except Sunday
1870	Lord of the Manor offered Staithes occupants of property the chance to purchase their holdings
21-Sep.1870	The coble 'Rachael' run down by steamship 'Thames' with crew of John Dawson, William Harrison & William Stout all drowned, John's son saved.
1871	x3 Staithes Fishermen drowned - Richard & Thomas Cole and William Thompson, when their coble Sea Venture capsized
1871	Staithes inhabitants 1306
22-Oct.1871	Prime Minister William Ewart Gladstone visited Staithes
1871	Boulby Alum Works closed
1873	Grinkle Miners cottages at Staithes lane End under construction
1874	Grinkle Mine opened
1875	Staithes Lifeboat House established on the site of old Alum Building
01-Jun-1875	Staithes first Lifeboat the 'Hannah Somerset', launch/naming ceremony
14-Nov.1875	The new Staithes Lifeboat slipway wrecked, Cod & Lobster flooded and Staith houses damaged during severe storms
1875	Staithes viaduct built
07-Aug. 1877	Laura Johnson the Dame to be was born
04-Jan. 1878	Opening of Staithes Board School at top of Staithes Bank, by C M Palmer
1880	The second & larger primitive Methodist Chapel opened (now the Heritage Centre)
08-Oct.1881	The 'Richard' a large fishing yawl lost with 9 hands including: Richard Thompson(master), brothers, Matthew & Joseph Thompson, Richard Ackwood, Isaac Verrill, William Crispin & John Newton (known as Dick Thompson's Storm)
1881	Staithes cobles reduced to 52 fishing boats & population was 1417
1881	Isaac Crake aged 10 fell to his death from Staithes Viaduct.
1882	The Cod and Lobster was washed away in severe storms
02-Dec.1883	Staithes station opened and first train ran on 3/12/83
31-Jul.1884	Bishop Lacey laid the foundation stone on Staithes Catholic Church

YEAR	EVENT
1884	Horse & Steeple racing in Race Course Field, between railway line and cliffs
1884	Staithes experienced severe storms and flooding
1885	Saxon coffin found when excavating for the new Railway, proving the existence of former Staithes Saxon Church
02-Jun.1885	Staithes Roman Catholic Mission Church formally opened - Church of Our Lady Star of the Sea.
Feb. 1886	Coal ship wrecked under the cliffs at Staithes & children missed school in order to gather it up
1886	Charles Mark Palmer received his baronetcy when he became Sir Charles
26-Dec.1887	The first Goods Train stopped at Staithes and delivered coble WY 123, 'Louise Becket'
14-Sep.1887	Staithes 1st Co-op store opened on the High Street
15-Aug.1888	Staithes Fishermen's and Seamen's Institute opened by Sir Charles Mark Palmer & Lady Palmer
27-Nov.1888	The lifeboat rescued 43 out of 44 cobles to safety during a severe storm, with the loss of John Crooks lifeboatman & one crewman.
30-Sep.1890	Artist George Weatherill died
1892	Lavinia Brown became a pupil teacher at the Board School Staithes at the age of 13 and remained there until 1944
1892	Piped water from Ellerby reservoir was supplied into Staithes to 15 strategically placed cast iron taps
14-Mar.1896	The crew of the coble WY 220 'Phylis' Joseph and Addison Verrill were rescued by Thomas Verrill (Tom Captain) & crew in the 'Mary Jane', (WY 146) after being struck by a huge wave in severe storms
23-May1896	Board of Trade medals were awarded to Thomas Verrill, Joseph Crispin, Robert Longster, George Webster & John Harrison for their gallant rescue of the 'Phylis' crew
1897	Laura Johnson & Harold Knights first visit to Staithes
1897	Bark House & Warehouse demolished to widen Chapel Yard
14-Jun. 1898	Staithes first Regatta held as part of the Staithes Fair
10-Jan. 1899	benefit Concert held in the Board School to raise funds for Staithes Cricket Club
06-Jun. 1899	Ocean Coble Race held with William Francis Verrill & crew in 'Martha & Elizabeth' winning
30-Sep.1899	Coble Knight Commander lost at sea, Francis(Frank) & William(Billy) Unthank & their father Francis(Frank) all drowned
02-Mar. 1900	A concert was held in the Fisherman's Institute for the Relief of Ladysmith
c1900	The new replacement Cod & Lobster Inn was built
1901	The Staithes Art Club formed with initial 20 members
Feb.1902	Coble 'Amey Robinson' lost with all hands including Robert Longster (Master), Joseph Crispin the two Board of Trade medal winners for rescuing life at sea for the earlier 'Phylis' rescue and James Tose
1903	Laura Johnson, artist married fellow artist Harold Knight in the old church in West Leake, Notts
1904	New Hall opened at the top of Websters Steps complete with library and billiard table - used for meetings, concerts etc and became the base for the Juvenile Temple Independent Order of Templars, The Hope of Staithes
Sep. 1905	The new Boulby Ironstone Mine opened and first train load of ironstone was extracted by the Skinningrove Iron Company
Nov. 1905	Miner's Demonstrations in Staithes following the Kinsley Evictions.
1906	Staithes 2nd Co-operative opened on site previously occupied by the Rodham's boat building yard
1906	The old central supported trestle wooden bridge across Roxby Beck(Abraham's Lane) replaced by the new iron girder bridge
Dec. 1906	'Tin City' was created at Boulby
1907	The first season at Middlesbrough for Staithes sporting hero Edward (Neddy or Fishy) Verrill.
15-Jun. 1907	SS Enterprise ran aground at Cowbar Steel
20-Sep. 1907	SS Whitewood became hard and fast on Cowbar Steel
1909	The last two Staithes Yawls finished service
11-Sep.1909	Mollie Verrill's bravery in the rescue of the ss Staithes earnt her the title of Grace Darling the Second.
21-Nov.1909	Isaac Verrill (the younger) died
1909	Artist JR Bagshawe spent a week in Staithes on Yawl True Love sketching the long lining
13-Nov. 1909	SS Skipjack wrecked on Cowbar Steel
21-Nov.1909	The Post Office increased the postal rate for postcards from halfpenny to one penny
16-Feb. 1912	Loss of Staithes fishing boat 'Pebba'
12-Feb. 1914	Two Staithes fishermen drowned from capsized cobles WY212 'Faith, Hope & Charity' and 'Field Hop'
20-Mar.1915	Palmers Memorial Miners Accident Hospital opened facing Staithes Lane End
13-Jul. 1916	The German U Boat UB39 incident involving William Francis Verrill & cobles Success, Mary Anne, Richard & Venus
06-Oct.1919	Grinkle Estate Sale including many Staithes properties
1920	Jet Mining ceased in Staithes
mid 1920's	Mains water was beginning to be introduced into Staithes
1922	Staithes Lifeboat House closed owing to decline of fishing industry & shortage of men to man it
1922	The new bridge at Dalehouse was built replacing the old bridge dating from 1745

YEAR	EVENT
1923	Mizpah was allegedly the first Staithes coble to be fitted with an engine
1924	Commenced in 1921 the new Piers were completed in Staithes harbour
19-Nov. 1924	SS Princess Clementine ran aground between Runswick and Staithes during strong gales
05-Sep.1925	Heavy storms tore away a section of the Staith and harbour wall damaged by rough seas
04-May-1926	Richard Verrill and shipmate Daniel Cole were drowned whilst serving on SS Vale of Pickering
1927	Boulby Ironstone mine closed for the final time
1928	John Trattles Cole launched the last coble to be built in Staithes 'The Star of Hope', from Granary Yard slipway.
09-Apr-1928	Ceremony on Easter Monday to mark the re-opening of Staithes Lifeboat Station
25-May-1929	ss Michalis Prois wrecked on rocks near Staithes
1929	William Mansfield ex of Grinkle Terrace was elected as Labour member of Parliament & held seat until 1931
22-May-1930	The Grinkle Mine ceased working for the last time
18-Jun. 1930	SS Aberdonian stranded at Staithes
17-04-1905	Grinkle Mine closed
1935	Staithes main sewage scheme commenced
1936	Electricity became established throughout Staithes
1938	Staithes Lifeboat Station closed once again
1939	Potash discovered in the area near Boulby
10-Jul. 1941	German heavy bomber plane Ju88A flew into a cliff near Cliff Farm, Staithes, killing all crew
11-May1944	SS Empire Heath was torpedoed with 58 killed out of a complement of 59, including x8 Staithes men
1944	The First Staithes May Procession and Crowning of Statue of Our Lady
13-Sep. 1945	Ann Elizabeth Rodham (nee Robinson) celebrated the grand old age of 100 years, with a Tea in the Wesleyan Chapel
1947	The old smokehouse (former Jane Ward's Kipper Curing House) demolished
1947	Grinkle Park residence of Charles Palmer became a Country House Hotel
18-Sep.1949	Wilfred Pickles visited Staithes as part of his Radio programme 'Have a Go'
1951	Only one full time fishing coble recorded in Staithes
1953	Rough seas and storms caused damage to the Staith and to the Cod & Lobster seafront pub.
1958	Staithes Railway Station closed
23-Sep-1959	Opening of Re-constructed organ in the High Street Methodist Church
1962	The Queen purchased a Cleveland Bay 'Mulgrave Supreme' from Dalehouse farm.
1969	Work commenced on the Boulby Potash site
1970	Dame Laura Knight died
1973	Boulby Mine commenced commercial production of potash
26.5.1973	Colin Harrison 'lost' as his boat 'Boy Colin' capsized. His 12-year-old son, Colin was thankfully saved.
31-Mar. 1978	Staithes Lifeboat Station re-opened & named as Staithes & Runswick Lifeboat Station.
1978	Four full time cobles fishing out of Staithes and four fishing seasonally
1978	Staithes Board School Centenary
1985	Staithes Fisherman's Choir formed, with their theme song 'Men O' Steers'
1985	Staithes Board School closed
1985	Staithes new Primary School in Seaton Close opened for boys aged 5-11 & a Nursery Dept for ages 3-5
28-Jan-1991	The original silver cup commemorating the Great Ocean Coble Race of 1866 was stolen from Hinderwell rectory
1994	'Staithes Now', artists exhibition held in Staithes
07-Jun-1995	Plaque commemorating the Great Ocean Coble Race of 1866 was unveiled at Seaton School by Willie Wright and Tom Verrill
1998	Former Board school demolished and new houses built on the site
1999	Former Bethel Chapel closed its doors
2005	Black Lion public house closed
2006	Staithes Gallery opened providing the town with a prestigious centre for Art
2010	Staithes Methodist Chapel held its last service
21-Sep. 2012	The inaugural Staithes festival of Arts & Heritage
May. 2013	Partial collapse of the beck walling and loss of brick shed, outside 'Fordside' due to actions of digger removing a large boulder
06-Sep. 2013	Dalehouse witnessed the worst flooding for a century and the bridge at Beckmeetings was lost.
13-Sep. 2013	Staithes new Art Centre opened in the former Wesleyan Chapel & the 2nd Staithes Festival of Arts & Heritage commenced
07-Oct. 2013	Staithes photographer Terry Lawson (the 'modern Morley') sadly passed away

ACKNOWLEDGEMENTS

The author would like to thank all those who found the time to offer valuable information for inclusion in this book, the loan of images and for the local warmth & stories that cannot be found by research alone.

Particular thanks is given to the following people:

- **Sue Turland** for her valuable help and 'legwork' pinpointing certain village cottages, their names new & old and sketches & photography that assisted my research.
- **John Cole** and **William Hinchley** for giving up their time to talk at great length and for proof reading the manuscript for historical and topographical correctness. John helped considerably with his knowledge of the cobles, the masters and the fishermen, together with newspaper & photographic images.
- **Eileen Huby** for her time and in depth knowledge regarding family history and general lineage of the Staithes families.
- **Neil Suckling** for access to important chapel papers & family images.
- **Willie Wright** for our exchange of images and chats/information throughout the years.
- **Helen Kippax** for loan of 1937 images.
- **James Longster** for his Rodham images/information & his 1953 storm composition
- **Terry Lawson** for the loan of certain pertinent images and his personally produced postcards and Ann Lawson for the copy of Laura Knight's letter.
- **Elaine and Gerard Welford** for their Dalehouse information & images
- **Alan Morrison** for his Dalehouse images
- **Pete Coney** for allowing photograph of Vera Marsay enamel sign.
- **Colin Bullamore** for swopping/loaning images
- **Robin Pierce** for help with scanning and map graphics
- **Filip Cieslik** his encouragement, exhibition and book sales venue in the former antique shop on the Hight Street.
- **Brian Noble** for supply of magic lantern slides.

Thanks to Leonard S. Hodkin of 28. Thoresby Road, Hillsborough, Sheffield for his excellent pen & ink handrawn postcard, from my collection. This was drawn in c1910 when he was only 14 years old, whilst attending Morley St. Council School, (what talent) and titled 'North Sea Fishermen'. Leornard was the son of Frederick William Hodkin who was an Electro Silver Plater and Leonard joined him as an apprentice at the age of 15.

I would also like to thank all those who took the time to talk such as; Billy Blackwell, Lawrence Wicks, Maurice Selby, Eileen Wright, Irene & James Longster, Ted & Sheila Howell, Neil Suckling, Peter Ecclestone, Marianne and Richard Lyth, Dot Coney, Joyce Woods, Ann Lawson, Elizabeth Tinker, Margaret Welford, Ann Brooks, Reg Firth, Dave Hanson and Colin Harrison

Apologies to anyone who I have missed.

BIBLIOGRAPHY

- Staithes – Chapters from the History of a Seafaring Town, by John Howard
- Yorkshire Fisherfolk by Peter Frank
- The Whitby Library reference books, newspapers and general records
- The Whitby Gazette & Northern Echo archives
- The internet for everything Staithes
- Oil Paint & Grease autobiography by Laura Knight
- The Magic of a Line, autobiography by Laura Knight
- The Co-operative Society archives & Wheatsheaf publications
- A History & Geology of Staithes by Jean & Peter Ecclestone
- The History of Cleveland by Rev John Graves
- The History & Antiquities of Cleveland by John Walker Ord
- Cleveland Ancient & Modern by Rev J.C. Atkinson
- T. Bulmer & Co's 1890 Directory of North Yorkshire
- Kelly's 1897 Directory of North Riding
- Staithes Tragedy and Triumph by John Howard
- William Francis Verrill of Staithes & the German U-Boat by John Howard
- A Staithes Tapestry – The Grat Ocean Coble race of 1866 by John Howard
- The Story of the Staithes & Runswick Lifeboats by Jeff Morris
- The Secret Staithes Diary by Enid Lucy Pease Robinson
- F.W. Jackson Exhibition Catalogue, with forward by Michael Cross
- Staithes & Port Mulgrave Ironstone by J.S. Owen
- Ancestry.co.uk
- The Staithes Group by Peter Philips
- Boulby Ironstone Mine, 'Window of the Earth' by Simon Chapman

Designed and printed by Northend, Sheffield. emma@northend.co.uk

All Rights Reserved. No part of this publication may be reproduced, stored in a retrieval system, or transmitted in any form, or by any means, electronic, mechanical, photocopying, recording or otherwise without the prior permission in writing of the Copyright holders, nor be otherwise circulated in any form or binding or cover other than in which it is published and without a similar condition being imposed on the subsequent publisher.

Rod Jewell has sole copyright on all the Magic Lantern Slide Photographs and many of the one-off photographs contained within this book, reproduction is prohibited without the author's permission.

© Rod Jewell, 2013

ISBN 978-0-9568366-6-3